Index

to the

Cherokee Freedmen Enrollment Cards

of the

Dawes Commission

1901-1906

Jo Ann Curls Page

HERITAGE BOOKS
2006

HERITAGE BOOKS
AN IMPRINT OF HERITAGE BOOKS, INC.

Books, CDs, and more—Worldwide

For our listing of thousands of titles see our website
at
www.HeritageBooks.com

Published 2006 by
HERITAGE BOOKS, INC.
Publishing Division
65 East Main Street
Westminster, Maryland 21157-5026

Copyright © 1996 Jo Ann Curls Page

Other books by the author:

Extract of the Rejected Applications of the
Guion Miller Roll of the Eastern Cherokee
Volumes 1-3

International Standard Book Number: 978-0-7884-0495-4

TABLE OF CONTENTS

INDEX TO THE CHEROKEE FREEDMEN ENROLLMENT CARDS OF THE DAWES COMMISSION, 1901 - 1906

INTRODUCTION

During my research I have looked at the Cherokee Freedmen enrollment cards on microfilm a number of times. The Cherokee Freedmen were African American slaves of the Cherokee Indians. At least one parent was an African American if a person is listed on the Freedmen enrollment cards.

The enrollment cards are very interesting to read. The cards list the name of each family member in the household and that person's age, sex, and relationship to the head of the family. Also included are the parents' names and references to enrollment on earlier rolls. Often the cards contain notations of births, deaths, and marriages. Some of the cards contain references to the race of the parents. They may state that a parent is a Cherokee, Choctaw or Creek Indian, a Cherokee, Choctaw or Creek Freedman, a white or a non-citizen.

This index was compiled using the enrollment cards created by the Dawes Commission to determine which former slaves of the Cherokee were entitled to Cherokee citizenship and a share in the land of the Cherokee Nation. Many of these former slaves were denied citizenship because they did not return to the Cherokee Nation by February of 1867. The treaty made with the Cherokee after the Civil War required that the former slaves were to become citizens of the Cherokee Nation if they returned to the Nation within 6 months. Many of the former slaves left the Cherokee Nation during the Civil War and went to Kansas and Texas. They did not know that they had to return by February of 1867 in order to have any rights as former slaves of the Cherokee.

There are three separate lists in this index. The first consists of Cherokee Freedmen approved by the Dawes Commission. Most of these names are on the Final Roll but some died before its approval and a few names were stricken from the roll. There are 4376 names. The second list consists of Cherokee

Freedmen rejected by the Dawes Commission and denied citizenship. Many of these people were former slaves or descendants of former slaves of the Cherokee. They did not prove to the Dawes Commission that they were back in the Cherokee Nation by the February of 1867 deadline. There are 2686 names. The third list contains the names of the children of Cherokee Freedmen that were born after the closing of the roll in 1905 but before its approval in 1906. Their names were added to enrollment cards in a supplementary roll made in 1906 called Cherokee Freedmen Minors. There are 712 names.

I attempted to copy the names and ages as they appear on the enrollment card. The original names on some cards are misspelled. Therefore, they will appear on the index misspelled. Some of the enrollees did not know their ages nor the name of one or both parents. If there was no information on the enrollment card regarding age or parents, the area is blank on the index. The number listed with each enrollee is the enrollment card number also called the census card number.

There is an index to the final roll available but it contains only the name of the enrollee and the Dawes roll number or final roll number which is different from the enrollment card number. The final roll must be searched in order to obtain the enrollment card number.

There is no index at all for the rejected enrollees. Each time you look for someone on the three rolls of microfilm you must search the entire roll looking at each card. I decided to copy each name and make an alphabetical index with the enrollment card number for each enrollee. Included are the ages of the enrollees at the time of enrollment and the name of the parents because there are enrollees with the same names.

This index has been very useful in locating many of my relatives. I was able to locate the enrollment cards of some of my married female relatives by looking at the parents of all the enrollees. I knew the names of their parents so I was able to find those elusive female relatives.

After you locate the enrollment card number you can look at the application for enrollment file. It has the same number as the enrollment card. The application for enrollment file contains the testimony of the applicant and his witnesses. Some of the files contain only a few pages and give little genealogical information but some are quite extensive. Some applicants mention aunts, uncles, cousins, grandparents, neighbors, occupations, where they lived and what they did during the Civil War, and when and how they returned to the Cherokee Nation after the Civil War. Some of these files contain marriage certificates and birth affidavits.

The enrollment card number or census card number is needed to find an enrollment card or an application for enrollment file. The enrollment cards and the application for enrollment files are both available on microfilm at the National Archives in Washington D.C. and at the Regional Archives at Ft. Worth, Texas. The microfilm is also available for rental or purchase from the American Genealogical Lending Library in Bountiful, Utah.

Hopefully, this index will help others find their Cherokee Freedmen relatives who lived in Indian Territory before it became the state of Oklahoma.

INDEX ONE

ENROLLEES APPROVED FOR THE FINAL ROLL

NATIONAL ARCHIVES PUBLICATION
MICROFILM
M1186 Rolls 23, 24, 25, 26

CARD#	NAME	AGE	PARENTS
1531	Aid Adair	2	Benj & Lizzie Adair
1039	Amy Adair	3	William & Emma Adair
1039	Arizona Adair	8	William & Emma Adair
1081	Bertha Adair	26	Mose Whitmire& Mariah Vanderfoot
1531	Cleveland Adair	4	Benj & Lizzie Adair
1039	Emma Adair	29	Henry Francis & Manerva Harris
1039	Ethel Adair	10	William & Emma Adair
1531	George Adair	6	Benj & Lizzie Adair
1039	Glenie Adair	2mos	William & Emma Adair
1039	Inola Adair	6	William & Emma Adair
1531	Isaac Adair	10	Benj & Lizzie Adair
1039	Lawrence Adair	5	William & Emma Adair
932	Leater Adair	1	Robert & Ida Adair
1531	Lizzie Adair	28	Frank & Martha Whitmire
1039	Nevada Adair	13	William & Emma Adair
1531	Ollie Adair	8	Benj & Lizzie Adair
932	Robert Adair	29	Amos Adair & Caroline Chambers
1039	Robert Adair	11	William & Emma Adair
1039	Wenona Adair	2	William & Emma Adair
1039	William Adair	35	Amos Adair & Caroline Chambers
1548	Albert Adams	15	George & Katie Adams
734	Babe Adams	1mo	Samuel & Hattie Adams
734	Beatrice Adams	3	Samuel & Hattie Adams
1548	Cora Adams	10	George & Katie Adams
1548	Cordelia Adams	2	George & Katie Adams
1548	Elias Adams	13	George & Katie Adams
1548	Ella Adams	5	George & Katie Adams
1548	Elmer Adams	8	George & Katie Adams
734	Eugene Adams	8	Samuel & Hattie Adams
1548	George Adams	19	George & Katie Adams
734	Georgia Adams	5	Samuel & Hattie Adams
734	Hattie Adams	30	George Lasley & Phillis Bean
1548	Katie Adams	35	William & Lettie Tucker
979	Squire Adams	23	Joe & Cora Adams
1548	Walter Adams	11	George & Katie Adams
66	Ada Alberty	2	George & Mintie Alberty
775	Addie Alberty	5	Lincoln Alberty & Mamie Davis
237	Amanda Alberty	45	Gus Buffington & Cinda Beck

3

153	Amelia Alberty	19	Jerry & Ruth Alberty
1526	Andrew Alberty	47	Mose & Charity Alberty
108	Arthur Alberty	9mos	Andrew Kirkum & Fannie Alberty
1526	Ben Alberty	3	Andrew & Lizzie Alberty
153	Bertha Alberty	15	Jerry & Ruth Alberty
108	Bertha Alberty	3	Bird Herron & Fannie Alberty
177	Boney Alberty	38	Dave & Martha Alberty
58	Carrie Alberty	16	David & Lucy Alberty
1526	Charity Alberty	10	Andrew & Lizzie Alberty
66	Charles Alberty	11	George & Mintie Alberty
66	Clarence Alberty	13	George & Mintie Alberty
66	Clifford Alberty	5mos	George & Mintie Alberty
199	Cora Alberty	22	Ed & Amanda Alberty
58	David Alberty	56	George Adair & Sallie Alberty
801	Dewey Alberty	3	Moses & Amanda Alberty
1526	Dollie Alberty	1	Andrew & Lizzie Alberty
1564	Easter Alberty	16	Josh & Josie Alberty
598	Easter Alberty	21	James & Rose Alberty
66	Ella Alberty	12	George & Mintie Alberty
204	Emery Alberty	23	Jerry & Ruth Alberty
58	Emiline Alberty	12	David & Lucy Alberty
66	Emma Alberty	6	George & Mintie Alberty
382	Emma Alberty	16	Sam Holt & Nellie Alberty
776	Emma Alberty	2	Sam Butler & Patsy Alberty
108	Fannie Alberty	20	Ed & Clara Alberty
66	Flora Alberty	10	George & Mintie Alberty
801	Gussie Alberty	5	Moses & Amanda Alberty
1526	Hattie Alberty	11	Andrew & Lizzie Alberty
153	Hattie Alberty	9	Jerry & Ruth Alberty
66	Jaby Alberty	9	George & Mintie Alberty
183	Jananna Alberty	18	Sally Alberty
1344	Jane Alberty	46	Zeb Beck & Nicey Alberty
1172	Jay Alberty	23	Andrew Alberty & Lucy Beck
587	Jennie Alberty	37	George & Rachel Johnson
153	Jerry Alberty	66	Mose & Sarah Alberty
596	Jerry Alberty	19	James & Rose Alberty
200	Jesse Alberty	10	Noah & Mary Alberty
183	Jessie Alberty	15	Sally Alberty
36	John Alberty	24	Ed & Amanda Alberty
184	John Alberty	21	Sallie Alberty

4

181	John Alberty	21mos	John & Lelia Alberty
202	Joshua Alberty	26	Jerry & Ruth Alberty
1564	Josie Alberty	43	Henry Rider & Betsy May
801	Juanita Alberty	7	Moses & Amanda Alberty
181	Lelia Alberty	21	Sallie Alberty
587	Lincoln Alberty	39	Em & Polly Alberty
1526	Lizzie Alberty	33	Peter & Elizabeth Meigs
776	Lono Alberty	14	Jim & Patsy Alberty
239	Louisa Alberty	21	Joe & Mag Rogers
58	Malinda Alberty	9	David & Lucy Alberty
587	Martha Alberty	11	Lincoln & Jennie Alberty
58	Mary Alberty	8	David & Lucy Alberty
66	Mintie Alberty	41	Butler & Sarah Vann
1526	Mollie Alberty	6	Andrew & Lizzie Alberty
801	Moses Alberty	31	Jerry & Ruth Alberty
66	Nancy Alberty	3	George & Mintie Alberty
1526	Ned Alberty	6mos	Andrew & Lizzie Alberty
382	Nellie Alberty	36	Jake Crapo & Lucy Holt
776	Nellie Alberty	7	Jim & Patsy Alberty
200	Noah Alberty	33	Jerry & Ruth Alberty
776	Oakley Alberty	9	Jim & Patsy Alberty
776	Patsy Alberty	35	Otter Alberty & Nancy Taylor
382	Pearl Alberty	12	Sam Holt & Nellie Alberty
596	Rose Alberty	46	Isom Nave & Martha Chouteau
153	Ruth Alberty	55	Willis & Lucinda Marcour
645	Ruth Alberty	32	Polly Alberty
801	Ruth Alberty	6	Moses & Amanda Alberty
183	Sally Alberty	40	Arthur Thompson & Jennie McCoy
1266	William Alberty	55	William West & Louisa Alberty
776	Willie Alberty	18	Jim & Patsy Alberty
347	James Aldrich	21	Amos & Rachel Aldrich
294	Jesse Aldrich	16	Amos Aldrich & Rachel Ward
294	Lewis Aldrich	15	Amos Aldrich & Rachel Ward
294	William Aldrich	19	Amos Aldrich & Rachel Ward
935	Amy Allen	22	Frank Ross
1177	Anna Allen	23	George & Rose Allen
831	Annie Allen	3	John & Lucy Allen
1179	Clinton Allen	14	George & Rose Allen
1179	Cora Allen	11	George & Rose Allen
163	Jane Allen	60	Hard & Fannie Vann

5

1179	Lincoln Allen	14	George & Rose Allen
831	Lucy Allen	21	Robert & Annica Foster
831	Robert Allen	5mos	John & Lucy Allen
1179	Rose Allen	49	William & Judy Ross
1178	William Allen	25	George & Rose Allen
293	Amos Alrid	23	Amos & Rachel Aldrich
293	Anne Alrid	1mo	Amos & Mary Alrid
536	Emma Alwell	25	George Davis & Mary Mackey
536	Fay Alwell	16mos	William & Emma Alwell
536	Ruth Alwell	5mos	William & Emma Alwell
536	Waldo Alwell	4	William & Emma Alwell
1139	Angeline Anderson	31	Isaac Colbert & Sallie Mathis
765	Mary Anderson	6wks	Jesse & Sarah Anderson
765	Sarah Anderson	20	Jerry & Ruth Alberty
957	Thomas Anderson	9	George Ross & Jane Anderson
728	Lulu Armstrong	21	Lewis & Ebey Lynch
438	Benson Arnsby	8mos	Lewis & Julia Arnsby
438	Lewis Arnsby	27	Henry Arnsby & Lucinda Riley
715	Cornelius Austin	32	Thomas Austin & Eliza Fountain
538	Elizabeth Austin	12	Steven & Emma Austin
538	Frank Austin	13	Steven & Emma Austin
538	Hannibal Austin	18	Steven & Emma Austin
538	Lula Austin	15	Steven & Emma Austin
715	Mary Austin	22	Nelson & Rose Moore
538	Robert Austin	19	Steven & Emma Austin
414	Melinda Baker	25	Pompey & Sarah Thompson
599	Sallie Baker	29	William Baker & Patsie Nivens
414	Willie Baker	4mos	Nathaniel & Melinda Baker
12	Thomas Baker	7	Nathaniel Baker & Mandy Harris
1240	Anderson Baldridge	29	John & Annie Baldridge
825	Charles Baldridge	10	Jack & Nancy Baldridge
1237	Charley Baldridge	10mos	William Thomas & Rose Baldridge
1237	Chudie Baldridge	8	William Thomas & Rose Baldridge
1241	Columbus Baldridge	27	John & Annie Baldridge
825	Dick Baldridge	14	Jack & Nancy Baldridge
299	Ellen Baldridge	20	Wheat Baldridge & Sallie
1241	Inola Baldridge	5	Columbus & Addie Baldridge
1237	Izetta Baldridge	17	Charley Ebb & Rose Baldridge
825	Jack Baldridge	46	Talawka Baldridge & Lettie Vann
1239	Jessie Baldridge	4	John Jr. & Bertha Baldridge

1238	John Baldridge	71	Silva Baldridge
825	John Baldridge	12	Jack & Nancy Baldridge
1239	John Jr. Baldridge	31	John & Annie Baldridge
825	Minnie Baldridge	16	Jack & Nancy Baldridge
1237	Parthena Baldridge	14	Charley Ebb & Rose Baldridge
825	Phoebe Baldridge	8	Jack & Nancy Baldridge
1237	Rose Baldridge	35	John & Annie Baldridge
1238	Russell Baldridge	18	John & Eliza Baldridge
825	Solomon Baldridge	6	Jack & Nancy Baldridge
299	Wheat Baldridge	67	Jack Hicks & Dinah Jack
1237	William Baldridge	11	William Thomas & Rose Baldridge
1345	Anna Ballard	15	John & Jennie Ballard
1345	Jeff Ballard	18	John & Jennie Ballard
1345	Jennie Ballard	42	Martha Alberty
1345	Malcolm Ballard	20	John & Jennie Ballard
1345	Spivey Ballard	16	John & Jennie Ballard
307	Louis Barden	15	Oscar Barden & Ibby McClure
307	Luny Barden	13	Pscar Barden & Ibby McClure
307	Oscar Barden	10	Oscar Barden & Ibby McClure
372	Billie Barker	23	Henry & Cynthia Barker
954	Clarence Barker	1wk	William & Susie Barker
954	Earnest Barker	1	William & Susie Barker
233	Harrison Barker	20	Henry Barker & Cynthia Blackwell
233	Henrietta Barker	9	Henry Barker & Cynthia Blackwell
233	Reedy Barker	15	Henry Barker & Cynthia Blackwell
954	Susie Barker	26	Jim & Siney Thomas
954	William Jr Barker	6	William & Susie Barker
789	Mintie Barlow	58	Andrew & Eliza Johnson
1410	Clara Barnes	27	Jane Claggett
1410	Jane Barnes	4	John & Clara Barnes
1385	Jennie Barnes	4	Robert & Sarah Barnes
1329	Lizzie Barnes	36	
345	McKinley Barnes	7mos	Joshua & Pollie Barnes
1385	Nola Barnes	9mos	Robert & Sarah Barnes
345	Pollie Barnes	19	Haywood & Savina Youngblood
1410	Precilla Barnes	5mos	John & Clara Barnes
1385	Robert Barnes	10days	Robert & Sarah Barnes
1385	Samuel Barnes	2	Robert & Sarah Barnes
1385	Sarah Barnes	30	Samuel & Nancy Starr
1410	William Barnes	16mos	John & Clara Barnes

653	Catch Barnett	6mos	Catch & Mary Barnett
653	Emma Barnett	3	Catch & Mary Barnett
1588	Jesse Barnett	6	Joe Barnett & Maud Riley
653	Joseph Barnett	10	Catch & Mary Barnett
653	Leroy Barnett	4	Catch & Mary Barnett
653	Mary Barnett	30	Eli & Linda Keys
653	Monday Barnett	9	Catch & Mary Barnett
653	Susie Barnett	4	Catch & Mary Barnett
725	Alexander Bean	12	Joseph & Amy Bean
1454	Alsea Bean	44	Reuben & Jennie Downing
361	Amanda Bean	12	Henry & Frances Bean
725	Amy Bean	45	Fred & Juno Martin
361	Anderson Bean	17	Henry & Frances Bean
1424	Andrew Bean	37	John & Clarinda Bean
1380	Arthur Bean	20	Tobias Bean
1420	Arthur Bean	58	Sandy & Rachel Bean
361	Bertha Bean	8	Henry & Frances Bean
55	Charlotte Bean	13	Anderson & Sarah Bean
351	Clara Bean	1	Patum & Eartha Bean
736	Clifton Bean	4	Lewis & Sarah Bean
1308	Debbie Bean	18	Dennis Bean & Mary Howell
579	Dennis Bean	42	
465	Dock Bean	26	Anderson & Sarah Bean
1454	Dovie Bean	17	Henry & Alsea Bean
351	Eartha Bean	24	James & Clara Smith
1454	Effie Bean	15	Henry & Alsea Bean
774	Eliza Bean	23	Lander & Ellis Bean
1589	Ellen Bean	23	Jess Vann & Emma Purtle
1301	Emma Bean	10	Henry Bean & Harriett Tucker
351	Emma Bean	4mos	Patum & Eartha Bean
1454	Ernest Bean	9	Henry & Alsea Bean
719	Ethel Bean	9	Joseph & Hattie Bean
725	Evylon Bean	2	Joseph & Amy Bean
361	Frances Bean	49	Simon & Sarah Sanders
736	Frank Bean	6mos	Lewis & Sarah Bean
897	George Bean	13	Jacob & Sallie Bean
820	Harvey Bean	1	Andrew & Malinda Bean
719	Hattie Bean	29	Dan & Susie Tucker
1301	Henrietta Bean	6	Henry Bean & Harriett Tucker
1397	Henry Bean	49	Nathan & Annie Bean

790	Ida Bean	35	Wilson & Patsy Martin
351	Ira Bean	3mos	Patum & Eartha Bean
719	Isaac Bean	12	Joseph & Hattie Bean
736	James Bean	7	Lewis & Sarah Bean
286	John Bean	7	Joe & Louisa Bean
799	John Bean	25	Jacob & Mahala Bean
719	Joseph Bean	30	Jake & Mahala Bean
1421	Joseph Bean	54	Sandy & Rachel Bean
744	Joshua Bean	29	Joe & Patsy Bean
1193	Leander Bean	51	Jack & Mary Bean
736	Lewis Bean	29	Jake & Mahala Bean
747	Lillie Bean	16	Arthur & Lucinda Bean
1424	Lottie Bean	18	John & Clarinda Bean
351	Louie Bean	3	Patum & Eartha Bean
286	Louisa Bean	40	Lewis Coody & Jeuwel Mackey
747	Lucinda Bean	50	Rufus & Lucy Vann
1501	Lucy Bean	23	George & Bettie Bean
286	Malinda Bean	17	Joe & Louisa Bean
820	Malinda Bean	26	George & Rachel Johnson
1502	Mary Bean	27	George & Bettie Bean
1454	Mary Bean	5	Henry & Alsea Bean
284	Minnie Bean	22	Joe & Louisa Bean
286	Murphy Bean	13	Joe & Louisa Bean
351	Patum Bean	26	Joe & Louisa Bean
55	Peggie Bean	11	Anderson & Sarah Bean
755	Phyllis Bean	46	Rufus & Lucy Vann
1424	Rector Bean	14	John & Clarinda Bean
725	Rosella Bean	14	Joseph & Amy Bean
1280	Ruby Bean	8	Rufus Bean & Bessie Chapman
1502	Samuel Bean	6	Fred LaFlore & Mary Bean
1424	Sandy Bean	20	John & Clarinda Bean
755	Sephenia Bean	4	Lander & Phyllis Bean
736	Sevier Bean	9mos	Lewis & Sarah Bean
725	Susan Bean	16	Joseph & Amy Bean
729	Thomas Bean	21	Jake & Mahala Bean
286	Thomas Bean	16	Joe & Louisa Bean
1380	Tobias Bean	63	Sandy & Rachel Bean
1454	Viola Bean	2	Henry & Alsea Bean
201	Walter Bean	21	Anderson & Sarah Bean
55	William Bean	14	Anderson & Sarah Bean

464	William Bean	21	Henry & Frances Bean
725	William Bean	8	Joseph & Amy Bean
755	William Bean	7	Lander & Phyllis Bean
1502	William Bean	11	Fred LaFlore & Mary Bean
346	Addie Beck	22	Thomas & Narcissa Cates
295	Amanda Beck	11	Dennis Beck & Eliza Sheppard
1382	Benjamin Beck	58	George & Sarah Grumgould
1407	Benjamin Beck	26	Maryland & Ibbie Beck
1399	Cora Beck	3mos	Nelson & Mina Beck
1404	Dallas Beck	22	Maryland & Ibbie Beck
1399	Dempsey Beck	9	Nelson & Mina Beck
930	Eliza Beck	19	Sam Whitmire & Ann Sanders
1399	Fanny Beck	20	Nelson & Mina Beck
1399	Florence Beck	12	Nelson & Mina Beck
346	Gertie Beck	18mos	Jim & Addie Beck
1406	Harvey Beck	10	Maryland & Mary Beck
1399	Hattie Beck	17	Nelson & Mina Beck
1398	Ida Beck	21	Nelson & Mina Beck
1406	Ida Beck	12	Maryland & Mary Beck
1399	James Beck	19	Nelson & Mina Beck
402	Jane Beck	25	James & Sarina Parris
363	Jennie Beck	60	Thomas & Sarah Duncan
346	Jim Beck	29	James & Jennie Beck
1382	John Beck	15	Benj & Bettie Beck
402	Joseph Beck	2	William & Jane Beck
1382	Josephine Beck	18	Benj & Bettie Beck
1399	Lewis Beck	3	Nelson & Mina Beck
1525	Luguittie Beck	14	Samuel & Mary Beck
833	Mary Beck	38	Andy & Millie Frye
1406	Maryland Beck	58	Jim & Lottie Beck
929	Minnie Beck	30	Campbell Taylor & Ann Sanders
257	Nathan Beck	25	James Hill & Lucy Beck
1100	Nelson Beck	45	James & Lottie Beck
1399	Nelson Jr. Beck	10	Nelson & Mina Beck
402	Sadie Beck	4	William & Jane Beck
1525	Samuel Beck	52	Jim & Lottie Beck
1399	Viola Beck	4	Nelson & Mina Beck
402	William Beck	29	Pack Hill & Lucy Beck
1337	Christy Beeson	2	Jesse & Mary Beeson
1337	Clifton Beeson	5	Jesse & Mary Beeson

10

1551	Malinda Beeson	24	William & Charlotte Tucker
1337	Mary Beeson	23	Jeff Rowe
1337	Mercy Beeson	4	Jesse & Mary Beeson
1335	Roxie Beeson	3	William Beeson & Lena Ward
1337	Sanford Beeson	7	Jesse & Mary Beeson
961	Susan Beeson	27	Mart & Bettie Whitmire
332	Ora Bell	1	Will Bell & Sarah Penn
418	Annie Benge	18	Isaac & Jennie Drew
430	Charles Benge	26	Isaac & Jennie Benge
418	Emma Benge	8	Isaac & Jennie Drew
430	Henrietta Benge	1	Charles & Mary Benge
418	Isaac Benge	51	Maximan & Darkey Benge
418	James Benge	12	Isaac & Jennie Drew
418	Jennie Benge	44	Poller & Katie Drew
418	Katie Benge	15	Isaac & Jennie Drew
418	Roger Benge	3	Isaac & Jennie Drew
642	Samuel Benge	8	Samuel Benge & Alice Walker
291	Will Benge	25	Ike Benge & Fannie Riley
315	Aaron Benton	17	Thomas & Amanda Benton
315	Amanda Benton	60	Jack & Rosie Campbell
316	Claude Benton	6	William Benton & Nealy Hill
315	Isaiah Benton	20	Thomas & Amanda Benton
348	James Benton	19	Thomas Benton & Tabby Deberry
348	Thomas Benton	12	Thomas Benton & Tabby Deberry
260	Viola Benton	6	George Bell & Rosetta Green
316	William Benton	24	Thomas & Amanda Benton
496	Mary Berlone	15	Joshua Caldwell & Nancy Logan
145	Charles Berry	25	Con Berry & Jane Mackey
1097	Arthur Bird	10	Levi & Sophia Bird
1097	Benjamin Bird	12	Levi & Sophia Bird
1097	Ella Bird	16	Levi & Sophia Bird
1097	George Bird	14	Levi & Sophia Bird
1098	Henry Bird	22	Levi & Sophia Bird
1097	Jesse Bird	19	Levi & Sophia Bird
841	Joanna Bird	38	Frances Patterson
1453	Bessie Birdsong	18	Dempsey Beck & Liza Elsey
419	Stephen Blackhawk	43	Blackhawk & Betsy Blackhawk
233	Cynthia Blackwell	40	Jeter & Frances Thompson
721	Squire Blair	75	Janie Blair
48	Sallie Blake	9	Charlie Blake & Nancy Tyner

678	Belle Blunt	14	George Blunt & Betsy McConnell
1113	Ella Blunt	17	Jackson Blunt & Eliza Thompson
678	Maude Blunt	16	George Blunt & Betsy McConnell
730	Monroe Blythe	50	Ben & Jemima Blythe
1256	Mary Boone	40	George Benge & Lydia Coody
1089	Alexander Boudinot	50	
1331	Alex Jr Boudinot	1	Alex & Mariah Boudinot
664	Jennie Boudinot	61	Rollie Hensley & Mamie Vann
1541	Mariah Boudinot	24	Cornelius & Celia Bacon
622	Eliza Bolin	21	John & Martha Irons
622	Harrison Bolin	3wks	Bud & Eliza Bolin
622	Klu Bolin	2	Bud & Eliza Bolin
559	Luther Bolin	5mos	Taylor Bolin & Lou Keys
1055	Susan Bowles	55	Gilbert & Jane Vann
1444	Doda Bowlin	8	John & Elizabeth Bowlin
1444	Elizabeth Bowlin	38	Amos & Georganna Thornton
1444	Eunice Bowlin	12	John & Elizabeth Bowlin
1444	Helen Bowlin	10	John & Elizabeth Bowlin
1444	Henrietta Bowlin	18	John & Elizabeth Bowlin
1444	Leonard Bowlin	3	John & Elizabeth Bowlin
1444	Sophia Bowlin	3mos	John & Elizabeth Bowlin
1444	William Bowlin	15	John & Elizabeth Bowlin
1473	Polly Boyd	46	Jake Morgan & Peggie Alberty
1013	Deatrus Bradford	7	Thomas & Fannie Bradford
1013	Fannie Bradford	37	Robert & Malissa Foster
1013	Frances Bradford	5	Thomas & Fannie Bradford
1013	Jennetta Bradford	11	Thomas & Fannie Bradford
1013	Lula Bradford	11mos	Thomas & Fannie Bradford
1013	Malissa Bradford	9	Thomas & Fannie Bradford
1013	Tessie Bradford	13	Thomas & Fannie Bradford
1013	Tola Bradford	2	Thomas & Fannie Bradford
188	Barney Brady	71	Sookie Griggs
569	Arena Brannon	7mos	Edgar & Henrietta Brannon
569	Henrietta Brannon	19	Isaac & Elmira Crossland
569	Mattie Brannon	1mo	Edgar & Henrietta Brannon
569	Ophelia Brannon	2	Edgar & Henrietta Brannon
807	Isaac Breakbill	7	John & Sophia Breakbill
807	Louie Breakbill	16	John & Sophia Breakbill
807	Mary Breakbill	3	John & Sophia Breakbill
807	Sophia Breakbill	36	Lewis & Chaney Rowe

807	Stella Breakbill	12	John & Sophia Breakbill
691	Charlotte Brewer	35	Bass & Violet Harlin
14	Clara Brewer	10	Robert & Sallie Brewer
14	Dennis Brewer	13	Robert & Sallie Brewer
249	Ezekiel Brewer	80	Adam & Fannie Brewer
14	Ezekiel Brewer	15	Robert & Sallie Brewer
425	Jackson Brewer	24	Kate Irons
249	Kemp Brewer	16	Ezekiel & Louisa Brewer
249	Louisa Brewer	54	Kemp Shipley
14	Robert Brewer	45	Russell Vann & Alsie Brewer
691	Rose Brewer	1wk	Charlotte Brewer
14	Sallie Brewer	35	Eli Laury & Millie
179	Samuel Brewer	30	Zeke & Louisa Brewer
501	Seenie Brewer	60	Jack Gilbert & Julia Carter
1077	Ada Brown	4	Anderson & Rebecca Brown
313	Alex Brown	13	Sam & Jennie Brown
1038	Amanda Brown	23	York & Frances Patterson
313	Amelia Brown	19mos	Sam & Jennie Brown
999	Anderson Brown	30	Jesse & Lucinda Brown
339	Anna Brown	26	Jack & Katie Brown
856	Annie Brown	7	Samuel & Ellen Brown
993	Aseney Brown	26	Jack Bean & Nancy Bryant
1012	Bettie Brown	30	Charles Taylor & Amanda Melton
1038	Beulah Brown	1	John & Amanda Brown
337	Birt Brown	2	William & Mary Brown
364	Charles Brown	20	Joe & Josephine Brown
313	Charles Brown	17	Sam & Jennie Brown
856	Charlie Brown	1	Samuel & Ellen Brown
214	Clarence Brown	6	William Brown & Pearl Starr
85	Clark Brown	17	Joe Brown & Sarah Thompson
1015	Clyde Brown	12	Mr. Rollocks & Sarah Brown
1038	Cora Brown	8mos	John & Amanda Brown
1077	Cora Brown	3	Anderson & Rebecca Brown
383	David Brown	22	Samuel & Jennie Brown
605	Dee Brown	2	Joseph & Lulu Brown
856	Dunk Brown	3	Samuel & Ellen Brown
1298	Edward Brown	30	William Brown & Jane Webb
526	Eli Brown	13	Henry & Jane Brown
541	Elizabeth Brown	3	David & Savilla Brown
856	Ellen Brown	28	Dunk & Chick Vann

526	Emma Brown	20	Henry & Jane Brown
337	Emma Brown	4mos	William & Mary Brown
688	Enious Brown	23	Sam & Jennie Brown
541	Ethel Brown	1	David & Savilla Brown
1019	Ethel Brown	17	George & Mahala Brown
383	Florence Brown	20	Elijah & Lydia Coody
845	Floyd Brown	7mos	John & Minnie Brown
526	George Brown	18	Henry & Jane Brown
1027	George Brown	10	Silas & Jane Brown
489	Gertrude Brown	11	Moses Brown & Georgia Foreman
313	Gracie Brown	8	Sam & Jennie Brown
526	Henry Brown	46	Peter & Fannie Loury
314	Henry Brown	2	James & Julia Brown
1298	Henry Brown	4	Edward & Mamie Brown
222	Herbert Brown	22	Joe & Josie Brown
1481	Howard Brown	1	William & Lettie Brown
1023	Israel Brown	33	Isaac & Lila Brown
314	James Brown	3	James & Julia Brown
526	Jane Brown	49	George & Mary Drew
314	Jeff Brown	5	James & Julia Brown
313	Jennie Brown	47	George & Gracie Crossland
1300	Jennie Brown	4	Charlie & Nellie Brown
1255	Jesse Brown	27	William & Jane Brown
314	Jesse Brown	4	James & Julia Brown
1010	Jesse Jr Brown	28	Jesse & Lucinda Brown
610	Joe Brown	5	Rufus Brown & Rachel Winters
605	Joe Brown	7wks	Joseph & Lulu Brown
314	John Brown	3mos	James & Julia Brown
426	John Brown	28	Jack & Katie Brown
988	John Brown	12	Jesse & Lucinda Brown
1448	Jonas Brown	61	Sarah Brown
605	Joseph Brown	31	Jack & Katie Brown
314	Julia Brown	24	George & Gracie Crossland
313	Julia Brown	15	Sam & Jennie Brown
427	Julie Brown	2mos	Richard & Clarie Brown
80	Julia Brown	3	Charlie Brown & Carrie Foster
325	Katie Brown	47	Joe Wolf & Fannie Fields
1298	Laura Brown	3mos	Edward & Mamie Brown
1481	Lettie Brown	33	Charles & Susan Pee
313	Lewis Brown	20	Sam & Jennie Brown

526	Lillie Brown	16	Henry & Jane Brown
553	Lillie Brown	17	Hugh Rogers & Sarah Nave
1015	Luther Brown	7	Mr. Rollocks & Sarah Brown
383	Lydie Brown	1	David & Florence Brown
1019	Mahala Brown	58	Charles & Mary Martin
489	Marcus Brown	5	Bud Trainor & Georgia Foreman
553	Marie Brown	2mos	Richard & Lillie Brown
383	Mary Brown	2mos	David & Florence Brown
33	Maud Brown	7	Mose Brown & Georgia Foreman
856	May Brown	5	Samuel & Ellen Brown
1300	Michael Brown	9mos	Charlie & Nellie Brown
605	Milton Brown	7mos	Joseph & Lulu Brown
845	Minnie Brown	18	Samuel Landrum & Sarah Norris
1038	Minnie Brown	3	John & Amanda Brown
313	Mollie Brown	11	Sam & Jennie Brown
1300	Moses Brown	5	Charlie & Nellie Brown
1300	Nellie Brown	26	Aaron & Queen Martin
1028	Pearl Brown	23	George & Mahala Brown
421	Peggie Brown	14	Joseph & Josephine Brown
993	Phillip Brown	4	Washington & Aseney Brown
989	Polly Brown	23	Jesse & Lucinda Brown
1077	Rebecca Brown	26	William & Mariah Musgrove
689	Rhoda Brown	49	Grace Grayson
993	Rhoda Brown	6	Washington & Aseney Brown
427	Richard Brown	21	Jack & Katie Brown
993	Richard Brown	8	Washington & Aseney Brown
1300	Roxie Brown	8	Charlie & Nellie Brown
225	Sallie Brown	35	Charles Chambers & Sophia Smith
528	Samuel Brown	26	Henry & Jane Brown
313	Sarah Brown	3	Sam & Jennie Brown
1015	Sarah Brown	35	Jesse & Lucinda Brown
541	Savilla Brown	26	George & Rose Rogers
1027	Silas Brown	30	George & Mahala Brown
1298	Stella Brown	2	Edward & Mamie Brown
845	Sylvester Brown	3mos	John & Minnie Brown
1027	Viola Brown	4	Silas & Jane Brown
314	William Brown	4mos	James & Julia Brown
337	William Brown	31	Henry & Jane Brown
992	William Brown	25	Jesse & Lucinda Brown
1300	William Brown	2	Charlie & Nellie Brown

1027	Willie Brown	13	Silas & Jane Brown
369	Dora Bruce	21	Lewis Drew & Nancy Cheeck
369	Ella Bruce	2	George & Dora Bruce
232	Annie Bruner	6	Joe & Emma Bruner
232	Emma Bruner	40	Ninna Thompson & Hannah Brown
232	Isabel Bruner	13	Joe & Emma Bruner
1534	Ella Bryant	15	Frank & Martha Whitmire
1185	Malinda Bryant	15	Israel & Mandy Bryant
1185	Mandy Bryant	35	Jess Rogers & Ruth Tucker
1185	Oscar Bryant	9	Israel & Mandy Bryant
842	Rosa Bryant	25	George & Nancy Bryant
764	Sophia Bryant	45	William Vann & Catherine McNair
59	Eliza Buckler	26	Henry Johnson & Lottie Ross
1247	Horace Buckner	20	John & Lizzie Buckner
1247	Lizzie Buckner	37	Ott Alberty & Nancy Taylor
1247	Walter Buckner	13	John & Lizzie Buckner
1247	Willie Buckner	15	John & Lizzie Buckner
823	Albert Buffington	3	Ernest & Saphronia Buffington
759	Aldrick Buffington	17mos	John & Mary Buffington
259	Ambrose Buffington	46	Harry Buffington
137	Ambrose Buffington	25	Josh Lowrey & Margaret Parrish
696	Augustus Buffington	70	Lucy Buffington
823	Augustus Buffington	6mos	Ernest & Saphronia Buffington
759	Bert Buffington	6	John & Mary Buffington
759	Clarence Buffington	12	John & Mary Buffington
9	Daisy Buffington	4mos	Henry & Mary Buffington
258	Dorcas Buffington	76	Chas Foreman & Patsy Busheyhead
1215	Ella Buffington	17	Henry Buffington & Matt Ridge
823	Ernest Buffington	22	Gus & Mary Buffington
759	Frank Buffington	14	John & Mary Buffington
539	Harry Buffington	36	Ambrose & Nancy Buffington
9	Henry Buffington	35	Henry & Paulina Buffington
759	Jesse Buffington	10	John & Mary Buffington
759	John Buffington	32	Gus & Mary Buffington
759	Mary Buffington	34	John & Maria Chase
696	Mary Buffington	65	
539	Nancy Buffington	36	George & Rose Rogers
1087	Ruth Buffington	2	Reuben & Lizzie Buffington
823	Saphronia Buffington	21	Andy & Millie Frye
759	Stella Buffington	8	John & Mary Buffington

759	Walter Buffington	13	John & Mary Buffington
99	William Buffington	40	Gus Buffington & Cinda Beck
722	Jennie Buford	31	Monroe & Annie Hardiman
722	Johnson Buford	14	Philip & Jennie Buford
722	Walter Buford	16	Philip & Jennie Buford
677	Annie Burgess	13	William Burgess & Sarah Roland
109	Carrie Burgess	10	John & Jennie Burgess
677	Charley Burgess	19	William Burgess & Sarah Roland
109	Cora Burgess	8	John & Jennie Burgess
109	Elizabeth Burgess	13	John & Jennie Burgess
677	Gilbert Burgess	10	William Burgess & Sarah Roland
109	Jennie Burgess	44	Fred & Caroline Davies
109	John Burgess	42	Burgess Foreman&Sopha Schrimsher
109	Johnnie Burgess	4	John & Jennie Burgess
677	Lola Burgess	16	William Burgess & Sarah Roland
109	Mattie Burgess	17	John & Jennie Burgess
109	Ola Burgess	15	John & Jennie Burgess
1074	Cora Burney	10mos	James & Mariah Burney
1074	James Burney	34	Bob Burney & Lucinda French
1533	Louisa Burney	11	James Burney & Sarah Allen
1074	Mariah Burney	22	William & Sarah Burgess
1074	Willie Burney	3	James & Mariah Burney
276	Kamita Burton	37	Rosewell & Mary Mackey
276	Nancy Burton	12	Samuel & Kamita Burton
16	Alice Butler	14	Samuel & Cynthia Butler
16	Annie Butler	8	Samuel & Cynthia Butler
16	Cynthia Butler	40	John Hollan
16	Elizabeth Butler	17	Samuel & Cynthia Butler
16	Ella Butler	19	Samuel & Cynthia Butler
669	Jerry Butler	43	Butler & Creecie McNair
864	John Butler	23	Samuel & Cynthia Butler
16	Joseph Butler	16	Samuel & Cynthia Butler
16	Lillie Butler	11	Samuel & Cynthia Butler
494	Lone Butler	12	Maxey Butler & Peggie Malven
71	Mary Butler	41	Caleb & Mariah Vann
494	Sam Butler	8	Maxey Butler & Peggie Malven
16	Samuel Butler	44	Butler & Patsy McNair
1394	Earnest Bursby	7	Elijah & Eliza Bursby
1394	Eliza Bursby	28	Dick & Willie Chambers
1394	Lela Bursby	11	Elijah & Eliza Bursby

1394	Pleas Bursby	9	Elijah & Eliza Bursby
483	Amanda Byrd	18	Alec Bean & Susie Byrd
483	Castella Byrd	5mos	Henry & Susie Byrd
483	Emma Byrd	10	Henry & Susie Byrd
483	Henrietta Byrd	19	Henry Byrd & Mary Rowe
483	John Byrd	16	Alec Bean & Susie Byrd
483	Lawrence Byrd	3	Henry & Susie Byrd
483	Malissa Byrd	12	Henry & Susie Byrd
483	Rose Byrd	14	Henry & Susie Byrd
483	Susie Byrd	7	Henry & Susie Byrd
483	Susie Byrd	35	Phelan Evans & Mary Walker
1029	Annie Cabbell	29	George & Mahala Brown
1029	Earnest Cabbell	2mos	Frank & Annie Cabbell
1029	Sophronia Cabbell	2	Frank & Annie Cabbell
1518	Henry Caesar	7	Ranson Caesar & Sarah Charman
1270	Mary Caesar	29	Hannah Brown
493	Corrine Caldwell	10	Joshua Caldwell & Nancy Logan
493	Sallie Caldwell	8	Joshua Caldwell & Nancy Logan
546	Earl Calvin	5	Gus & Sarah Calvin
546	Lillian Calvin	2	Gus & Sarah Calvin
546	Pearl Calvin	3	Gus & Sarah Calvin
546	Sarah Calvin	23	Henry & Frances Bean
846	Albert Campbell	15	Charles & Emma Campbell
317	Alena Campbell	21	Thomas & Amanda Benton
663	Alfred Campbell	15	Joe Campbell & Lizzie Wilson
317	Amanda Campbell	4	Thomas & Alena Campbell
20	Charles Jr. Campbell	23	Charlie & Emma Campbell
846	Charles Campbell	60	Dinah Campbell
966	Clara Campbell	3	Henry Campbell & Julia Vann
317	Dora Campbell	17mos	Thomas & Alena Campbell
772	Edna Campbell	53	Lewis & Chaney Rowe
837	Edward Campbell	50	Jack & Rose Campbell
317	Elijah Campbell	2mos	Thomas & Alena Campbell
846	Emma Campbell	51	Tobe & Mary Looney
1107	George Campbell	29	Charley & Emma Campbell
827	Grace Campbell	4	James & Mary Campbell
966	Hannah Campbell	5	Henry Campbell & Julia Vann
353	Jackson Campbell	8mos	Joseph & Mary Campbell
827	James Campbell	26	Charley & Emma Campbell
966	Jessie Campbell	2mos	Henry Campbell & Julia Vann

846	John Campbell	19	Charles & Emma Campbell
353	Joseph Campbell	35	Jack & Rose Campbell
20	Lillie Campbell	4mos	Charles Campbell Jr.
128	Lottie Campbell	60	Edmund Ross & Charlotte Campbell
837	Martha Campbell	40	William & Matilda Love
649	Mary Campbell	45	Fannie Loury
846	Mary Campbell	11	Charles & Emma Campbell
570	Octavia Campbell	13	B.C. & Susie Campbell
570	Ora Campbell	10	B.C. & Susie Campbell
570	Osa Campbell	11	B.C. & Susie Campbell
570	Peggie Campbell	16	B.C. & Susie Campbell
570	Susie Campbell	39	Nathan & Rosanna Melton
827	Viva Campbell	5	James & Mary Campbell
846	Walter Campbell	25	Charles & Emma Campbell
1350	Annie Canard	16	Andrew Rider&Elizabeth Williamson
1373	Eliza Carbin	26	Robert Foster & Bettie Robinson
1373	Hattie Carbin	5	Sanford & Eliza Carbin
1373	Henry Carbin	3	Sanford & Eliza Carbin
1373	Ruby Carbin	4wks	Sanford & Eliza Carbin
359	Ellis Carr	13	Jack Carr & Emma Price
359	Milton Carr	11	Jack Carr & Emma Price
1090	Laura Carson	20	Eli & Patience Vann
1186	Louvena Carson	8mos	Thomas & Sallie Carson
1401	Mary Carson	41	Mose Harlin & Katie Red
1090	Nona Carson	5mos	Jason & Laura Carson
1186	Sallie Carson	19	Israel & Mandy Bryant
556	Andy Carter	31	Luke & Maria Carter
556	Andy Carter	3	Andy & Florence Carter
194	Angeline Carter	21	Bart Wilson & Frances McNack
659	Arch Sr. Carter	56	Mose & Amy Starr
659	Arch Jr. Carter	16	Arch Sr. & Sarah Carter
194	Cornelius Carter	3	Joseph & Angeline Carter
557	David Carter	19	Luke & Maria Carter
556	Elnora Carter	5	Andy & Florence Carter
556	Florence Carter	26	Los Catis & Narcissa Dalton
194	Frances Carter	4mos	Joseph & Angeline Carter
452	Frances Carter	1	Mose & Oma Carter
558	Fred Carter	7	Rachel Carter
1264	Henry Carter	23	John Carter & Peggie Francis
1154	Isabelle Carter	32	Nelson Carter

452	Jennetta Carter	3	Mose & Oma Carter
452	Jesse Carter	4	Mose & Oma Carter
558	John Carter	11	Rachel Carter
659	Johnson Carter	20	Arch & Sarah Carter
194	Joseph Carter	28	Arch & Sarah Carter
194	Lila Carter	5	Joseph & Angeline Carter
601	Luke Carter	49	Richard Carter & Mary Lipe
1302	Lydia Carter	48	Edmond Vann & Mary Stover
557	Mary Carter	16	Luke & Maria Carter
659	Matilda Carter	17	Arch & Sarah Carter
611	Minnie Carter	21	Arch & Sarah Carter
452	Mose Carter	31	Arch & Sarah Carter
1152	Nelson Carter	55	Jennie McCoy
452	Oma Carter	22	Bart & Lydia Thompson
452	Peggie Carter	7	Mose & Oma Carter
659	Sarah Carter	54	Anderson & Lydia Lowrey
556	William Carter	1	Andy & Florence Carter
110	Clarence Cates	8	Thomas Cates & Narcissa Dalton
110	Dora Cates	12	Thomas Cates & Narcissa Dalton
110	Ernest Cates	14	Thomas Cates & Narcissa Dalton
110	Henrietta Cates	16	Thomas Cates & Narcissa Dalton
110	Lucy Cates	18	Thomas Cates & Narcissa Dalton
110	Maud Cates	10	Thomas Cates & Narcissa Dalton
221	Thomas Cates	21	Thomas & Narcissa Cates
349	Caroline Charles	80	
938	Caroline Chambers	49	Anna Watie
1017	Charles Chambers	70	John & Hester Chambers
1175	Charles Chambers	2	Ed & Mary Chambers
1323	Dick Chambers	35	Charles Chambers & Sidney West
1005	Dora Chambers	31	Robert & Melissa Foster
933	Ed Chambers	22	Charles & Caroline Chambers
1209	Ella Chambers	23	Al & Millie Smith
1096	Elnora Chambers	3	Emanuel & Samatha Chambers
1096	Emanuel Chambers	21	Charles & Caroline Chambers
1036	Frances Chambers	3	Grant Chambers & Julia Dickson
1128	Grant Chambers	34	John & Jane Chambers
1426	Henry Chambers	34	Charles Chambers & Katie Blackwell
1471	Jack Chambers	54	Nicey Chambers
934	Leroy Chambers	1	Matt & Allie Chambers
934	Matt Chambers	25	Charles & Caroline Chambers

933	Meriland Chambers	9mos	Ed & Mary Chambers
1005	Minnie Chambers	8	Henry & Dora Chambers
934	Oliver Chambers	5mos	Matt & Allie Chambers
907	William Chambers	3mos	Clora White
189	Anna Chase	22	John & Mariah Chase
550	Arthur Chase	11	John & Ruth Chase
550	Charles Chase	5	John & Ruth Chase
146	Fannie Chase	15	John & Maria Chase
146	Henry Chase	18	John & Maria Chase
146	Maria Chase	51	Jesse & Lydia Lowrey
550	Ruth Chase	26	Joshua & Betsy Sheppard
1518	Jim Chatman	4	Will & Sarah Chatman
1518	Julia Chatman	2	Will & Sarah Charman
1518	Nannie Chatman	10mos	Will & Sarah Chatman
1518	Sarah Chatman	24	Henry Smith & Sidney West
1275	Rocky Childers	30	Isaac James & Nancy Sheppard
512	Greely Choate	16	Edward & Josie Choate
512	Josie Choate	30	Sukey Williams
512	Sherman Choate	18	Edward & Josie Choate
668	Carrie Chouteau	11	William & Rose Chouteau
1253	Cornelius Chouteau	8	John Chouteau & Mary Ross
1137	Eli Chouteau	28	Jesse & Katie Chouteau
668	Ellen Chouteau	15	William Marcum & Rose Chouteau
1135	John Chouteau	50	Jesse & Katie Chouteau
1253	Joshua Chouteau	10	John Chouteau & Mary Ross
1271	Louisa Chouteau	85	Mose Mackey
597	Martha Chouteau	80	Nat & Rose Alberty
668	Rose Chouteau	30	William & Hannah Vann
1271	Samuel Chouteau	55	Tobie & Clara Chouteau
1182	Tobe Chouteau	33	Jesse & Katie Chouteau
668	William Chouteau	30	Jesse & Katie Chouteau
1253	William Chouteau	14	John Chouteau & Mary Ross
1449	Susie Chukelate	102	
1317	Alexander Claggett	6	John & Nancy Claggett
1057	Charles Claggett	8mos	Charles & Ruth Claggett
1317	Elizabeth Claggett	12	John & Nancy Claggett
1317	Isabell Claggett	10	John & Nancy Claggett
1409	Jane Claggett	57	Ben Vann & Mary Taylor
1317	Josie Claggett	3	John & Nancy Claggett
1317	Mariah Claggett	7	John & Nancy Claggett

1057	Millie Claggett	8	Charles & Ruth Claggett
1317	Nancy Claggett	30	Andy & Ibbie Daniels
1317	Nancy Claggett	1	John & Nancy Claggett
1057	Ralph Claggett	3	Charles & Ruth Claggett
1409	Rose Claggett	16	
1057	Ruth Claggett	25	Andy & Millie Frye
1057	Tessie Claggett	7	Charles & Ruth Claggett
1317	Willie Claggett	14	John & Nancy Claggett
1265	Appelina Clark	5	Ben & Rosa Clark
1265	Beatrice Clark	11	Ben & Rosa Clark
1265	Jettie Clark	5	Ben & Rosa Clark
1265	Ocie Clark	8	Ben & Rosa Clark
881	Rachel Clay	17	Buck & Eliza Ledman
379	Anthony Clifton	65	Alex Benge & Maria Bark
1481	Richard Clinch	13	Henry Clinch & Lettie Brown
1223	Sophronia Coats	56	Spence Bell & Patsy Martin
1250	Bunk Coker	55	Ben & Annie Coker
1197	Annie Colbert	5	Henry & Jennie Colbert
1500	Dan Colbert	4mos	John & Maggie Colbert
1197	Elzora Colbert	8	Henry & Jennie Colbert
1197	Jennie Colbert	30	Nelson & Fannie Carter
1197	Louisa Colbert	6	Henry & Jennie Colbert
1500	Maggie Colbert	23	Lone & Cherry Landrum
1197	McKinley Colbert	3	Henry & Jennie Colbert
1198	Rosa Colbert	25	Charles Smith & Winnie Reeves
1197	Kizer Colbert	1	Henry & Jennie Colbert
849	Rosie Coleman	23	Will Davis & Nannie Vann
24	Abraham Collins	18	Reuben & Chaney Collins
344	Blanche Collins	22	Haywood & Savina Youngblood
24	Frank Collins	17	Reuben & Chaney Collins
24	Martha Collins	12	Reuben & Chaney Collins
441	Alex Coody	32	Morris Stidhaw & Lydia Coody
101	Elijah Coody	55	Sharp & Nancy Coody
101	Henry Coody	18	Elijah & Lydia Coody
1002	James Coody	15	Jackson & Josephine Coody
76	Joseph Coody	6	William Coody & Josephine Hall
1002	Josephine Coody	33	Robert & Melissa Foster
441	Katis Coody	25	Daniel & Rose Roach
101	Lydia Coody	57	
1339	Susan Coody	100	

447	William Coody	27	Elijah & Lydia Coody
1279	William Jr. Coody	2mos	William & Jennetta Coody
368	Leon Cooper	24	Lee Cooper
334	William Cooper	29	Lee Cooper & Sarah Ross
726	Eddie Cordrey	14	Rufus & Mary Cordrey
726	Jeffie Cordrey	10	Rufus & Mary Cordrey
726	Rufus Cordrey	41	Tom Cordrey & Jennie Boudinot
726	Toby Cordrey	12	Rufus & Mary Cordrey
297	Addie Cornish	30	Arron & Letha Johnson
230	Bessie Cotton	1	Robert & Cynthia Cotton
230	Cynthia Cotton	26	Jesse Foreman & Julia Crapo
230	Elizabeth Cotton	3	Robert & Cynthia Cotton
230	Jesse Cotton	2	Robert & Cynthia Cotton
230	Killring Cotton	10mos	Robert & Cynthia Cotton
230	Taylor Cotton	5	Robert & Cynthia Cotton
230	Wisdom Cotton	4	Robert & Cynthia Cotton
1047	Annie Cox	3	Willis & Sarah Cox
1047	Dora Cox	8mos	Willis & Sarah Cox
1047	Lizzie Cox	4	Willis & Sarah Cox
1047	Sarah Cox	50	Jack Smith & Lila Brown
223	Daisy Crapo	15	Jacob & Judy Crapo
223	Diley Crapo	8	Jacob & Judy Crapo
223	Jacob Crapo	65	
223	Judy Crapo	49	Rufus Fields & Diley Foreman
542	Addison Cravens	9	Harvey & Lucinda Cravens
542	Harvey Cravens	14mos	Harvey & Lucinda Cravens
542	Lela Cravens	7	Harvey & Lucinda Cravens
542	Lucinda Cravens	35	Jerry & Ellen Foreman
542	Roland Cravens	6	Harvey & Lucinda Cravens
248	Annie Crawford	4	Mark & Lena Crawford
25	Beatrice Crawford	2	Charlie & Janie Sanders
248	David Crawford	7mos	Mark & Lena Crawford
248	Frank Crawford	5	Mark & Lena Crawford
248	Jessie Crawford	12	Mark & Lena Crawford
248	John Crawford	10	Mark & Lena Crawford
248	Lena Crawford	39	Johnson & Lila Vann
248	Thomas Crawford	8	Mark & Lena Crawford
1229	Alice Crippin	16	Benj Lephfew & Eliza Watson
1522	Anthony Crittenden	57	Moses Crittenden & Emily Weaver
1522	John Crittenden	1mo	Anthony & Jane Crittenden

1522	Josie Crittenden	15	Anthony & Jane Crittenden
1522	Lucy Crittenden	9	Anthony & Jane Crittenden
1522	Steve Crittenden	7	Anthony & Jane Crittenden
1522	William Crittenden	12	Anthony & Jane Crittenden
1259	Mary Crittendon	35	Emily Weaver
48	Lydia Crockett	59	Caleb & Sallie Vann
431	Andrew Crossland	9	Lewis Crossland & Sarah Nalls
412	Andy Crossland	75	Isaac & Malinda Jack
575	Elena Crossland	14	Isaac & Elmira Crossland
575	Elmira Crossland	44	Andy Daugherty & Rosanna Melton
431	Fannie Crossland	7	Lewis Crossland & Sarah Nalls
273	George Crossland	69	George Stidman & Nellie Thompson
1267	George Crossland	37	George & Grace Crossland
212	George Crossland	2	Lewis & Sallie Crossland
273	Grace Crossland	51	Lem McDaniel & Sarah Rogers
1145	Henry Crossland	22	George & Gracie Crossland
575	Isaac Crossland	46	Andy & Sarah Crossland
212	John Crossland	13	Lewis Crossland & Sarah Nalls
667	Jonas Crossland	22	George & Grace Crossland
1267	Joseph Crossland	1	George Crossland
575	Leota Crossland	11	Isaac & Elmira Crossland
212	Lewis Crossland	35	George & Gracie Crossland
212	Lila Crossland	5mos	Lewis & Sallie Crossland
575	Lincoln Crossland	9	Isaac & Elmira Crossland
212	Martha Crossland	5	Lewis & Sallie Crossland
575	Rosanna Crossland	15	Isaac & Elmira Crossland
575	Samuel Crossland	17	Isaac & Elmira Crossland
328	Samuel Crossland	38	Andy & Dina Mackey
278	Simon Crossland	24	Eli Crossland & Hannah Wright
212	Willie Crossland	7	Lewis & Sallie Crossland
232	Jane Crossley	17	Sam Crossley & Emma Bruner
229	Frank Crutchfield	10	Will Crutchfield & Alice Smith
1583	Beatrice Curls	5mos	Riley & Nancy Curls
1583	Clarence Curls	1	Riley & Nancy Curls
1583	Edward Curls	7	Riley & Nancy Curls
1583	George Curls	4	Riley & Nancy Curls
1583	James Curls	6	Riley & Nancy Curls
1582	Julius Curls	34	James Curls & Millie McNair
1583	Riley Curls	32	James Curls & Millie McNair
1583	Stephenia Curls	3	Riley & Nancy Curls

1583	Willie Curls	9	Riley & Nancy Curls
1236	Harrison Curry	25	John & Charlotte Curry
1234	Joseph Curry	30	John & Charlotte Curry
1208	Addie Curtis	40	Jack & Susan Benge
1208	Leander Curtis	6	George & Addie Curtis
110	Narcissa Dalton	45	Harry & Darcus Buffington
1020	Alberty Daniels	1mo	Jesse & Hattie Daniels
1321	Charles Daniels	41	Andy & Ibbie Daniels
1429	Enoch Daniels	33	George & Eliza Daniels
1436	Ethel Daniels	11	Thomas Daniels & Celia Kirkpatrick
1419	Frances Daniels	40	Turk Vann & Minta Barlow
1316	Frank Daniels	17	Andrew & Ibbie Daniels
829	Frank Daniels	40	Burl Daniels & Eliza Hilderbrand
1419	George Daniels	40	Toney & Cynthia Daniels
1438	George Daniels		Thomas Daniels & Celia Kirkpatrick
1419	Henry Daniels	11	George Daniels & Sadie Ives
1316	Ibbie Daniels	60	Thomas Ridge & Peggie Vann
1020	Jesse Daniels	24	Louis & Amanda Daniels
1322	Jonas Daniels	24	Andy & Ibbie Daniels
1319	Josephine Daniels	18	Andy & Ibbie Daniels
1429	Laura Daniels	19	Cornelius & Laura Ridge
875	Lewis Daniels	56	James Mackey & Winnie Drew
1320	Lewis Daniels	27	Andy & Ibbie Daniels
1318	Lucinda Daniels	28	Andy & Ibbie Daniels
1429	Marshall Daniels	1mo	Enoch & Laura Daniels
1316	Martha Daniels	12	James & Ellen Daniels
134	Mish Daniels	18	Ran Lovely & Chaney Richardson
134	Nannie Daniels	8mos	Tobe & Mish Daniels
1419	Nathan Daniels	13	George Daniels & Sadie Ives
875	Patsy Daniels	42	Sam & Katie Vann
1429	Ralph Daniels	6mos	Enoch & Laura Daniels
1319	Thomas Daniels	19	Andy & Ibbie Daniels
875	William Daniels	4	Lewis & Patsy Daniels
829	Willie Daniels	18	Frank & Lizzie Daniels
220	Charles Dansby	14	Walter Dansby & Mandy Foreman
326	Walter Dansby	35	Charles & Sukey Dansby
142	Abe Davis	40	Caroline Davis
936	Bertie Davis	16	William & Emma Davis
1199	Carl Davis	3	Joe & Belle Davis
936	Carrie Davis	2	William & Emma Davis

1199	Charles Davis	11days	Joe & Belle Davis
936	Chester Davis	15	William & Emma Davis
1016	Coren Davis	1mo	Herman & Peggy Davis
1199	Dan Davis	8	Joe & Belle Davis
775	Elizabeth Davis	1	Hiram & Mamie Davis
936	Emma Davis	43	Isaac Glass & Betsy Whitmire
142	Fannie Davis	37	Morris & Mary Walker
142	Fannie Davis	10	Abe & Fannie Davis
936	Henry Davis	9	William & Emma Davis
514	Isaac Davis	9	Lee & Eliza Davis
1201	James Davis	21	Joe & Belle Davis
936	Jennette Davis	12	William & Emma Davis
142	Jennie Davis	14	Abe & Fannie Davis
1199	Joe Davis	46	Tom Faught & Betsy Davis
142	John Davis	16	Abe & Fannie Davis
1200	John Davis	24	Joe & Belle Davis
1200	John Jr Davis	13mos	John & Katie Davis
936	Joseph Davis	19	William & Emma Davis
1199	Joseph Davis	10	Joe & Belle Davis
936	Julia Davis	14	William & Emma Davis
143	Julia Davis	46	Bug Denbug & Patsy Goss
1202	Lizzie Davis	20	Joe & Belle Davis
936	Lottie Davis	3mos	William & Emma Davis
947	Lovie Davis	22	Will Davis & Amy Bean
775	Mamie Davis	21	Wash Nave & Betsy Blunt
142	Mary Davis	18	Abe & Fannie Davis
514	Napoleon Davis	7	Lee & Eliza Davis
936	Oscar Davis	7	William & Emma Davis
1016	Peggy Davis	16	Sam Welch & Lucy Hill
343	Phillis Davis	27	Field & Mary Evans
388	Rachel Davis	10mos	John Davis & Florence Thomas
1199	Sadie Davis	18	Joe & Belle Davis
42	Sarah Davis	68	Henry & Rachel Riley
142	Susan Davis	12	Abe & Fannie Davis
1199	Thomas Davis	13	Joe & Belle Davis
936	William Jr Davis	18	William & Emma Davis
1199	Willie Davis	16	Joe & Belle Davis
987	Mary Dawn	68	Katie Vann
1248	Andrew Day	15	William Day & Laura Garlington
1248	Clarence Day	5	William Day & Laura Garlington

1248	Ella Day	11	William Day & Laura Garlington
1248	Lena Day	8	William Day & Laura Garlington
1461	Charley Dean	7	Fred Dean & Rodia Wade
839	Amanda Deckman	24	William & Lutitia Downing
839	Charles Deckman	4	John & Amanda Deckman
81	Fannie Delwood	26	Dred & Caroline Foreman
81	Maggie Delwood	8	Thomas & Fannie Delwood
81	Richard Delwood	3	Thomas & Fannie Delwood
81	Wren Delwood	6mos	Thomas & Fannie Delwood
1367	Patsy Demumber	31	Jake & Sarah Martin
30	Ada Dennis	14	Junius Dennis & Patsy Johnson
958	Annie Dennis	16	Alfred Dennis & Mary Groves
595	Fannie Dennis	2	Jim Dennis & Carrie Thompson
958	James Dennis	17	Alfred Dennis & Mary Groves
958	John Dennis	7	Alfred Dennis & Mary Groves
38	Junius Dennis	28	Junius & Patsy Dennis
595	Rosa Dennis	4	Jim Dennis & Carrie Thompson
1156	Charley Derrick	2	Edward & Josie Derrick
1156	Eddie Derrick	6	Edward & Josie Derrick
1156	Henrietta Derrick	10	Edward & Josie Derrick
1156	Jennie Derrick	14	Edward & Josie Derrick
1156	Josie Derrick	35	Rider & Jennie Sanders
1156	Katie Derrick	12	Edward & Josie Derrick
1131	Lucian Derrick	4	David & Nannie Derrick
1156	Minnie Derrick		Edward & Josie Derrick
1156	Nellie Derrick	16	Edward & Josie Derrick
1156	William Derrick	4	Edward & Josie Derrick
1036	Effie Dickson	6	Albert & Julia Dickson
149	Eustace Dickson	2	George & Mattie Dickson
1036	Julia Dickson	29	York & Frances Patterson
149	Mattie Dickson	24	William & Peggie Hudson
411	William Diges	16	Steward & Rachel Diges
187	Clem Dixon	16mos	Nathaniel & Mary Dixon
814	Letha Dixon	13	Joe & Eliza Dixon
187	Nathaniel Dixon	26	Henderson Dixon&Charlotte Johnson
814	Wiley Dixon	9	Joe & Eliza Dixon
507	Catherine Dotson	8	Mark & Eliza Dotson
507	Creed Dotson	11	Mark & Eliza Dotson
573	Dewey Dotson	2	John & Mary Dotson
507	Eliza Dotson	42	Moses Ross & Pauline Eagle

507	Frances Dotson	1	Mark & Eliza Dotson
573	John Dotson	5	John & Mary Dotson
573	Mary Dotson	23	Nathan & Rosa Melton
573	Nathaniel Dotson	7mos	Nathan & Rosa Melton
507	Nora Dotson	5	Mark & Eliza Dotson
895	Asa Downing	4	William & Lutitia Downing
1257	Cladonia Downing	4	Tom Downing & Mary Kelly
895	Cora Downing	7	William & Lutitia Downing
781	Dorothea Downing	4	James Galbert & Luvinia Downing
780	Emanuel Downing	17	Zebedee & Jennie Downing
824	Georgie Downing	5mos	Alexander Davis & Martha Downing
783	Henry Downing	25	Zebedee & Jennie Downing
1543	Hurbert Downing	6wks	Walter & Rachel Downing
1482	Inez Downing	15mos	John Downing & Mary Lane
780	Jennie Downing	43	Rosa Chism
895	Joel Downing	11	William & Lutitia Downing
895	John Downing	14	William & Lutitia Downing
895	Judie Downing	17	William & Lutitia Downing
1326	Leegustus Downing	3	Johnson & Mary Downing
895	Lucian Downing	9	William & Lutitia Downing
781	Luvinia Downing	28	Zebedee & Jennie Downing
780	Lydia Downing	7	Zebedee & Jennie Downing
780	Maggie Downing	15	Zebedee & Jennie Downing
824	Martha Downing	31	Lewis & Chaney Rowe
1326	Mary Downing	20	Charley & Chaney Graves
1503	Mary Downing	38	Jake & Sarah Martin
1503	Mary Downing	18	Elias & Mary Downing
824	Maudie Downing	2	Alexander Davis & Martha Downing
1158	Thomas Downing	23	William & Lutitia Downing
824	Oliver Downing	3	Alexander Davis & Martha Downing
1086	Susan Downing	20	William & Lutitia Downing
782	Walter Downing	21	Zebedee & Jennie Downing
780	Zebedee Downing	46	Reuben & Jennie Downing
1221	Aginora Drew	12	James & Becky Drew
488	Amanda Drew	20	James & Ellen Drew
520	Annie Drew	5	James & Lucy Drew
471	Benjamin Drew	23	Pollard & Katie Drew
1221	Beulah Drew	4	James & Becky Drew
1221	Cassie Drew	8	James & Becky Drew
517	Charlie Drew	16	George & Lottie Drew

521	Colbert Drew	22	James & Ellen Drew
488	Cornelia Drew	23	James & Ellen Drew
520	Delia Drew	13	James & Ellen Drew
651	DeWitt Drew	3	Jack Bailey & Louisa Drew
525	Dinah Drew	75	
1270	Ethel Drew	13	Stephen Drew & Mary Caesar
651	Frederick Drew	10	Sam & Louisa Drew
516	Gano Drew	6	Thomas & Ruth Drew
517	George Drew	40	George & Diana Drew
390	Hannah Drew	17	Lewis & Nancy Drew
516	Henrietta Drew	3mos	Thomas & Ruth Drew
520	Hester Drew	6	James & Lucy Drew
520	Ida Drew	18	James & Ellen Drew
208	Isaac Drew	21	Josh & Rose Drew
520	James Drew	50	George & Diana Drew
439	James Drew	46	Pollard & Katie Drew
517	Jane Drew	11	George & Lottie Drew
161	Jennie Drew	23	Joshua & Rosa Drew
517	Jesse Drew	12	George & Lottie Drew
651	Jesse Drew	12	Sam & Louisa Drew
520	Jimmie Drew	16	James & Ellen Drew
390	John Drew	22	Lewis & Nancy Drew
629	Joshua Drew	42	George & Diana Drew
516	Katie Drew	3	Thomas & Ruth Drew
517	Lem Drew	7mos	Charley Wright & Lewis Drew
520	Lena Drew	10	James & Ellen Drew
629	Leo Drew	6	Joshua & Susan Drew
517	Lewis Drew	17	George & Lottie Drew
517	Lottie Drew	40	Charles & Maria Mackey
651	Louisa Drew	43	Eli & Malinda Keys
518	Lucy Drew	25	George & Lottie Drew
629	Lucy Drew	11mos	Joshua & Susan Drew
208	Luella Drew	9mos	Isaac & Mary Drew
1221	Malissa Drew	15	James & Becky Drew
629	Maria Drew	3	Joshua & Susan Drew
630	Mary Drew	22	Cato & Rachel Vann
1221	Matt Drew	18	James & Becky Drew
629	Minnie Drew	2	Joshua & Susan Drew
641	Moses Drew	39	Pollard & Katie Drew
516	Nip Drew	13	Thomas & Ruth Drew

651	Odessa Drew	6	Sam & Louisa Drew
630	Peachie Drew	9mos	Henry & Mary Drew
629	Rosa Drew	7	Joshua & Susan Drew
516	Ruth Drew	40	Caleb & Sallie Vann
176	Sallie Drew	25	Joshua & Rosa Drew
516	Sallie Drew	10	Thomas & Ruth Drew
651	Savanah Drew	8	Sam & Louisa Drew
629	Susan Drew	24	Jake & Lucy Crapo
516	Thomas Drew	45	Pollard & Katie Drew
602	Ella Duncan	20	Phil Duncan & Mary Mackey
1037	Ella Duncan	28	York & Frances Patterson
1037	George Duncan	5mos	Charlie & Ella Duncan
1037	Ida Duncan	8	Charlie & Ella Duncan
1037	James Duncan	6	Charlie & Ella Duncan
1037	Luvenia Duncan	2	Charlie & Ella Duncan
628	Tilden Duncan	22	Phil Duncan & Jane Mackey
473	Charles Eagle	50	John & Pauline Eagle
473	Pauline Eagle	80	
1306	Eliza Eastman	33	Jerry & Abbie Vann
1306	Lee Eastman	15	Isaac & Eliza Eastman
1306	Lewis Eastman	9	Isaac & Eliza Eastman
1306	Mary Eastman	5	Isaac & Eliza Eastman
1306	Ollie Eastman	6	Isaac & Eliza Eastman
1306	Pearl Eastman	8	Isaac & Eliza Eastman
1306	Roberta Eastman	4mos	Isaac & Eliza Eastman
701	Johnanna Eaton	8	Tom & Nettie Eaton
701	Nina Eaton	6	Tom & Nettie Eaton
701	Phil Eaton	4	Tom & Nettie Eaton
701	Stephen Eaton	14	Tom & Nettie Eaton
701	Tom Eaton	39	Phil Barker & Rachel Eaton
1237	Madeline Ebb	3mos	Rose Baldridge
336	Mollie Edwards	22	Peter Humphries & Sarah Ross
218	Annie Elliott	24	Simon & Katie Fields
636	George Elliorr	9mos	Robert & Mary Elliott
636	Mary Elliott	29	Jack Walker & Polly Ross
218	Pennie Elliott	5mos	William & Annie Elliott
636	Robert Elliott	18mos	Robert & Mary Elliott
218	William Elliott	6wks	William & Annie Elliott
574	Augustus Ellis	11	William Ellis & Rosetta Melton
511	William Ellis	38	Sandy & Becky Ellis

1499	Dora Escoe	22	Lone & Cherry Landrum
529	David Evans	20	Fielding Evans & Mary Walker
530	Fannie Evans	17	Fielding Evans & Mary Walker
884	Henrietta Evans	10	Will & Jennie Evans
529	Henry Evans	16	Fielding Evans & Mary Walker
884	James Evans	6	Will & Jennie Evans
884	Jennie Evans	28	Lewis & Betsy Whitmire
506	Malinda Evans	31	Fielding Evans & Mary Walker
530	Martha Evans	2	John Chouteau & Fannie Evans
529	Mary Evans	13	Fielding Evans & Mary Walker
604	William Evans	32	Fielding Evans & Mary Walker
548	Ab Fields	49	Joe Wolfe & Fannie Fields
392	Adda Fields	14	Rockwell & Lydia Fields
454	Anna Fields	8	Mike & Carrie Fields
548	Archie Fields	10	Ab & Sallie Fields
454	Carrie Fields	28	Stick Ross & Martha Pack
392	Charles Fields	12	Rockwell & Lydia Fields
454	Clyde Fields	2	Mike & Carrie Fields
548	Diana Fields	19	Ab & Sallie Fields
690	Edward Fields	3	Thomas & Vinnie Fields
261	Ernest Fields	11	Simon & Kate Fields
261	Frank Fields	17	Simon & Kate Fields
690	Grum Fields	2mos	Thomas & Vinnie Fields
261	James Fields	14	Simon & Kate Fields
391	James Fields	23	Rockwell & Lydia Fields
1151	Jerry Fields	62	Mike & Rachel Daniels
454	Jeta Fields	11	Mike & Carrie Fields
548	Joab Fields	17	Ab & Sallie Fields
548	John Fields	13	Ab & Sallie Fields
686	John Sr Fields	33	Simon & Kate Fields
1161	John Jr Fields	5	John & Nellie Fields
261	Kate Fields	53	Jack Pack & Martha Nave
690	Kella Fields	2	Thomas & Vinnie Fields
392	Keller Fields	20	Rockwell & Lydia Fields
548	Levi Fields	2	Ab & Sallie Fields
548	Lula Fields	11	Ab & Sallie Fields
548	Lydia Fields	14	Ab & Sallie Fields
392	Lydia Fields	55	George & Diana Drew
1161	Maggie Fields	7	John & Nellie Fields
1161	Mary Fields	1	John & Nellie Fields

454	Mike Fields	31	Jerry & Ann Fields
220	Mike Fields	66	Will & Julia Williams
548	Mose Fields	8	Ab & Sallie Fields
690	Nellie Fields	5	Thomas & Vinnie Fields
220	Oma Fields	60	Charlie Thompson & Nancy Mackey
392	Rockwell Fields	70	Joe Wolfe & Fannie Fields
454	Ross Fields	6	Mike & Carrie Fields
548	Sallie Fields	39	George & Diana Drew
392	Samuel Fields	17	Rockwell & Lydia Fields
548	Turner Fields	6	Ab & Sallie Fields
690	Vinnie Fields	23	William Starr
690	Willie Fields	7	Thomas & Vinnie Fields
454	Willie Fields	4	Mike & Carrie Fields
1437	Eva Finley	27	Thomas Daniels & Celia Kirkpatrick
1437	Frank Finley	3days	Tim & Eva Finley
1437	Haydee Finley	2	Tim & Eva Finley
84	Mary Fleeks	24	Wash & Lydia Sheppard
952	Alice Flowers	17	Tone Rider & Annie Escoe
952	Viola Flowers	1	Joe & Alice Flowers
1557	Castella Flynn	3	Dennis & Sarah Flynn
1557	Fannie Flynn	11	Dennis & Sarah Flynn
1557	Gracie Flynn	1	Dennis & Sarah Flynn
1557	Joseph Flynn	17	Dennis & Sarah Flynn
1557	Nettie Flynn	6	Dennis & Sarah Flynn
1557	Oliver Flynn	20	Dennis & Sarah Flynn
1557	Sarah Flynn	40	Joseph & Mary Riley
1557	Serena Flynn	8	Dennis & Sarah Flynn
800	Eliza Folsom	38	Lewis & Chaney Rowe
283	Bessie Ford	9	William & Julia Ford
122	Bessie Ford	2	John & Lutetia Ford
1190	Clarence Ford	2	Luther & Florence Ford
283	Daniel Ford	12	William & Julia Ford
1190	Fannie Ford	3	Luther & Florence Ford
1190	Florence Ford	30	Junius & Patsy Dennis
1190	Henry Ford	6	Luther & Florence Ford
1439	Jackson Ford	1	William & Nona Ford
122	John Ford	6mos	John & Lutetia Ford
122	Lutetia Ford	21	George & Philis Pettit
87	Luther Ford	9	Luther Ford & Lucy Sanders
283	Mary Ford	5	William & Julia Ford

1439	Nona Ford	20	Harrison Foreman& Lizzie Hornback
1094	Ollie Ford	22	Mit Buffington
283	Virgin Mary Ford	5	William & Julia Ford
283	William Ford	3	William & Julia Ford
77	Willie Ford	12	John & Carrie Ford
223	Aaron Foreman	20	Jesse Foreman & Judy Crapo
459	Abe Foreman	32	Stephen & Dilah Foreman
640	Addie Foreman	5	Jacob & Leah Foreman
640	Albert Foreman	8	Jacob & Leah Foreman
83	Albert Foreman	14	Albert & Judia Foreman
306	Alfronie Foreman	8	Allen & Amanda Foreman
306	Allen Foreman	26	Jerry & Ellen Foreman
640	Andrew Foreman	10	Jacob & Leah Foreman
306	Antone Foreman	19mos	Allen & Amanda Foreman
1495	Benjamin Foreman	29	Jess Foreman & Judy Crapo
324	Benjamin Foreman	21	Richard & Sallie Foreman
576	Benjamin Foreman	26	Jerry & Ellen Foreman
322	Birdie Foreman	3	Richard & Sallie Foreman
83	Caroline Foreman	13	Albert & Judia Foreman
75	Caroline Foreman	60	Cyrus & Winnie Ross
916	Caroline Foreman	40	Jack & Rose Campbell
308	Carrie Foreman	8	Jerry & Hannah Foreman
1330	Charles Foreman	50	Jefferson & Becky Foreman
405	Clora Foreman	50	George & Cassie Landrum
911	Cora Foreman	24	Daniel & Patsy Roach
911	Dennis Foreman	6	Robert Foreman & Fannie Goldsby
300	Dewey Foreman	2	Zack & Mattie Foreman
83	Eddie Foreman	10	Albert & Judia Foreman
1349	Etha Foreman	1	Benj Foreman & Maggie Harris
265	Floyd Foreman	2	Thomas Crapo & Carrie Harris
322	Freeland Foreman	9	Richard & Sallie Foreman
489	Georgia Foreman	26	George Goldsby & Ellen Lynch
83	Grover Foreman	5	Albert & Judia Foreman
136	Gus Foreman	11	Will Foreman & Lou Sheppard
911	Harrison Jr Foreman	3wks	Robert & Cora Foreman
916	Harrison Foreman	48	Ed Drew & Martha Chouteau
308	Jackson Foreman	15	Jerry & Hannah Foreman
640	Jacob Foreman	40	Stephen & Deliah Foreman
480	James Foreman	26	Steve & Dilah Foreman
322	Jane Foreman	19	Richard & Sallie Foreman

308	Jerry Foreman	70	Jerry & Rhoda Foreman
306	Jerry Foreman	4	Allen & Amanda Foreman
272	Jesse Foreman	36	Jesse & Mary Foreman
549	Jesse Foreman	25	Harrison Foreman & Tabby Depy
489	John Foreman	27	Harrison & Caroline Foreman
83	Judia Foreman	33	Dred & Caroline Foreman
308	Kizzie Foreman	19	Jerry & Hannah Foreman
640	Leah Foreman	30	Alex Crapo & Martha Vann
322	Lela Foreman	7	Richard & Sallie Foreman
640	Lelia Foreman	12	Jacob & Leah Foreman
640	Lillie Foreman	13	Jacob & Leah Foreman
911	Linnie Foreman	4	Robert & Cora Foreman
405	Luster Foreman	58	Nancy White
322	Mattie Foreman	18	Richard & Sallie Foreman
1352	Mattie Foreman	7	John Foreman & Maggie Haynes
83	Maude Foreman	9	Albert & Judia Foreman
1040	Minnie Foreman	26	Harrison & Caroline Foreman
308	Nancy Foreman	6	Jerry & Hannah Foreman
322	Nora Foreman	13	Richard & Sallie Foreman
300	Rhoda Foreman	7	Zack & Mattie Foreman
322	Richard Foreman	48	Ben & Jane Foreman
640	Robert Foreman	3	Jacob & Leah Foreman
911	Robert Foreman	25	Harrison & Caroline Foreman
300	Roscoe Foreman	11	Zack & Mattie Foreman
322	Sallie Foreman	44	Robert Webber & Jennie Beck
308	Sarah Foreman	1	James Jackson & Kizzie Foreman
300	Sheridan Foreman	15	Zack & Mattie Foreman
1349	Silvester Foreman	6	Benj Foreman & Maggie Harris
458	Wesley Foreman	23	Jesse & Judie Foreman
1162	William Foreman	3	Abe & Lizzie Foreman
308	Willie Foreman	2mos	James Jackson & Kizzie Foreman
348	Zachariah Foreman	17	Harrison Foreman & Tabby Deberry
300	Zack Foreman	53	Jerry & Rhodie Foreman
300	Zack Jr. Foreman	8	Zack & Mattie Foreman
916	Zack Foreman	18	Harrison Foreman&Mary Hutchinson
97	Amanda Foster	72	Lucy Bell
1395	Annie Foster	7	Thomas & Nellie Foster
1376	Armstead Foster	39	Randall Foster & Eliza Phillips
1008	Arthur Foster	8	Phillip & Annie Foster
1008	Asa Foster	3	Phillip & Annie Foster

80	Carrie Foster	19	Cy & Lucinda Johnson
997	Carrie Foster	6	Jerry & Sarah Foster
1006	Charles Foster	20	Lucinda Foster
997	Clara Foster	12	Jerry & Sarah Foster
1004	Clara Foster	44	Melissa Foster
997	Clarence Foster	9	Jerry & Sarah Foster
995	Clem Foster	12	Edward & Jennie Foster
997	Cora Foster	7mos	Jerry & Sarah Foster
995	Edward Foster	45	Jerry & Julia Foster
1007	Frank Foster	26	Sam Ross & Lucinda Lane
832	George Foster	16	Robert & Amnica Foster
1008	George Foster	18	Phillip & Annie Foster
1476	George Foster	16	Randall & Louvina Foster
995	Idella Foster	9	Edward & Jennie Foster
1004	James Foster	17	Aaron Starr & Clara Foster
1061	James Foster	8	Thomas & Nellie Foster
995	Jennie Foster	40	Dave & Lucinda French
997	Jerry Foster	50	Squire & Louisa Adair
1003	John Foster	17	Charles Fletcher & Lucinda Lane
1004	John Foster	9	Wash Lynch & Clara Foster
1170	John Foster	33	Sarah Burgess
1373	John Foster	10	Will Tucker & Eliza Carbin
995	Lillie Foster	18	Edward & Jennie Foster
1373	Louis Foster	13	Will Tucker & Eliza Carbin
1001	Malissa Foster	70	William & Sarah Blackwell
1004	Maude Foster	20	Horace Tinnon & Clara Foster
995	Pearlie Foster	14	Edward & Jennie Foster
1001	Percy Foster	46	Robert & Eliza Foster
1008	Phillip Foster	48	Robert Foster
1078	Phillis Foster	21	Randal & Luvinia Foster
995	Quinnie Foster	6	Edward & Jennie Foster
1079	Sarah Foster	24	Randall & Luvinia Foster
1550	Sarah Foster	33	William & Lottie Tucker
995	Stella Foster	16	Edward & Jennie Foster
1061	Thomas Foster	34	Randle & Viney Foster
1008	Walter Foster	14	Phillip & Annie Foster
1035	Beatrice Francis	7mos	Jack & Lela Francis
1035	Jack Francis	26	Henry Francis & Manerva Harris
1262	Peggie Francis	43	Henry & Hannah Melton
1194	Annie Franklin	30	Walker & Alcie Johnson

1307	Bessie Frazier	17	Blue & Jennie Thompson
1567	Mariah Freeman	21	Callis & Emma West
1124	Aleck French	16	Wash & Charlotte French
1129	Charles French	3	James & Clara French
1129	Clara French	22	Rab & Rhoda Rogers
1000	David French	72	Dave & Charlotte French
1124	David French	12	Wash & Charlotte French
1124	Easter French	9	Wash & Charlotte French
927	Eli French	31	David & Lucinda French
1463	Emeline French	19	William & Mariah French
1249	James French	27	William & Mariah French
636	James French	11	James French & Mary Elliott
636	Thomas French	8	James French & Mary Elliott
1268	Walter French	20	Wash French & Louisa Gaskin
1124	Wash French	40	David French & Easter Green
1124	William French	18	Wash & Charlotte French
802	Andy Fry	66	Fry & Harriett Fry
802	Henrietta Fry	16	Andy & Milly Fry
802	Milly Fry	64	Mary Bean
1390	Andrew Frye	4mos	Leander & Mary Frye
817	Leander Frye	29	Andy & Millie Frye
582	Rosa Frye	16	Joe Frye & Carrie Lowe
1483	Allie Fulsom	10	Jess & Eliza Fulsom
1483	Charley Fulsom	12	Jess & Eliza Fulsom
1483	Gertie Fulsom	6	Jess & Eliza Fulsom
1483	Jess Fulsom	32	Jennie Boudinot
483	Lee Funkhauser	3	Lee Funkhauser & Amanda Byrd
1281	Eliza Gaines	61	Edmond Vann & Mary Stover
1248	Laura Garlington	30	Samuel Meigs & Amanda Meads
267	Willie Garnett	5mos	Jerry Garnett & Sallie McConnell
1343	Maud Garrett	24	Tom Buffington & Jane Alberty
1067	Ada Gaskins	18	William & Louisa Gaskins
1067	Ida Gaskins	11	William & Louisa Gaskins
1067	Joella Gaskins	19	William & Louisa Gaskins
1067	John Gaskins	14	William & Louisa Gaskins
1067	Levi Gaskins	6	William & Louisa Gaskins
1067	Lola Gaskins	1	William & Louisa Gaskins
1067	Louisa Gaskins	38	Robert Webber & Lucinda French
1067	Minnie Gaskins	3mos	John Murrell & Joella Gaskins
632	Carrie Gentry	19	John Gentry & Maria Sanders

633	George Gentry	27	John Gentry & Maria Sanders
1049	Ada Gibson	13	Ransom & Sarah Gibson
1578	Carrie Gibson	27	Mose & Jane Riley
858	Clifford Gibson	9	Mose & Susie Gibson
1049	Cynthia Gibson	3	Will & Sarah Gibson
1049	Harvey Gibson	14	Ransom & Sarah Gibson
1049	Myrtle Gibson	7	Will & Sarah Gibson
1049	Pearlie Gibson	11	Ransom & Sarah Gibson
858	Reed Gibson	4	Mose & Susie Gibson
858	Roy Gibson	7	Mose & Susie Gibson
1049	Sarah Gibson	35	Ed & Reah Vann
1049	Sedalia Gibson	8	Will & Sarah Gibson
858	Susie Gibson	30	Mose & Maria Whitmire
1492	John Gilds	18	Mack Gilds & Melvina Williams
552	Ella Givens	20	Horace Tennant & Sarah Nave
433	Austin Glass	10	John Glass & Sarah Reed
433	Bertha Glass	3	Joseph Glass & Sarah Reed
433	Bettie Glass	11	John Glass & Sarah Reed
969	Douglas Glass	19	Robert & Elizabeth Glass
433	Eli Glass	4	Joseph Glass & Sarah Reed
969	Elizabeth Glass	55	Armstead Nave & Dina Vann
436	Ellen Glass	36	Pollard & Katie Drew
482	Fannie Glass	23	Henry & Jane Brown
443	Fox Glass	51	John & Sookie Glass
969	Henry Glass	8	Robert & Elizabeth Glass
969	Ida Glass	11	Robert & Elizabeth Glass
443	John Glass	19	Fox & Lucy Glass
1072	John Glass	23	Robert & Elizabeth Glass
606	Joseph Glass	38	Joseph & Easter Glass
433	Joseph Jr. Glass	9	John Glass & Sarah Reed
443	Katie Glass	13	Fox & Lucy Glass
969	Lena Glass	17	Robert & Elizabeth Glass
1110	Lewis Glass	21	Robert & Lizzie Glass
1431	Louis Glass	47	Joe & Esther Glass
443	Lucy Glass	50	Parlor & Katie Drew
969	Luvina Glass	13	Robert & Elizabeth Glass
443	Marthy Glass	11	Fox & Lucy Glass
443	Minnie Glass	16	Fox & Lucy Glass
969	Nancy Glass	15	Robert & Elizabeth Glass
481	Neal Glass	24	John Glass & Ruth Wright

513	Philip Glass	56	Sookie Glass
1071	Randall Glass	26	Robert & Elizabeth Glass
969	Robert Glass	55	Jos Glass & Susie Marson
482	Samuel Glass	30	Phil & Rachel Glass
964	Susie Glass	5	James Burney & Angeline Whitmire
1230	Lonie Gnash	11mos	Lemuel Gnash
262	Matilda Goff	53	Robert & Mariah Ross
32	Clarence Goldsby	23	George Goldsby & Ellen Lynch
898	Luther Goldsby	21	George Goldsby & Ellen Lynch
898	Nina Goldsby	4	Luther & Fannie Goldsby
898	Roberta Goldsby	2	Luther & Fannie Goldsby
1324	Andy Graves	15	Charley & Chaney Graves
1324	Chaney Graves	44	Andy Frye & Chaney Ross
1325	Eli Graves	24	Charley & Chaney Graves
1324	Fred Graves	11	Charley & Chaney Graves
1324	Georgia Graves	5	Charley & Chaney Graves
1324	Harry Graves	18	Charley & Chaney Graves
1325	Jefferson Graves	1	Eli & Edna Graves
1324	Lillie Graves	13	Charley & Chaney Graves
1325	Mabel Graves	3	Eli & Edna Graves
1324	Martha Graves	8	Charley & Chaney Graves
1324	Nellie Graves	17	Charley & Chaney Graves
545	Delia Gray	1mo	Charlie & Susie Gray
545	Julia Gray	5	Charlie & Susie Gray
545	Lucinda Gray	2	Charlie & Susie Gray
545	Susie Gray	21	Lizzie Crossland
1350	Callie Grayson	11	Robert Grayson & Elizabeth Williams
1523	Gertrude Grayson	9	Armstead Foster & Louisa Grayson
409	Aleck Green	24	William & Easter Green
393	Charlie Green	2mos	Gilford & Georgia Green
393	Clarence Green	2mos	Gilford & Georgia Green
289	Easter Green	60	Alex Benge & Mariah Bark
393	Georgia Green	29	Rockwell & Lydia Fields
260	Rosetta Green	27	Harrison Foreman & Amanda Benton
469	Betsie Griffin	33	Gracie Musgrove
469	Josie Griffin	12	Nathan & Betsie Griffin
469	Nathan Griffin	47	
923	Ben Grimmett	66	Len Rowe & Silva Grimmett
56	Clark Grimmet	48	Henderson Grimmet & Amy Smith
182	John Grimmet	22	Clark & Mandy Grimmet

215	Mary Grimmet	19	Benj & Fannie Grimmet
580	Benj Jr Grimmett	48	
1125	Ellis Grimmett	50	Jack Ratcliff & Sylvia Grimmett
1125	Ellis Jr Grimmett	19	Ellis & Charlotte Grimmett
1116	Ethel Grimmett	14	Henderson & Peggy Grimmett
1116	Evans Grimmett	16	Henderson & Peggy Grimmett
1242	Frances Grimmett	3mos	Benj & Maggie Grimmett
1116	Frank Grimmett	9	Henderson & Peggy Grimmett
1116	George Grimmett	5	Henderson & Peggy Grimmett
1497	Harry Grimmett	10	William Grimmett & Hattie Adair
67	Henderson Grimmett	24	Bob & Maude Grimmett
1116	Henderson Grimmett	37	Ben & Clarinda Grimmett
1116	Mamie Grimmett	2	Henderson & Peggy Grimmett
67	Mary Grimmett	27	Fred & Sophie Schrimsher
1192	Peggie Grimmett	46	Rhoda Reynolds
67	Philip Grimmett	7mos	Henderson & Mary Grimmett
67	Richard Grimmett	20mos	Henderson & Mary Grimmett
1192	Sandy Grimmett	20	Clark & Peggie Grimmett
1112	Squirrel Grimmett	22	Ben & Clarinda Grimmett
1242	Susan Grimmett	2mos	Benj & Maggie Grimmett
1126	William Grimmett	27	Ellis & Lizzie Grimmett
58	Willie Grimmett	1	John Grimmett & Carrie Alberty
1479	John Groomer	9	George Groomer & Della Still
1479	Willie Groomer	13	George Groomer & Della Still
1289	Dona Grooms	7	Guss & Eliza Grooms
1289	Leuretha Grooms	3	Guss & Eliza Grooms
1289	Martha Grooms	11	Guss & Eliza Grooms
1289	Peter Grooms	5	Guss & Eliza Grooms
958	Carrie Groves	3	John & Mary Groves
958	Mary Groves	50	Joe Tucker & Ruth Rogers
607	Alice Gunter	13	John & Rosa Gunter
607	Fannie Gunter	16	John & Rosa Gunter
1213	Henry Gunter	31	Jeff & Elizabeth Gunter
1213	Isaac Gunter	27	Jeff & Elizabeth Gunter
607	Jesse Gunter	7	John & Rosa Gunter
607	John Gunter	5	John & Rosa Gunter
1545	John Gunter	44	Jeff Gunter
434	Lewis Jr. Gunter	12	Lewis & Rachel Gunter
1165	Lewis Gunter	32	Jeff Gunter & Lizzie Crossland
434	Lucy Gunter	18mos	Lewis & Rachel Gunter

434	Myrtle Gunter	8	Lewis & Rachel Gunter
434	Rachel Gunter	50	Pollard & Katie Drew
607	Richard Gunter	1	John & Rosa Gunter
607	Rosa Gunter	40	Jesse & Patsie Roach
607	Rosanna Gunter	9	John & Rosa Gunter
607	Tuxie Gunter	11	John & Rosa Gunter
487	Beulah Haddox	20	Frank & Julia Vann
1313	Charley Hailstock	24	Jim Hailstock & Eliza Dodson
436	David Hale	10	Abraham Hale & Ellen Glass
436	Ellis Hale	8	Abraham Hale & Ellen Glass
436	Richard Hale	14	Abraham Hale & Ellen Glass
432	Dave Hall	4	William & Lizzie Hall
76	Georgianna Hall	2mos	Richard Thompson & Josephine Hall
76	Jewiel Hall	4	James & Josephine Hall
280	John Hall	22	John Hall & Louisa Thompson
76	Josephine Hall	24	John & Eliza Hall
432	Josie Hall	8	William & Lizzie Hall
432	Lizzie Hall	35	Rosewell & Mary Mackey
492	Annie Hamilton	23	Roswell & Nan Mackey
492	Nanie Hamilton	9mos	Price & Annie Hamilton
492	Roswell Hamilton	4	Price & Annie Hamilton
492	Squirrel Hamilton	3	Price & Annie Hamilton
1346	Lena Hanks	21	Frank Blade & Jennie Ballard
1068	Effie Hardman	2	Joseph & Adeline Hardman
1068	Joseph Hardman	26	Monroe Hardman & Anica Foster
706	Celia Hardrick	25	Alex & Rosa Rowe
706	James Hardrick	7	Silas & Celia Hardrick
706	Julia Hardrick	3	Silas & Celia Hardrick
706	Lewis Hardrick	4mos	Silas & Celia Hardrick
706	Perry Hardrick	8	Silas & Celia Hardrick
706	Rosa Hardrick	5	Silas & Celia Hardrick
1393	Mary Hardrick	28	Jack & Jane Baldridge
1393	Precilla Hardrick	5mos	Nelson & Mary Hardrick
784	Rosanna Hardrick	75	Mike Watie & Hannah Gans
676	Caroline Harlan	22	Abe & Fannie Davis
676	Muly Harlan	27	Bass & Violet Harlan
676	Willie Harlan	6mos	Muly & Caroline Harlan
59	Eulia Harland	9	Harry Harland & Eliza Buckler
90	Bass Harlin	64	Jesse Roach & Mary Harlin
674	Benjamin Harlin	24	Thomas & Lucy Harlin

279	Charlotte Harlin	21	William & Sarah Burgess
240	Charlotte Harlin	5	Solomon Harlin & Malinda Rogers
92	Clem Harlin	25	Bass & Violet Harlin
92	Eddy Harlin	9mos	Clem & Jennette Harlin
90	Georgian Harlin	6	Bass & Susan Harlin
484	Harry Harlin	27	Thomas & Lucy Harlin
675	Howard Harlin	22	Thomas & Lucy Harlin
643	Jane Harlin	22	Fielding Lewis & Mary Walker
162	John Harlin	33	Thomas & Lucy Harlin
279	Joseph Harlin	27	Thomas & Lucy Harlin
672	Kinney Harlin	14	Thomas & Lucy Harlin
672	Kizzie Harlin	18	Thomas & Lucy Harlin
279	Leanna Harlin	4mos	Joseph & Charlotte Harlin
618	Levi Harlin	9	Solomon & Sarah Harlin
162	Mary Harlin	27	Ben & Edia Ross
92	Mitchell Harlin		Clem & Jennette Harlin
279	Myrtle Harlin	3mos	Joseph & Charlotte Harlin
672	Nelson Harlin	16	Thomas & Lucy Harlin
16	Samuel Harlin	2	Ben Harlin
618	Sarah Harlin	27	Wat & Margaret Parris
618	Solomon Harlin	32	Bass & Violet Harlin
618	Solomon Jr Harlin	7	Solomon & Sarah Harlin
672	Thomas Harlin	57	Joe Riley & Mary Harlin
618	Walter Harlin	8	Solomon & Sarah Harlin
279	William Harlin	2	Joseph & Charlotte Harlin
1305	Jordan Harper	22	Jordan Harper & Lydia Carter
1304	Robert Harper	27	Jordan Harper & Lydia Carter
265	Carrie Harris	20	Stephen & Delilah Foreman
1292	Carrie Harris	16	Henry Nash & Eliza Gaines
1292	Delilah Harris	3mos	Alex & Carrie Harris
216	Eddie Harris	8mos	John & Sallie Harris
1233	Irene Harris	12	Nelson & Mary Harris
12	John Harris	2	William & Mandy Harris
778	Julia Harris	7	William Harris & Matilda Vann
1233	Mary Harris	33	John Curry & Charlotte Vann
1033	Minerva Harris	40	Jack & Rose Campbell
1233	Olive Harris	10	Nelson & Mary Harris
1233	Rheta Harris	8	Nelson & Mary Harris
216	Sallie Harris	25	Thomas & Narcissa Cates
1470	Thomas Harris	52	Reuben Still

12	William Harris	4	William & Mandy Harris
216	Willie Harris	2wks	John & Sallie Harris
1486	Freeman Harrison	7	John & Susie Harrison
1486	Johnnie Harrison	2mos	John & Susie Harrison
1486	Susie Harrison	36	Rose Archie
609	Euna Hayes	13	Abe Hayes & Malinda Parker
1354	Bert Henderson	24	Edward & Rachel Henderson
1056	Emma Henderson	33	Andrew Hollins & Susan Bowles
1056	Lennie Henderson	6	Russ & Emma Henderson
1402	Henry Henderson	40	Katie Kernel
1504	Russell Henderson	30	Ed & Rachel Henderson
1412	Charlotte Henry	43	Mike Whitmire & Rhoda Thompson
91	Rolla Henson	100	Bass & Jennie McIntosh
693	Albert Hicks	7	Robert & Martha Hicks
693	Clarence Hicks	17	Robert & Martha Hicks
693	Ella Hicks	12	Robert & Martha Hicks
209	Howard Hicks	11	Jack Hicks & Martha Vann
693	Jesse Hicks	10	Robert & Martha Hicks
693	Martha Hicks	49	Gilbert & Caroline Vann
261	Mary Hicks	9	John & Phoebe Hicks
209	Ora Hicks	8	Jack Hicks & Martha Vann
1488	Peggy Hicks	60	Robert Drew & Delila Ratliff
693	Robert Hicks	38	Jesse Hicks & Sophia Schrimpsher
693	Robert Hicks	15	Robert & Martha Hicks
261	Wash Hicks	9	John & Phoebe Hicks
693	William Hicks	18	Robert & Martha Hicks
1375	Fannie Hight	50	Irving & Phoebe Vann
1593	Alma Hill	18	George & Amanda Hill
1454	Alsea Hill	5	Reuben & Lucinda Hill
1562	Amanda Hill	29	Johnson Webber & Margaret Ward
1024	Cynthia Hill	12	Reuben Hill & Jane Vann
1562	Della Hill	11	George & Amanda Hill
1309	Donie Hill	13	Watis & Finis Hill
1562	Flossie Hill	9	George & Amanda Hill
610	Harrison Hill	7	Nathaniel Hill & Rachel Winters
1454	Isaac Hill	1	Reuben & Lucinda Hill
1450	James Hill	30	Allen & Lucy Hill
1510	Jess Hill	16	Charley Hill & Anna Johnson
1454	Lucinda Hill	24	Henry Sidney & Alsea Bean
1014	Lucy Hill	50	Jim & Lottie Beck

551	Martha Hill	11	Harrison Hill & Minnie Lang
215	Mary Hill	40	Ben & Eliza Grimmet
658	Nancy Hill	20	Daniel Roach & Rose Gunter
1510	Paulina Hill	42	Jesse Foreman & Peggie Sheppard
658	Perlien Hill	2	John & Nancy Hill
1562	Sadie Hill	8	George & Amanda Hill
658	Thomas Hill	4mos	John & Nancy Hill
1062	Jesse Holmes	3	John & Daisy Holmes
656	Alexander Holt	48	Fox & Lydia Holt
533	Edmund Holt	21	Alex Holt & Harriett Johnson
626	George Holt	22	Aleck Holt & Harriett Johnson
381	James Holt	18	Alex & Lucy Holt
381	Lucy Holt	50	
1456	Alfred Hopkins	4	Alfred & Delilah Hopkins
1456	Charlie Hopkins	3mos	Alfred & Delilah Hopkins
1456	Delilah Hopkins	32	Robert Vann & Flora Murrell
1456	Florence Hopkins	16	Alfred & Delilah Hopkins
1456	Gussie Hopkins	10	Alfred & Delilah Hopkins
1456	Ira Hopkins	13	Alfred & Delilah Hopkins
1456	Johnnie Hopkins	8	Alfred & Delilah Hopkins
1456	Lena Hopkins	2	Alfred & Delilah Hopkins
1456	Lucinda Hopkins	12	Alfred & Delilah Hopkins
1456	Nancy Hopkins	6	Alfred & Delilah Hopkins
1118	Randolph Hopkins	15	Alfred Hopkins & Flora Nave
1219	Beatrice Howell	4mos	George & Maria Howell
1219	Beulah Howell	4	George & Maria Howell
1219	Emma Howell	1	George & Maria Howell
1219	Georgeann Howell	9	George & Maria Howell
1219	Iola Howell	3	George & Maria Howell
1219	Maria Howell	33	Jerry & Ellen Foreman
1219	Mary Howell	7	George & Maria Howell
396	Sarah Howell	21	Rockwell & Lydia Fields
133	Annie Hudson	17	William & Peggie Hudson
1333	Emmett Hudson	10	William & Eliza Hudson
133	Fannie Hudson	20	William & Peggie Hudson
151	Frank Hudson	26	William & Peggie Hudson
1333	Ida Hudson	2	William & Eliza Hudson
1333	Ivory Hudson	5mos	William & Eliza Hudson
1333	Levi Hudson	8	William & Eliza Hudson
133	Maggie Hudson	15	William & Peggie Hudson

133	Peggie Hudson	51	Jack & Martha Pack
1332	Peter Hudson	75	Henry Blackburn & Celia Hudson
890	Susan Hudson	40	Joe Wolfe & Fannie Fields
1333	Wilburn Hudson	4	William & Eliza Hudson
1333	William Hudson	43	Peter & Charity Hudson
100	William Hudson	29	William & Phoebe Hudson
1382	Pearl Huff	20	Benj & Bettie Beck
962	Arthur Hughes	16	Charles & Martha Hughes
962	Calvin Hughes	4	Charles & Martha Hughes
1310	Charles Hughes	48	Johnson Thompson & Rosa Johnson
962	Emmett Hughes	6	Charles & Martha Hughes
962	John Hughes	13	Charles & Martha Hughes
962	Lee Hughes	15	Charles & Martha Hughes
962	Lola Hughes	8	Charles & Martha Hughes
962	Luella Hughes	11	Charles & Martha Hughes
962	Martha Hughes	35	John & Ellen Landrum
1310	Walter Hughes	19	Charles Hughes & Phoebe Grim
1293	Ella Humes	28	Sandy & Rosa Mingo
1446	Ada Humphrey	19	Jeff & Sallie Humphrey
572	Altha Humphrey	40	Jerry & Sookie Foreman
567	Ida Humphrey	15	Jerry & Altha Humphrey
567	Jerry Humphrey	44	Dick Humphrey & Rosanna Melton
568	Johanna Humphrey	21	Jerry & Altha Humphrey
1446	Sallie Humphrey	60	Charles Timberlake & Katie Nave
567	Susie Humphrey	19	Jerry & Altha Humphrey
638	Julia Humphreys	25	Dick Humphreys & Lou Alberty
235	Emily Humphries	75	Samuel Russell & Annie Hall
229	James Humphry	19	Peter Humphry & Alice Smith
229	Peggie Humphry	14	Peter Humphry & Alice Smith
229	Phillip Humphry	12	Peter Humphry & Alice Smith
766	Mary Hunter	24	Jacob & Mahala Bean
766	Roosevelt Hunter	6wks	William & Mary Hunter
567	Troy Huston	4mos	Tom Huston & Susie Humphrey
135	Harry Ireland	9	John Ireland & Lucy Stanton
135	Henry Ireland	10	John Ireland & Lucy Stanton
135	Mattie Ireland	7	John Ireland & Lucy Stanton
24	Albert Irons	13	John & Martha Irons
285	Alice Irons	15	Ned & Julia Irons
424	Andy Irons	35	Pompey & Abbie Rogers
285	Emma Irons	12	Ned & Julia Irons

24	Emma Irons	3mos	John & Martha Irons
126	Etha Irons	5	Alex & Lydia Irons
285	Henderson Irons	3	Ned & Julia Irons
285	Jeff Irons	5	Ned & Julia Irons
243	Jenanna Irons	22	Joe Ross & Susie Vann
24	Joanna Irons	9	John & Martha Irons
24	John Irons	45	Pomp & Monk Rogers
126	Johnnie Irons	2	Alex & Lydia Irons
424	Josie Irons	23	Joseph & Catherine Rogers
285	Julia Irons	38	Margaret
126	Lydia Irons	27	Charles & Mary Nave
24	Martha Irons	41	Will Lynch & Lydia Tucker
126	Mary Irons	8	Alex & Lydia Irons
285	Ned Irons	44	Prince Worsely & Rachel Irons
285	Pollie Irons	10	Ned & Julia Irons
24	Robert Irons	15	John & Martha Irons
24	Will Irons	17	John & Martha Irons
243	Susie Irons	5mos	George & Jenanna Irons
1411	Mamie Irven	25	Alex & Jane Claggett
1411	Minerva Irven	4	Samuel & Mamie Irven
1411	Richard Irven	2	Samuel & Mamie Irven
117	Minnie Ivory	12	Calvin Ivory & Belle Roberson
327	Fannie Jackson	18	Jack & Katie Brown
327	John Jackson	8mos	William & Fannie Jackson
1119	Mary Jackson	42	Robert & Rose Drew
1276	Allen James	23	Isaac James & Nancy Sheppard
1277	Archie James	22	Benj. James & Nancy Sheppard
1273	Benjamin James	19	Benj James & Nancy Sheppard
1276	John James	6mos	Allen & Eva James
1276	Reuben James	3mos	Allen & Eva James
249	Gabriel Jamison	4	Robert & Catherine Jamison
1205	William Jamison	24	Gabriel Jamison & Emma Thompson
112	Dollie Jenkins	8	George & Margaret Jenkins
112	Glennie Jenkins	5	George & Margaret Jenkins
112	Johnnie Jenkins	7	George & Margaret Jenkins
112	Mamie Jenkins	2	George & Margaret Jenkins
112	Margaret Jenkins	28	Hector Vann & Hilda Williams
112	Maybel Jenkins	3mos	George & Margaret Jenkins
1518	Evaline Jimison	10	Robert Jimison & Sarah Chatman
79	Ada Johnson	12	Cy & Lucinda Johnson

1467	Admiral Johnson	2	Seymour Johnson & Fannie Fairchild
106	Albert Johnson	43	Moses & Mary Johnson
1574	Alfred Johnson	8	Harrison & Delilah Johnson
1574	Allie Johnson	15	Harrison & Delilah Johnson
578	Alsie Johnson	80	George Blackwood & Celia Still
748	Amanda Johnson	59	Andrew & Eliza Johnson
1230	Amanda Johnson	50	Jake & Judy Adair
461	Andrew Johnson	24	Nicey Johnson
769	Andy Johnson	21	Fog & Sidney Johnson
1288	Annie Johnson	5	Lewis & Malinda Johnson
241	Annie Johnson	3	George Irons & Jane Ray
1575	Arch Johnson	6	Jim & Lottie Johnson
1168	Arthur Johnson	3	Israel & Susie Johnson
1288	Belle Johnson	10	Lewis & Malinda Johnson
555	Ben Johnson	25	Mose & Mary Johnson
106	Benjamin Johnson	6	Albert & Cynthia Johnson
978	Benjamin Johnson	13	Will & Mary Johnson
1230	Catherine Johnson	18	Reuben & Amanda Johnson
128	Charlotte Johnson	18	Henry Johnson & Lottie Campbell
366	Clara Johnson	13	Fog & Harriett Johnson
79	Cy Johnson	41	Toby & Adaline Johnson
79	Cy Johnson	6	Cy & Lucinda Johnson
1464	David Johnson	35	Dave & Jane Starr
1574	Delilah Johnson	38	Riley & Maria McNair
1574	Della Johnson	4	Harrison & Delilah Johnson
205	Della Johnson	2	Ellis Eldridge & Elizabeth Johnson
445	Dinah Johnson	48	Johnson Meigs & Rosanna Ross
79	Dora Johnson	8	Cy & Lucinda Johnson
205	Elizabeth Johnson	22	Tobe Johnson & Vic Thompson
1574	Ella Johnson	3	Harrison & Delilah Johnson
468	Emmett Johnson	13	Aaron & Ellen Johnson
406	Ernest Johnson	11	Nathan & Martha Johnson
1168	Ethel Johnson	9	Israel & Susie Johnson
1288	Eva Johnson	8	Lewis & Malinda Johnson
753	Evan Johnson	25	Walker & Frances Johnson
1168	Fannie Johnson	12	Israel & Susie Johnson
366	Fog Johnson	58	Johnson Rowe & Eliza Johnson
140	Frank Johnson	28	Moses & Julia Johnson
1168	Frank Johnson	15	Israel & Susie Johnson
341	George Johnson	18	Murrel & Maartha Johnson

1472	George Johnson	6	Frank & Laura Johnson
1230	Hallie Johnson	15	Reuben & Amanda Johnson
586	Hannah Johnson	7	John & Mamie Johnson
894	Hannah Johnson	45	Jess Gunter & Sophia Campbell
366	Harriett Johnson	37	Jack & Annie Pack
1574	Harrison Johnson	10mos	Harrison & Delilah Johnson
79	Harry Johnson	14	Cy & Lucinda Johnson
978	Harvey Johnson	9	Will & Mary Johnson
406	Henry Johnson	3mos	Nathan & Martha Johnson
205	Hattie Johnson	6	Sam'l Thompson Elizabeth Johnson
1168	Hattie Johnson	7	Israel & Susie Johnson
261	Henry Johnson	11	Evans & Lucy Johnson
113	James Johnson	20	Lewis & Hester Johnson
867	James Johnson	20	Sam & Sarah Johnson
1168	Jay Johnson	14	Israel & Susie Johnson
1574	Jesse Johnson	12	Harrison & Delilah Johnson
468	Joanna Johnson	4	Peter Bean & Minnie Johnson
586	John Johnson	24	George & Rachel Johnson
125	John Johnson	26	Mose Johnson & Julia Davis
125	John H. Johnson	1	John & Irene Johnson
406	John Johnson	4	Nathan & Martha Johnson
406	Joseph Johnson	2	Nathan & Martha Johnson
3	Joseph Johnson	47	Adaline Johnson
54	Julia Johnson	19	Moses & Mary Johnson
1288	Julia Johnson	5mos	Lewis & Malinda Johnson
1472	Laura Johnson	26	George & Martha McNair
406	Laurie Johnson	14	Nathan & Martha Johnson
141	Leander Johnson	30	Moses & Julia Johnson
106	Leander Johnson	9	Albert & Cynthia Johnson
406	Leon Johnson	6	Nathan & Martha Johnson
113	Lewis Johnson	50	Mose & Mary Johnson
113	Lewis Jr. Johnson	11	Lewis & Frances Johnson
1288	Lewis Johnson	1	Lewis & Malinda Johnson
468	Lillybelle Johnson	4mos	Jesse Vann & Minnie Johnson
1288	Lizzie Johnson	12	Lewis & Malinda Johnson
1288	Lottie Johnson	15	Lewis & Malinda Johnson
1575	Lottie Johnson	42	Riley & Maria McNair
113	Louella Johnson	17	Lewis & Hester Johnson
54	Louisa Johnson	14	Moses & Mary Johnson
79	Lucinda Johnson	43	John & Carisby Bean

1575	Luford Johnson	9	Jim & Lottie Johnson
1574	Luman Johnson	14	Harrison & Delilah Johnson
30	Maggie Johnson	18	Tobe & Charlotte Johnson
1288	Malinda Johnson	28	William Nash & Eliza Gaines
53	Malinda Johnson	46	Henderson Grimmett & Amy Pettit
341	Martha Johnson	42	Jess & Katie Vann
406	Martha Johnson	30	Arch & Sarah Carter
54	Mary Johnson	15	Moses & Mary Johnson
106	Mary Etta Johnson	3mos	Albert & Cynthia Johnson
468	Minnie Johnson	22	Aaron & Ellen Johnson
1168	Minnie Johnson	18	Israel & Susie Johnson
54	Moses Johnson	46	Tobe Starr & Mariah Johnson
54	Moses Jr. Johnson	17	Moses & Mary Johnson
224	Murrell Johnson	51	Andrew & Eliza Johnson
753	Murrell Johnson	4	Evan & Sallie Johnson
1472	Nancy Johnson	4	Frank & Laura Johnson
406	Nathan Johnson	30	George Benge & Adaline Johnson
141	Nettie Johnson	1	Leander & Minnie Johnson
1230	Nettie Johnson	12	Reuben & Amanda Johnson
461	Nicey Johnson	40	Adaline Johnson
1574	Nola Johnson	6	Harrison & Delilah Johnson
30	Patsy Johnson	49	Mary Mayes
894	Pearl Johnson	15	Robert & Hannah Johnson
79	Percy Johnson		Cy & Lucinda Johnson
1288	Peter Johnson	4	Lewis & Malinda Johnson
1575	Rebecca Johnson	11	Jim & Lottie Johnson
1230	Reuben Johnson	11	Reuben & Amanda Johnson
1288	Reuben Johnson	3	Lewis & Malinda Johnson
30	Samuel Johnson	20	Tobe & Charlotte Johnson
53	Sandy Johnson	56	Richard Whitmire & Mariah Johnson
54	Sandy Johnson	12	Moses & Mary Johnson
113	Sanford Johnson	13	Lewis & Hester Johnson
54	Sarah Johnson	8	Moses & Mary Johnson
79	Sarah Johnson	3	Cy & Lucinda Johnson
867	Sarah Johnson	47	George & Peggie Landrum
848	Seymour Johnson	23	Cye Johnson & Silva Thompson
1230	Simuel Johnson	7	Reuben & Amanda Johnson
1230	Solomon Johnson	23	Reuben & Amanda Johnson
742	Susan Johnson	38	Turk Vann & Minta Barlow
79	Tobe Johnson	20	Cy & Lucinda Johnson

54	Tobe Johnson	10	Moses & Mary Johnson
30	Tobe Johnson	44	Tobe Starr & Mariah Brady
30	Viola Johnson	1	Maggie Johnson
403	Walter Johnson	22	Nicey Johnson
1575	Wilbert Johnson	7	Jim & Lottie Johnson
174	William Johnson	21	Lewis & Hester Johnson
586	Zadie Johnson	5mos	John & Mamie Johnson
1230	Zilla Johnson	9	Reuben & Amanda Johnson
749	Alice Jones	35	Walter & Amanda Johnson
98	Alice Jones	29	Ed & Amanda Alberty
497	Andrew Jones	28	Freeland Jones & Nancy Logan
1251	Anna Jones	7	Jacob Lipe & Lula Jones
1164	Bettie Jones	45	Peggie Bolden
408	Callis Jones	35	Callis & Eliza Jones
1286	Centralia Jones	1	Spencer & Georgia Jones
493	Charles Jones	20	Fielding Jones & Nancy Logan
1286	Charlie Jones	12	Spencer & Georgia Jones
1217	Cynthia Jones	14	Isom & Rachel Jones
305	Eliza Jones	63	Mose & Maria Starr
1286	Ellen Jones	15	Spencer & Georgia Jones
837	Eva Jones	15	Edward & Martha Campbell
1084	George Jones	19	Sam & Sarah Webber
1286	Georgia Jones	36	William Nash & Eliza Gaines
866	Harriet Jones	12	Dave & Mary Jones
1206	Helen Jones	7	Armstead & Sophia Jones
1206	Henry Jones	14	Armstead & Sophia Jones
407	Jack Jones	29	Callis & Eliza Jones
282	Jeanette Jones	3	Sam & Mary Jones
1286	John Jones	16	Spencer & Georgia Jones
1217	Laura Jones	10	Isom & Rachel Jones
1084	Lettie Jones	3	Kirk & George Jones
1206	Lorene Jones	2	Eddie Watkins
1251	Lula Jones	20	Armstead & Sophia Jones
866	Mary Jones	26	Willis & Martha Martin
1286	McKinley Jones	3	Spencer & Georgia Jones
1206	Nora Jones	16	Armstead & Sophia Jones
1206	Ola Jones	11	Armstead & Sophia Jones
749	Oscar Jones	16	Monroe & Alice Jones
598	Owen Jones	5	Robert Jones & Easter Alberty
1217	Rachel Jones	46	John & Dianah Morgan

344	Reedy Jones	4	Jack Jones & Blanche Collins
1286	Roxie Jones	4	Spencer & Georgia Jones
389	Sherman Jones	8mos	William Jones & Mary Robbins
1206	Sophia Jones	45	George & Peggie Landrum
1286	Susie Jones	9	Spencer & Georgia Jones
1206	Timothy Jones	9	Armstead & Sophia Jones
1286	Walter Jones	5	Spencer & Georgia Jones
282	Wilburn Jones	6	Sam & Mary Jones
498	William Jones	24	Freeland Jones & Nancy Logan
749	Willie Jones	12	Monroe & Alice Jones
1206	Willie Jones	2	Armstead & Sophia Jones
1183	Katie Kell	50	Lucy Rider
1257	Mary Kelly	21	Allen & Cynthia Lynch
535	Alexander Kemp	31	Alex Kemp & Delila Smith
535	Christie Kemp	22	John & Causby Bean
535	Clarence Kemp	15mos	Alex & Christie Kemp
535	Florence Kemp	2	Alex & Christie Kemp
535	Willie Kemp	4	Alex & Christie Kemp
1359	Jane Kernel	67	Dave Brown & Charlotte Nave
1403	Katie Kernel	70	John & Harriett Vann
868	Abraham Keys	40	Eli & Linda Keys
292	Alice Keys	13	Frank & Linda Keys
652	Amanias Keys	2	Lewis Smith & Ellen Keys
559	Annie Keys	4	George & Maria Keys
559	Bettie Keys	2	George & Maria Keys
559	Callie Keys	8	George & Maria Keys
651	Charles Keys	18	Jim Stephens & Louisa Drew
960	Charles Keys	38	Isaac Keys & Delilah Brown
1030	Charles Keys	14	John Keys & Fannie Lowrey
868	Ella Keys	12	Abraham & Mary Keys
652	Ellen Keys	22	Rap Hawkins & Louisa Keys
292	Elnora Keys	10	Frank & Linda Keys
631	Florence Keys	5mos	George & Lizzie Keys
292	Frank Keys	36	Eli & Julia Keys
631	George Keys	42	Eli & Malinda Keys
960	Hannah Keys	35	Henry & Mariah Rider
650	Henry Keys	24	Joe Rogers & Louisa Drew
960	Jessie Keys	16	Charles & Hannah Keys
653	John Keys	14	John Hicks & Mary Barnett
868	John Keys	9	Abraham & Mary Keys

959	John Keys	45	Isaac Keys & Delilah Brown
959	Johnetha Keys	8	John & Eliza Keys
583	Jonas Keys	43	Eli & Linda Keys
960	Lillie Keys	17	Charles & Hannah Keys
631	Lizzie Keys	22	John & Silla Gentry
559	Lou Keys	16	George & Maria Keys
559	Maria Keys	40	William Lynch & Lydia Tucker
292	Martha Keys	22	Richard & Nellie Humphries
559	Mary Keys	17	George & Maria Keys
959	Minnie Keys	15	John & Eliza Keys
559	Rosella Keys	12	George & Maria Keys
651	Samuel Keys	14	Sam & Louisa Drew
959	Stella Keys	10	John & Eliza Keys
292	Susan Keys	17	Frank & Linda Keys
868	Willie Keys	16	Abraham & Mary Keys
1566	Ada Kilpatrick	23	Callie & Emma West
1566	Easter Kilpatrick	2	Ada Kilpatrick
1566	Ivy Kilpatrick	7	Ada Kilpatrick
1566	Warren Kilpatrick	4	Ada Kilpatrick
1042	Florence King	26	John & Maria Gentry
627	Mary King	39	Daniel & Ruth Snow
627	Willie King	11	George & Mary King
44	Benjamin Kirby	8	Sherman & Rhoda Kirby
44	Mary Kirby	7	Sherman & Rhoda Kirby
44	Peggy Kirby	5	Sherman & Rhoda Kirby
44	Rhoda Kirby	30	Wyly Polsom & Peggie Grim
44	Susanna Kirby	2	Sherman & Rhoda Kirby
342	Maud Kircum	22	Murrel & Martha Johnson
342	William Kircum	3	Andy & Maud Kircum
956	Cora Kirk	9	Silas & Ruth Kirk
956	Edwin Kirk	7	Silas & Ruth Kirk
956	Gertie Kirk	5	Silas & Ruth Kirk
956	Herbert Kirk	2	Silas & Ruth Kirk
956	Nora Kirk	11	Silas & Ruth Kirk
956	Ruth Kirk	38	Tobe & Mary Looney
956	Silas Kirk	40	Emily Kirk & Polly Alberty
1554	Thomas Kirk	40	Robert Kirk & Emily Weaver
1436	Celia Kirkpatrick	50	George & Cassie Landrum
350	Robert Laflace	37	Robert Laflace & Caroline Charles
743	Albert Landrum	19	Spencer & Martha Landrum

714	Alice Landrum	29	Arthur & Lula Bean
702	Arch Landrum	70	Jesse & Winnie Ratliff
485	Benjamin Landrum	16	William & Charity Landrum
877	Benjamin Landrum	12	John & Mary Landrum
877	Betsy Landrum	15	John & Mary Landrum
750	Caroline Landrum	60	Griffin & Celia Daniels
485	Cassie Landrum	9	William & Charity Landrum
874	Celia Landrum	3mos	William & Lucy Landrum
485	Charity Landrum	40	Dred & Caroline Foreman
1498	Cherry Landrum	38+	Jordan & Delilah Thompson
714	Cicero Landrum	9	Sherman & Alice Landrum
7	Daniel Landrum	36	George & Caroline Landrum
877	Eva Landrum	4	Andy & Ella Landrum
877	George Landrum	19	John & Mary Landrum
1498	George Landrum	23	Lone & Cherry Landrum
743	Gertie Landrum	4	Spencer & Martha Landrum
971	Harry Landrum	23	John & Mary Landrum
1529	James Landrum	14	Sam Landrum & Mattie McNair
1498	Jesse Landrum	18	Lone & Cherry Landrum
761	Jincy Landrum	66	Jim & Chlora Landrum
714	John Landrum	6	Sherman & Alice Landrum
877	John Landrum	59	George & Peggie Landrum
1356	Joseph Landrum	49	John Rowe & Emily Vann
714	Lavina Landrum	12	Sherman & Alice Landrum
877	Lon Landrum	6	Andy & Ella Landrum
1498	Lone Landrum	45	George & Cassie Landrum
771	Lovie Landrum	18	Nelson Thompson & Sidney Johnson
838	Major Landrum	37	Reed & Mary Landrum
1498	Mamie Landrum	8	Lone & Cherry Landrum
877	Mary Landrum	55	Major Wright & Peggie Whitmire
1498	Minnie Landrum	12	Lone & Cherry Landrum
877	Nelson Landrum	17	John & Mary Landrum
743	Obee Landrum	9	Spencer & Martha Landrum
771	Odoth Landrum	6mos	Charley & Lovie Landrum
1498	Pearl Landrum	6	Lone & Cherry Landrum
878	Polly Landrum	33	John & Mary Landrum
1498	Reed Landrum	16	Lone & Cherry Landrum
896	Sam Landrum	42	George Landrum&CarolineMcIntosh
714	Sherman Landrum	36	George & Caroline Landrum
743	Spencer Landrum	35	Arch & Winnie Landrum

485	William Landrum	40	George & Cassie Landrum
874	William Landrum	31	George & Caroline Landrum
702	Winnie Landrum	70	Lucy Musrat
739	Della Lane	2	Dry & Florence Lane
739	Florence Lane	22	Spencer Landrum & Mary Rowe
1003	George Lane	8	David & Lucinda Lane
1418	James Lane	20	George Lane & Florence Meigs
1003	Lucinda Lane	46	Melissa Foster
1482	Mary Lane	30	Charles & Susan Pee
1482	Millie Lane	3	Reuben & Mary Lane
1594	Pearlie Lane	9	Mitchell & Ada Lane
834	Susan Lane	30	Andy & Millie Frye
551	Minnie Lang	29	Joseph & Martha Watie
165	Eliza Langston	50	Jack & Eliza Smith
17	Charles Lasley	19	Columbus & Peggy Lasley
17	Columbus Lasley	53	Columbus & Hannah Lasley
17	Columbus Jr. Lasley	5	Columbus & Peggy Lasley
983	Cynthia Lasley	11	George & Jane Lasley
152	Edward Lasley	14	Andy & Lucy Lasley
17	Florence Lasley	10	Columbus & Peggy Lasley
152	Frank Lasley	10	Andy & Lucy Lasley
18	Hannah Lasley	91	
152	James Lasley	8	Andy & Lucy Lasley
983	Jane Lasley	49	Daniel Phillips & Mary Don
152	John Lasley	12	Andy & Lucy Lasley
1466	John Lasley	40	John Lasley & Rachel Whitmire
211	Lewis Lasley	26	George & Jane Lasley
983	Logan Lasley	16	George & Jane Lasley
152	Lucy Lasley	42	Jess & Hannah Hilderbrand
1315	Lula Lasley	22	Reuben & Carrie Nave
17	Mary Lasley	16	Columbus & Peggy Lasley
17	Nellie Lasley	4	Columbus & Peggy Lasley
17	Ola Lasley	8	Columbus & Peggy Lasley
17	Peggy Lasley	48	Mose & Nancy Ross
21	William Lasley	26	Columbus & Peggy Lasley
211	Zola Lasley	3	Lewis & Lula Lasley
760	Charley Ledman	4	Buck & Eliza Ledman
760	Eliza Ledman	36	Gus & Mary Buffington
760	Hannah Ledman	9	Buck & Eliza Ledman
760	James Ledman	19	Buck & Eliza Ledman

760	John Ledman	11	Buck & Eliza Ledman
760	Josephine Ledman	13	Buck & Eliza Ledman
760	Mary Ledman	2	Buck & Eliza Ledman
760	Roy Ledman	15	Buck & Eliza Ledman
760	Viola Ledman	7	Buck & Eliza Ledman
42	Alzie Lee	7	Jourdan & Lizzie Lee
532	Clarence Lee	18	Robbin Thompson & Lizzie Lee
387	Jesse Lee	15	Jourdan & Lizzie Lee
387	Maggie Lee	13	Jourdan & Lizzie Lee
387	Millie Lee	11	Jourdan & Lizzie Lee
1114	Ed Leek	36	Ed & Elizabeth Leek
1043	Elizabeth Leek	65	Pompey & Lucinda Wright
951	Henry Leek	31	Ed & Elizabeth Leek
1442	Samuel Leek	13	Albert Leek & Elizabeth May
1452	Solomon Leek	6	Ed Leek & Aggie Harris
820	Alfred LeFlore	8	Fred LeFlore & Malinda Bean
1229	Frank Lephfew	14	Benj Lephfew & Eliza Watson
1229	Liddie Lephfew	11	Benj Lephfew & Eliza Watson
1229	Lizzie Lephfew	8	Benj Lephfew & Eliza Watson
770	Annie Lett	14	Tobe & Mary Lynch
1066	Eddie Lett	1mo	James & Minerva Lett
1066	Leona Lett	1	James & Minerva Lett
1066	Minerva Lett	24	Sam & Sarah Webber
1066	Odie Lett	3	James & Minerva Lett
994	Rebecca Lett	18	Jesse & Lucinda Brown
312	Addie Lewis	6mos	William & Emma Lewis
312	Annie Lewis	3	William & Emma Lewis
166	Dollie Lewis	10	Jacob & Alice Lewis
437	Edna Lewis	21	Dan & Ruth Snow
312	Emma Lewis	28	George & Gracie Crossland
437	Estella Lewis	3	Albert & Edna Lewis
312	George Lewis	7	William & Emma Lewis
1176	Ida Lewis	18	George & Rose Allen
166	Jacob Lewis	44	Thomas Ridge & Peggie Vann
166	Mary Lewis	13	Jacob & Alice Lewis
384	Moses Lewis	22	Jack & Nellie Lewis
166	Nellie Lewis	9mos	Wallace McNack
166	Pearl Lewis	17	Jacob & Nellie Lewis
220	Pearl Lewis	8	William Lewis & Mandy Foreman
1253	Richard Lewis	20	Jacob Lewis & Mary Ross

166	Sylva Lewis	55	York Still & Sarah Starr
1176	William Lewis	7wks	Barton & Ida Lewis
269	Thomas Linsey	7	Walter & Mary Linsey
554	Mary Lipe	62	Riley & Amy Carter
1104	Albert Little	2mos	Frank & Mary Little
1104	George Little	14	Frank & Mary Little
1104	Martha Little	12	Frank & Mary Little
1104	Mary Little	31	George & Mary Brown
493	Nancy Logan	50	
638	Lula Lorens	9	Catch Lorens & Julia Humphreys
638	Simpson Lorens	11	Catch Lorens & Julia Humphreys
244	Jennie Lott	4	William & Nigger Lott
244	William Lott	2	William & Nigger Lott
1103	Anna Love	27	Eli & Jane Nave
1103	Della Love	3mos	Frank & Anna Love
1103	Earnest Love	8	Frank & Anna Love
1103	Emma Love	3	Frank & Anna Love
1244	Flora Love	21	George & Martha McNair
1103	Lillie Love	6	Frank & Anna Love
387	James Lovely	20	Rand Lovely & Lizzie Lee
398	Bertha Lowe	5mos	William & Lillie Lowe
582	Carrie Lowe	36	Samuel Jones & Rose Webber
804	Eda Lowe	40	Phebe Hilderbrand
398	Evalina Lowe	11mos	William & Lillie Lowe
1036	Leroy Lowe	16	Tom Lowe & Julia Dickson
398	Lillie Lowe	26	Tassie Rogers & Mary Robbins
398	Ransom Lowe	2	William & Lillie Lowe
1030	Augustus Lowrey	25	Green & Fannie Lowrey
15	Elias Lowrey	4	Nelson & Fannie Lowrey
15	Ella Lowrey	17	Nelson & Fannie Lowrey
1054	Ellen Lowrey	23	George & Susie Melton
1111	George Lowrey	24	Green & Hattie Lowrey
654	Jesse Lowrey	44	Jesse & Lydia Lowrey
15	Jessie Lowrey	11	Nelson & Fannie Lowrey
15	Mary Lowrey	7	Nelson & Fannie Lowrey
15	Nelson Lowrey	40	Jesse & Lydia Lowrey
15	Ruth Lowrey	9	Nelson & Fannie Lowrey
1196	Geneva Luckey	4	Louis & Harriett Luckey
1196	Harriett Luckey	27	James & Siney Thomas
661	Ada Luther	14	Jack & Lizzie Luther

711	Anderson Lynch	17	Lewis & Ibbie Lynch
791	Anderson Lynch	64	William & Peggie Lynch
661	Anna Luther	17	Jack & Lizzie Luther
507	Jack Luther	18	Jack Luther & Eliza Dotson
700	Allen Lynch	61	Bosen & Mila Lynch
1391	Amanda Lynch	6mos	Charles & Ary Lynch
475	Amy Lynch	31	Leon Wolfe & Judy Taylor
1228	Andrew Lynch	25	Allen & Cynthia Lynch
1538	Calvin Lynch	3	William & Alice Lynch
717	Charles Lynch	40	Simon & Nancy Lynch
723	Corine Lynch	3mos	William & Mary Lynch
1538	Early Lynch	5	William & Alice Lynch
710	Edey Lynch	55+	Vina Lynch
1258	Edward Lynch	29	Allen & Cynthia Lynch
33	Ellen Lynch	42	Luge & Tempe Beck
1263	Elmer Lynch	9	George Lynch & Caroline Francis
694	Elzira Lynch	4mos	Simon Lynch & Martha Williams
1391	Emily Lynch	8	Charles & Ary Lynch
727	Evans Lynch	24	Lewis & Ebey Lynch
982	Florence Lynch	7	George & Matilda Lynch
1329	Garfield Lynch	19	Charles Lynch & Lizzie Barnes
1261	George Lynch	27	Joseph Lynch & Peggie Francis
711	Ibbie Lynch	70	Rufus & Lucy Vann
982	Iola Lynch	5	George & Matilda Lynch
731	James Lynch	4	Lincoln & Neatie Lynch
826	John Lynch	39	Allen & Harriett Lynch
709	Josephine Lynch	4	Andrew & Mary Lynch
711	Lewis Lynch	45	Simon & Edey Lynch
731	Lincoln Lynch	29	Simon & Nancy Lynch
1210	Margaret Lynch	22	Isaac & Rhoda Bean
723	Maria Lynch	10	William & Alice Lynch
1481	Martha Lynch	18	Tobe Lynch & Lettie Brown
709	Mary Lynch	25	William & Lutitia Downing
982	Matilda Lynch	30	Frank & Susan Ross
475	Nancy Lynch	14	Charlie & Amy Lynch
1422	Neatie Lynch	24	Sam & Rachel Vann
710	Simon Lynch	70	Griffin & Celia Daniels
741	Simon Jr. Lynch	23	Simon & Nancy Lynch
731	Spicie Lynch	1	Lincoln & Neatie Lynch
763	Tobe Lynch	46	John & Peggie Lynch

711	Willard Lynch	15	Tobe & Katie Lynch
723	William Lynch	32	Simon & Nancy Lynch
723	William Jr. Lynch	8	William & Alice Lynch
819	William Lynch	80	
792	Delsie Lyons	10	Ned & Mariah Lyons
792	James Lyons	4	Ned & Mariah Lyons
792	Katie Lyons	1	Ned & Mariah Lyons
792	Mahala Lyons	3	Ned & Mariah Lyons
792	Nancy Lyons	21	John & Mary Landrum
1283	Frank Mabry	1mo	
1283	Mary Mabry	18	Henry Nash & Eliza Gaines
252	Anna Mackey	14	Ellis & Peggy Mackey
252	Battice Mackey	18	Ellis & Peggy Mackey
273	Bertha Mackey	6mos	Elias & Mulsie Mackey
252	Columbus Mackey	8	Ellis & Peggy Mackey
370	Dennis Mackey	42	Roswell & Mary Mackey
282	Dinah Mackey	51	George Jenkins & Betsy Baldridge
41	Eli Mackey	20	Roswell & Mary Mackey
88	Eli Mackey	9	Crocket & Jane Mackey
252	Ellis Mackey	50	Parler & Katie Drew
213	Emma Mackey	12	Ned & Hannah Mackey
359	Emma Mackey	7mos	Rufus & Mary Mackey
252	Ernestine Mackey	3	Ellis & Peggy Mackey
491	Eva Mackey	13	Rosewell & Nan Mackey
252	George Mackey	20	Ellis & Peggy Mackey
1435	James Mackey	51	George & Maria Mackey
88	Jane Mackey	48	Charles & Katie Nave
680	John Mackey	26	Roswell Mackey & Sylvia Thompson
88	Kate Mackey	5	Crocket & Jane Mackey
213	Lula Mackey	19	John Vann & Sallie Crossland
613	Lula Mackey	17	Crocket & Jane Mackey
252	Martha Mackey	12	Ellis & Peggy Mackey
252	Mary Mackey	7mos	Ellis & Peggy Mackey
359	Mary Mackey	15	Ned Mackey & Emma Price
88	Mary Mackey	12	Crocket & Jane Mackey
1490	Minnie Mackey	27	James Hopkins & Janie Simmons
273	Mulsie Mackey	17	George & Grace Crossland
491	Nan Mackey	47	George & Cassie Landrum
252	Nancy Mackey	16	Ellis & Peggy Mackey
213	Ned Mackey	39	Roswell & Mary Mackey

213	Ned Jr. Mackey	6wks	Ned & Lula Mackey
1187	Peggie Mackey	40	Rawling & Martha Batice
282	Perry Mackey	54	Charlie Thompson & Nancy Mackey
41	Roswell Mackey	79	Mose & Hannah Mackey
41	Roswell Jr. Mackey	18	Roswell & Mary Mackey
508	Roswell Mackey	50	Joshua Mackey & Malinda Smith
460	Rufus Mackey	29	Charles Mackey & Juda Crapo
252	Sallie Mackey	5	Ellis & Peggy Mackey
213	Sallie Mackey		Ned & Lula Mackey
213	Sampson Mackey	10	Ned & Hannah Mackey
1490	Tommie Mackey	1	Taylor & Minnie Mackey
213	William Mackey	14	Ned & Hannah Mackey
900	Stephen Macum	17	Stephen Macum & Rutha Scott
924	Barney Madden	8	John & Mattie Madden
924	John Madden	39	William & Melinda Madden
924	John Jr Madden	4	John & Mattie Madden
732	Malinda Madden	50	Betsey Whitmire
924	Myrtle Madden	5mos	John & Mattie Madden
924	William Madden	9	John & Mattie Madded
926	William Jr Madden	23	William & Malinda Madden
915	Rosaline Maken	20mos	Thomas & Henrietta Maken
915	Thomas Maken	21	John & Rutha Maken
494	Peggie Malven	27	Seymour Matthew & Nan Mackey
1515	Daisy Manley	3mos	Joseph & Kate Manley
1515	Frank Manley	13	Joseph & Kate Manley
1515	Ida Manley	15	Joseph & Kate Manley
1515	Joseph Jr. Manley	6	Joseph & Kate Manley
1515	Kate Manley	34	Robert & Margaret Webber
1515	Lela Manley	8	Joseph & Kate Manley
1515	Sarah Manley	9	Joseph & Kate Manley
1515	Willie Manley	4	Joseph & Kate Manley
623	Beulah Markham	13	William & Cora Markham
623	Callie Markham	4	William & Cora Markham
623	Clarence Markham	7	William & Cora Markham
623	Clementine Markham	1	William & Cora Markham
623	Cora Markham	32	Johnson & Lila Vann
563	Ethel Markham	9	Sig & Mary Markham
563	Jesse Markham	2mos	Sig & Mary Markham
1555	Joe Markham	5	John & Charlotte Markham
1555	John Markham	39	Emery Kirk & Polly Markham

623	Legus Markham	5	William & Cora Markham
623	Mattie Markham	9	William & Cora Markham
563	Myra Markham	4	Sig & Mary Markham
563	Nancy Markham	11	Sig & Mary Markham
563	Nealy Markham	2	Sig & Mary Markham
534	Oscar Markham	33	Willis & Mariah Markham
563	Sig Markham	38	Alex & Violet Markham
563	William Markham	6	Sig & Mary Markham
623	William Markham	36	Fred & Julia Markham
301	Susan Marshall	24	Perry Mackey & Harriet Woodard
1294	Aaron Martin	67	Mike & Nellie Stutts
1368	Aaron Martin	25	Jake & Sarah Martin
919	Ada Martin	8	Aaron & Gracie Martin
268	Alex Martin	49	Martin & Gracie Vann
1296	Alice Martin	26	Guss & Jane Alberty
1591	Allen Martin	3wks	Samuel & Melvina Martin
786	Andrew Martin	2	Mike & Ida Martin
70	Annie Martin	5	Sipio Barnett & Patsy Martin
1425	Annie Martin	13	July & Josephine Martin
738	Arthur Martin	31	George & Sallie Martin
919	Augustus Martin	3mos	Willie & Gracie Martin
786	Bennie Martin	1mo	Mike & Ida Martin
712	Bessie Martin	12	Isaac Martin & Martha Grubbs
1425	Betsy Martin	2	July & Josephine Martin
873	Blunt Martin	23	Wilson & Patsy Martin
1372	Caroline Martin	8	Sam & Viney Martin
751	Carrie Martin	19	George & Sallie Martin
767	Carrie Martin	20	Jacob & Mahala Bean
1425	Carrie Martin	14	July & Josephine Martin
1369	Catherine Martin	3	John & Jennie Martin
1235	Cecil Martin	7	John & Ostella Martin
695	Clara Martin	4mos	Frank & Addie Martin
746	Clarence Martin	2	Joseph & Malinda Martin
919	Claude Martin	3	Willie & Gracie Martin
1301	Clem Martin	15	Nelson Hardrick & Harriett Tucker
1296	Clifton Martin	5	George & Alice Martin
1540	Cora Martin	17	Israel & Melvina Martin
773	Della Martin	3	Houston & Lucy Martin
268	Dinah Martin	57	George & Sarah Jefferson
1296	Ethel Martin	3	George & Alice Martin

873	Felix Martin	7	Blunt Martin & Martha Lyons
767	Frances Martin	2	Joseph & Carrie Martin
787	Frances Martin	13	Aaron & Cora Martin
695	Frank Martin	27	Wilson & Patsy Martin
1369	Frank Martin	1	John & Jennie Martin
724	Fred Martin	43	Fred & Juno Martin
1296	George Martin	38	Aaron & Queen Martin
268	Gracie Martin	18	Alex & Dinah Martin
919	Gracie Martin	26	Joe & Cora Adams
474	Helen Martin	6	Fed Martin & Carrie McCoy
786	Henrietta Martin	7	Mike & Ida Martin
1493	Herman Martin	3	Joshua & Ella Martin
1493	Hester Martin	1	Joshua & Ella Martin
786	Ida Martin	22	Joseph & Cora Adams
1235	Ira Martin	9	John & Ostella Martin
712	Isaac Martin	39	Frederick & Juno Martin
1299	Israel Martin	37	Aaron & Queen Martin
1371	Jacob Martin	24	Fred & Betsy Martin
697	James Martin	27	Wilson & Patsy Martin
724	James Martin	1	Fred & Jennie Martin
825	James Martin	2	Linzy Martin & Minnie Baldridge
1296	Jane Martin	1	George & Alice Martin
1369	Jerome Martin	11	John & Jennie Martin
70	Jerry Martin	56	Fred Martin & Susie Roe
1482	Jessie Martin	13	Tobe Martin & Mary Lane
1423	Joe Martin	23	Warren & Martha Martin
1537	John Martin	12	John Towers & Rachel Martin
1369	John Martin	35	Jake & Sarah Martin
1367	John Martin	15	Jim Martin & Patsy Demumber
457	Johnson Martin	22	Alex & Dinah Martin
268	Joseph Martin	13	Alex & Dinah Martin
746	Joseph Martin	20	Tobe Martin & Susie Johnson
1297	Joshua Martin	21	Aaron & Queen Martin
1493	Joshua Sr. Martin	24	Jake & Sarah Martin
1493	Julia Martin	5	Joshua & Ella Martin
1425	July Martin	42	Aaron & Queen Martin
805	Juno Martin	95	Jesse & Phillis Ross
756	Katy Martin	30	Rufus & Lucy Vann
1371	Lady Martin	4mos	Jacob & Bertha Martin
1299	Laura Martin	5	Israel & Lizzie Martin

756	Lee Martin	6	Lewis & Katy Martin
1299	Lizzie Martin	30	Henry Nash & Eliza Gaines
724	Lola Martin	7	Fred & Jennie Martin
713	Lora Martin	8	George & Mary Martin
1299	Lottie Martin	1	Israel & Lizzie Martin
1299	Louis Martin	8	Israel & Lizzie Martin
697	Luberta Martin	23	Jack & Nancy Baldridge
773	Lucy Martin	23	William & Rachel Vann
552	Lucy Martin	22	Ive Barker & Sarah Nave
268	Lucy Martin	9	Alex & Dinah Martin
786	Luvenia Martin	10	Mike & Ida Martin
1299	Maggie Martin	12	Israel & Lizzie Martin
1296	Martha Martin	11	George & Alice Martin
713	Mary Martin	28	William & Rachel Vann
1295	Michael Martin	34	Aaron & Queen Martin
1372	Mose Martin	12	Sam & Viney Martin
1235	Myrrh Martin	2mos	John & Ostella Martin
1482	Myrtle Martin	16	Tobe Martin & Mary Lane
796	Nancy Martin	9	Arthur & Nicey Martin
1372	Nannie Martin	2	Sam & Viney Martin
788	Nathaniel Martin	24	Tobe & Jennie Martin
787	Nealey Martin	9	Aaron & Cora Martin
724	Nelson Martin	20	Fred & Jennie Martin
796	Nicey Martin	28	Simon & Nancy Lynch
1365	Ocie Martin	19	Jake & Sarah Martin
1482	Ora Martin	8	Tobe Martin & Mary Lane
919	Oscar Martin	1	Willie & Gracie Martin
1235	Ostella Martin	28	John & Charlotte Curry
1372	Patsy Martin	5	Sam & Viney Martin
70	Patsy Martin	20	Jerry & Ellen Martin
1424	Pearlie Martin	2	Fred Martin & Lottie Bean
268	Peggie Martin	14	Alex & Dinah Martin
787	Phoebe Martin	7	Aaron & Cora Martin
724	Prisilla Martin	9	Fred & Jennie Martin
786	Ray Martin	3	Mike & Ida Martin
1235	Roy Martin	5	John & Ostella Martin
713	Ruie Martin	6	George & Mary Martin
1372	Sam Martin	32	Jake & Sarah Martin
1365	Sarah Martin	60	Mike & Nellie Martin
268	Sarah Martin	6	Alex & Dinah Martin

773	Sedalia Martin	1	Houston & Lucy Martin
724	Solomon Martin	18	Fred & Jennie Martin
1369	Susan Martin	7	John & Jennie Martin
1482	Susan Martin	10	Tobe Martin & Mary Lane
724	Sylvester Martin	14	Fred & Jennie Martin
287	Thomas Martin	24	Alex & Dinah Martin
1425	Wesley Martin	4	July & Josephine Martin
70	Willie Martin	5	Jerry & Mary Martin
1408	William Martin	40	Joe Martin & Jane Claggett
50	Florence Mathews	19	Lige Meadows & Mary Sumpter
50	Samie Mathews	6mos	William & Florence Mathews
217	Charlie Mayberry	1	Thomas & Ellen Mayberry
217	Ellen Mayberry	26	Joshua & Betsy Sheppard
217	George Mayberry	2mos	Thomas & Ellen Mayberry
217	Thomas Mayberry	8	Thomas & Ellen Mayberry
217	Willie Mayberry	4	Thomas & Ellen Mayberry
217	Zora Mayberry	6	Thomas & Ellen Mayberry
114	Gippy Mayes	17	Joshua & Katie Mayes
234	Joshua Mayes	12	Joshua Mayes & Hannah McWaters
114	Katie Mayes	45	Russell & Alcie Vann
114	Mack Mayes	9	Joshua & Katie Mayes
234	Robert Mayes	14	Joshua Mayes & Hannah McWaters
234	Samuel Mayes	11	Joshua Mayes & Hannah McWaters
234	Willie Mayes	17	Joshua Mayes & Hannah McWaters
340	Amanda Mayfield	18	Robert & Minnie Mayfield
1388	Bennie Mayfield	4mos	Charles & Lizzie Mayfield
193	Betsy Mayfield	40	Nellie Mayfield
1388	Beulah Mayfield	9	Charles & Lizzie Mayfield
1388	Charles Mayfield	33	Ceasar Mayfield & Nancy Starr
123	Clarietta Mayfield	2	Emberry & Joana Mayfield
123	Cleveland Mayfield	3mos	Emberry & Joana Mayfield
340	Curry Mayfield	16	Robert & Minnie Mayfield
1388	Emanuel Mayfield	12	Charles & Lizzie Mayfield
4	George Mayfield	35	Amos & Susan Mayfield
123	Joana Mayfield	24	Wash & Lydia Shepp
1157	Johnnie Mayfield	5	John Mayfield & Gular Miller
735	Louisa Mayfield	16	Thomas & Nicey Mayfield
193	Luke Mayfield	5	Roland & Betsy Mayfield
1388	McKinly Mayfield	4	Charles & Lizzie Mayfield
1388	Nathaniel Mayfield	2	Charles & Lizzie Mayfield

735	Nicey Mayfield	66	Ben & Ibby Bean
1388	Royal Mayfield	6	Charles & Lizzie Mayfield
116	Sallie Mayfield	23	Ike & Louisa Nivens
228	Mary Mayo	40	Jesse Foreman & Mary Vann
307	Ary McClure	3	William & Ibby McClure
307	Cornelius McClure	7	William & Ibby McClure
307	Henry McClure	5	William & Ibby McClure
307	Ibby McClure	34	Nathan & Rosanna Melton
307	Leo McClure	3mos	William & Ibby McClure
678	Betsy McConnell	47	Henry & Amy Vann
267	Elnora McConnell	7	Jack & Sallie McConnell
860	Pearlie McConnell	9	Jack & Sallie McConnell
267	Sallie McConnell	34	Bass & Violet Harlin
860	Violet McConnell	11	Jack & Sallie McConnell
474	Austin McCoy	1	Waddie & Carrie McCoy
474	Carrie McCoy	23	Andy & Millie Frye
269	Cornelius McCoy	8	James McCoy & Mary Linsey
1447	John McCoy	40	Frank & Sylva Alberty
474	Viola McCoy	17mos	Waddie & Carrie McCoy
474	Waddie McCoy	25	Waddie McCoy & Harriett Woodard
417	Andrew McCrackin	35	George & Rose McCrackin
599	Bessie McCullough	9	Frank McCullough & Sallie Baker
1400	Samuel McCurtain	40	Jack McCurtain & Katie Kernel
89	Frank McDade	3	Frank & Mollie McDade
89	Luster McDade	9mos	Frank & Mollie McDade
89	Mollie McDade	19	Andy & Emily Tyner
1246	Jake McDaniel	40	Dennis McDaniel & Lucy Smith
232	Peggie McDaniels	11mos	Emma Bruner
232	Sophie McDaniels	18	Jake McDaniels & Emma Bruner
1303	Allie McElroy	24	Jordan Harper & Lydia Carter
1204	Jane McGilbey	50	Ben Grimmett & Eliza Blain
1153	Dice McIntosh	36	Tobe McIntosh & Cinda
37	Robert McIntosh	9	Fred McIntosh & Josephine Sheppard
1155	Will McIntosh	19	Governor McIntosh & Bettie Rogers
37	William McIntosh	12	Dave McIntosh&Josephine Sheppard
1386	Cassie McLain	4	Felix & Nellie McLain
1386	Leo McLain	9	Felix & Nellie McLain
1386	Maxie McLain	7	Felix & Nellie McLain
1386	Nellie McLain	28	Samuel & Nancy Starr
1386	Rosa McLain	2mos	Felix & Nellie McLain

63	Adam McNack	5	Adam & Frances McNack
63	Bertha McNack	15	Adam & Frances McNack
63	Charles McNack	13	Adam & Frances McNack
63	David McNack	11	Adam & Frances McNack
63	Fannie McNack	17	Adam & Frances McNack
63	Frances McNack	60	Stephen & Susie Hilderbrand
63	Jerry McNack	2	Adam & Frances McNack
63	Jessie McNack	7	Adam & Frances McNack
63	Lewis McNack	9	Adam & Frances McNack
63	Wallace McNack	19	Adam & Frances McNack
698	Columbus McNair	51	Lauda & Ann McNair
1245	Dinah McNair	18	George & Martha McNair
1529	Mattie McNair	30	James Hailstock & Nancy Vann
698	Morris McNair	13	Columbus & Cora McNair
1243	Sarah McNair	24	George & Martha McNair
1517	Sabra McQueen	37	Charles Chambers & Sidney West
234	Ermon McWaters	9mos	Sherman & Hannah McWaters
234	Hannah McWaters	30	Daniel & Lottie Vann
234	Sherman McWaters	9mos	Sherman & Hannah McWaters
50	Joseph Meadows	17	Lige Meadows & Mary Sumpter
50	Julia Meadows	14	Lige Meadows & Mary Sumpter
448	Anna Meigs	18	Samuel & Ida Meigs
448	Christine Meigs	15	Samuel & Ida Meigs
448	Cora Meigs	10	Samuel & Ida Meigs
448	Ellen Meigs	11	Samuel & Ida Meigs
448	Ida Meigs	42	Steve & Christine Perry
448	James Meigs	3	Samuel & Ida Meigs
448	Johnson Meigs	13	Samuel & Ida Meigs
893	LeeElla Meigs	6mos	Flemming & Mattie Meigs
448	Leroy Meigs	5	Samuel & Ida Meigs
893	Mattie Meigs	20	William & Susan Hudson
448	Minnie Meigs	9	Samuel & Ida Meigs
448	Rebecca Meigs	8	Samuel & Ida Meigs
448	Robert Meigs	19	Samuel & Ida Meigs
448	Samuel Meigs	50	Johnson & Rosanna Meigs
448	Stephen Meigs	1	Samuel & Ida Meigs
1011	Amanda Melton	57	Cy & Sylvia Baldridge
1374	Bessie Melton	13	Henry Melton & Matilda Gibson
1581	Elizabeth Melton	17	Harrison & Delilah Johnson
1581	Elnora Melton	7mos	Bud & Elizabeth Melton

1011	George Melton	56	Peter & Judy Melton
1011	George Jr Melton	12	George & Susan Melton
904	Henry Melton	65	Joe Melton & Sophia Brown
1374	Iola Melton	7	Henry Melton & Matilda Gibson
1374	Joe Melton	12	Henry Melton & Matilda Gibson
148	John Melton	64	Wash Melton & Betsy Thompson
1052	Judy Melton	3	Jesse Daniels & Victoria Melton
687	Leve Melton	29	Nathan & Rosie Melton
565	Lillie Melton	7	Nathan & Rosanna Melton
904	Minta Melton	65	Robert & Rachel Vann
565	Nathan Melton	30	Nathan & Rosanna Melton
571	Nathan Melton	63	Lell Melton & Peggie Gunter
1212	Peter Melton	25	George & Susan Melton
571	Rosanna Melton	63	Jerry & Susie Brown
574	Rosetta Melton	32	Nathan & Rose Melton
904	Sallie Melton	45	Root Vann & Minta Melton
904	Steve Melton	23	Sallie Melton
1052	Victoria Melton	21	George & Susan Melton
1381	Willie Melton	11	Love & Sarah Melton
1445	Charles Merrell	6mos	Lewis & Mattie Merrell
1445	Cora Merrell	4	Lewis & Mattie Merrell
1445	Ethel Merrell	6	Lewis & Mattie Merrell
931	George Merrell	26	Dennis & Sarah Merrell
1445	Mattie Merrell	32	Andy Merrell & Sallie Humphrey
1445	Sadie Merrell	9	Lewis & Mattie Merrell
1445	Willie Merrell	12	Lewis & Mattie Merrell
671	Delana Midleton	3	Tobe & Cassie Midleton
671	Neal Midleton	5	Tobe & Cassie Midleton
671	Tobe Midleton	38	Jennie Vann
380	Effie Milam	7mos	Frank & Rosella Milam
220	Mike Milam	11	Frank Milam & Mandy Foreman
380	Rosella Milam	23	Samuel & Julia Webber
1573	Charles Miller	10	William Miller & Fannie Scott
1539	Clarence Miller	5	Simon & Dora Miller
1539	Dora Miller	23	William & Carrie Richardson
1138	Frank Miller	40	Caben Miller & Nancy Sheppard
1157	Gular Miller	28	John & Maria Chase
378	Jennie Miller	45	Banjo & Hannah Lasley
1539	Jerald Miller	3	Simon & Dora Miller
869	Lula Miller	28	Charles Smith & Sarah Johnson

1539	Vine Miller	7	Simon & Dora Miller
1485	Mary Miller	44	Mike Whitmire & Rhoda Thornton
5	Annie Minnus	42	Stephen Ross & Emily Humphry
1324	Albert Minsy	3	James Minsy & Nellie Graves
762	Kittie Mitchell	21	Luster & Clora Foreman
762	Mildred Mitchell	1	David & Kittie Mitchell
1143	Katie Monday	50	George & Cassie Landrum
1469	Thomas Moon	50	Anderson Taylor & Chaney Rowe
810	Alexander Moore	5	Nelson & Rosa Moore
862	Delbert Moore	4mos	Readus & Emma Moore
810	Ella Moore	16	Nelson & Rosa Moore
862	Emma Moore	20	Richard & Sallie Foreman
811	Emily Moore	26	Nelson & Rosa Moore
821	Feriby Moore	34	James & Rhoda Davis
146	Frank Moore	8	John & Julia Moore
811	Helen Moore	3	Harvey Martin & Emily Moore
811	Herbert Moore	6	John Buffington & Emily Moore
810	John Moore	8	Nelson & Rosa Moore
812	Lewis Moore	21	Nelson & Rosa Moore
810	Lucy Moore	18	Nelson & Rosa Moore
810	Nelson Moore	48	Anderson & Chaney Moore
862	Readus Moore	28	Lewis Armstead & Rose Moore
810	Rosa Moore	48	Jack & Rachel Musgrove
810	Sophia Moore	14	Nelson & Rosa Moore
810	Thomas Moore	11	Nelson & Rosa Moore
797	Annie Morgan	6	Henry & Lucy Morgan
797	Ella Morgan	7	Henry & Lucy Morgan
797	Lucy Morgan	25	Gus & Mary Buffington
797	Oscar Morgan	10	Henry & Lucy Morgan
263	Alice Morris	39	James Johnson & Caroline Starr
835	April Morris	1mo	David & Sarah Morris
263	Callie Morris	11	Charles & Alice Morris
263	Charles Morris	14	Charles & Alice Morris
1338	Charlie Morris	61	Major Donohoe & Jane Morris
835	Crowder Morris	5	David & Sarah Morris
835	David Morris	10	David & Sarah Morris
912	Elinor Morris	1	Wyly & Mary Morris
986	Eliza Morris	25	Eli & Patience Vann
835	Hoolie Morris	8	David & Sarah Morris
912	John Morris	4	Wyly & Mary Morris

263	Joshua Morris	7	Charles & Alice Morris
835	Louisa Morris	4	David & Sarah Morris
263	Maggie Morris	8	Charles & Alice Morris
912	Mary Morris	24	Ed & Matty Campbell
835	Octa Morris	12	David & Sarah Morris
263	Rosa Morris	2	Charles & Alice Morris
263	Sarah Morris	4	Charles & Alice Morris
835	Sarah Morris	36	Thomas Parks & Eliza Hilderbrand
263	Susan Morris	17	Charles & Alice Morris
263	William Morris	13	Charles & Alice Morris
835	WyJay Morris	2	David & Sarah Morris
888	Aggie Muldrow	29	Frank & Susan Ross
921	Arrell Mundis	3	Jesse & Sarah Mundis
921	Carl Mundis	5	Jesse & Sarah Mundis
921	Lydia Mundis	1mo	Jesse & Sarah Mundis
921	Nellie Mundis	6	Jesse & Sarah Mundis
921	Sarah Mundis	28	Aaron & Sarah Whitmire
880	Emma Munson	13	Henry Munson & Peggy Williams
929	Josie Munson	13	Henry Munson & Minnie Beck
880	Lewis Munson	10	Henry Munson & Peggy Williams
1392	Flora Murrell	67	Soney Brown & Sarah Ross
969	Jenetta Murrell	6wks	George Murrell & Nancy Glass
990	Alex Musgrove	5	Rider & Lizzie Musgrove
1063	Annie Musgrove	2mos	Willie & Susie Musgrove
609	Eddie Musgrove	12	Daniel Musgrove & Malinda Parker
1432	Ella Musgrove	20	Robert & Finis Carter
990	George Musgrove	4	Rider & Lizzie Musgrove
1024	George Musgrove	60	John & Katie Vann
1064	Judy Musgrove	26	Boney & Peggy Vann
990	Leoda Musgrove	8	Rider & Lizzie Musgrove
990	Lula Musgrove	2	Rider & Lizzie Musgrove
990	Mary Musgrove	7	Rider & Lizzie Musgrove
1024	Rebecca Musgrove	60	Jim & Dilsa Beck
990	Rider Musgrove	33	George Vann & Mary Dawn
1063	Susie Musgrove	23	George Nave & Aggie Rogers
1064	William Musgrove	36	George & Becky Musgrove
1460	Willie Musgrove	36	Tuck & Ruth Musgrove
431	Sarah Nalls	30	Daniel & Patsy Roach
1287	Allie Nash	13	John & Luella Nash
1290	Berry Nash	22	John Nash & Eliza Gaines

1291	Edward Nash	21	Henry Nash & Eliza Gaines
1287	Jesse Nash	12	John & Luella Nash
1287	John Nash	35	Henry Nash & Eliza Gaines
1285	Julia Nash	38	Miller George & Eliza Gaines
1287	Lucy Nash	6	John & Luella Nash
1287	Ollie Nash	8	John & Luella Nash
996	Albert Nave	13	Wash Nave & Maggie Roach
1102	Aleck Nave	16	Lewis & Mary Nave
1062	Amanda Nave	18	George Nave & Aggie Rogers
1222	Arthur Nave	15	John Nave & Laura Cloid
1025	Artie Nave	26	John & Lucinda Nave
798	Benjamin Nave	37	Charles & Elmira Nave
1314	Carrie Nave	43	Robert Webber & Lucinda French
813	Charity Nave	14	Larn Greenway & Laura Rowe
138	Charles Nave	5	Cornelius & Florence Nave
1314	Clem Nave	3	Noah Alberty & Carrie Nave
138	Cornelius Nave	32	Charles & Mary Nave
1362	Dave Nave	50	Wash & Maria Nave
138	Dora Nave	8	Cornelius & Florence Nave
95	Edward Nave	29	Charles & Mary Nave
1092	Eli Nave	53	Mose Nave
1314	Ella Nave	14	Reuben & Carrie Nave
1075	Ellen Nave	43	Robin Webber & Lucinda French
1101	Ellis Nave	30	Eli & Jane Nave
1102	Elnora Nave	10	Lewis & Mary Nave
1075	Emmett Nave	6	Dave & Ellen Nave
1102	Ethel Nave	17	Lewis & Mary Nave
1075	Evaline Nave	8	Dave & Ellen Nave
138	Florence Nave	31	Bob & Malinda Smith
1034	Frances Nave	17	Wash Nave & Rachel Pennington
1364	George Nave	37	Wash & Maria Nave
1065	George Nave	45	Armstead Nave & Dinah Vann
1075	George Nave	20	Dave & Ellen Nave
1314	Georgia Nave	12	Reuben & Carrie Nave
1053	Gertie Nave	8mos	Ulysses & Maggie Nave
1092	Harvey Nave	11	Wesley Nave
1314	Henrietta Nave	8	Reuben & Carrie Nave
1092	Jane Nave	55	Martha Johnson
1059	John Nave	47	George Nave & Amanda Melton
1075	John Nave	10	Dave & Ellen Nave

899	Jordan Nave	12	Roland Nave & Sarah Reese
1075	Keller Nave	18	Dave & Ellen Nave
1075	Laura Nave	15	Dave & Ellen Nave
1314	Lena Nave	20	Reuben & Carrie Nave
1070	Lewis Nave	56	Armstead Nave & Diana Vann
128	Lily Nave	15	Bud Nave & Lottie Campbell
1034	Luella Nave	14	Wash Nave & Rachel Pennington
1053	Maggie Nave	21	Manuel & Nancy Taylor
138	Margaret Nave	7mos	Cornelius & Florence Nave
1075	Mariah Nave	12	Dave & Ellen Nave
1102	Mary Nave	36	Eli & Jane Nave
1314	Mattie Nave	10	Reuben & Carrie Nave
88	Mattie Nave	12	Henry & Matt Starr
1102	Myrtle Nave	6	Lewis & Mary Nave
1314	Osie Nave	18	Reuben & Carrie Nave
1076	Peggie Nave	8mos	George & Emma Nave
1363	Reuben Nave	45	Wash & Maria Nave
1314	Sherman Nave	4	James Williams & Lena Nave
1075	Sherman Nave		Dave & Ellen Nave
138	Thomas Nave	10	Cornelius & Florence Nave
1053	Ulysses Nave	22	Dave & Ella Nave
1053	Velmafey Nave	1mo	Ulysses & Maggie Nave
1361	Wash Jr. Nave	43	Wash & Maria Nave
88	Will Nave	13	Henry & Matt Starr
138	William Nave	3	Cornelius & Florence Nave
1314	Willie Nave	16	Reuben & Carrie Nave
855	Cora Nelson	16	Edward & Jennie Nelson
855	Eddie Nelson	11	Edward & Jennie Nelson
855	Elizabeth Nelson	14	Edward & Jennie Nelson
70	Idelia Nelson	1	Patsy Martin
855	Jennie Nelson	38	Crockett Vann & Susan Bowles
855	Lola Nelson	4	Edward & Jennie Nelson
855	William Nelson	2	Edward & Jennie Nelson
855	Zacharia Nelson	18	Edward & Jennie Nelson
253	Clifford Nero	3mos	Richard & Rosa Nero
500	Jesse Nero	3mos	A.L. & Sarah Nero
253	Nancy Nero	3	Richard & Rosa Nero
500	Roger Nero	2	Abraham & Sarah Nero
253	Rosa Nero	24	Morris & Nancy Sheppard
500	Sarah Nero	25	Freeland Jones & Nancy Logan

253	Willie Nero	4	Richard & Rosa Nero
31	Alexander Nivens	60	John Shaw & Judia Rogers
31	Amelia Nivens	10	Alexander & Mary Nivens
237	Bertie Nivens	13	Rufus Nivens & Amanda Alberty
31	Charles Nivens	18	Alexander & Mary Nivens
118	Dennis Nivens	1mo	July & Sallie Nivens
118	Hanson Nivens	2	July & Sallie Nivens
169	Harrison Nivens	22	Alex & Mary Nivens
111	Harry Nivens	20	Isaac & Louisa Nivens
111	Isaac Nivens	60	Billy Postoak & Lizzie Smith
118	Jessie Nivens	3	July & Sallie Nivens
31	John Nivens	16	Alexander & Mary Nivens
31	June Nivens	12	Alexander & Mary Nivens
118	July Nivens	25	Isaac & Louisa Nivens
118	Lila Nivens	4	July & Sallie Nivens
31	Mary Nivens	48	Callis Jones & Susie Thompson
591	Rufus Nivens	33	Mose & Patsy Nivens
31	Samuel Nivens	20	Alexander & Mary Nivens
611	Thomas Nivens	6	Callis Nivens & Minnie Carter
118	Webb Nivens		July & Sallie Nivens
31	Wheeler Nivens	13	Alexander & Mary Nivens
34	Annie Nivins	24	Anderson & Sarah Bean
35	Callis Nivins	24	Alex & Mary Nivins
35	Clifford Nivins	7mos	Callis & Emma Nivins
35	Dewey Nivins	2	Callis & Emma Nivins
35	Emma Nivins	19	Junius & Patsy Dennis
34	Flora Nivins	2	Richard & Annie Nivins
34	Josie Nivins	4	Richard & Annie Nivins
35	Nellie Nivins	5mos	Callis & Emma Nivins
34	Richard Nivins	27	Alex & Mary Nivins
34	Sada Nivins	9mos	Richard & Annie Nivins
1425	Queen Nolen	16	July & Josephine Martin
1121	Charles Owens	2wks	Squire & Lizzie Owens
1121	Erman Owens	1	Squire & Lizzie Owens
1121	Ernest Owens	11	Squire & Lizzie Owens
1121	Livius Owens	13	Squire & Lizzie Owens
1121	Lizzie Owens	34	Frank & Susan Ross
1121	Lloyd Owens	7	Squire & Lizzie Owens
1393	Rebecca Owens	11	Jerry Owens & Mary Hardrick
1121	Susan Owens	9	Squire & Lizzie Owens

1393	Susie Owens	7	Jerry Owens & Mary Hardrick
1121	Zelia Owens	3	Squire & Lizzie Owens
104	Addie Pack	14	Frank & Julia Pack
104	Frank Pack	40	Jack & Martha Pack
507	George Pack	13	Frank Pack & Eliza Dotson
103	Henry Pack	28	Jack & Martha Pack
1148	Joseph Pack	46	Silas Pack
104	Lizzie Pack	19	Frank & Julia Pack
1405	Lottie Pack	30	Maryland & Ibbie Beck
455	Martha Pack	68	
104	Okla Pack	11	Frank & Julia Pack
400	William Pack	21	Frank & Julia Pack
357	Jackson Paine	33	Wallace & Martha Paine
65	Leonard Parker	2	Anderson & Samantha Parker
609	Malinda Parker	28	Jake & Lucy Crapo
609	Nona Parker	3	Spain Parker & Malinda Parker
609	Ola Parker	7mos	Spain Parker & Malinda Parker
65	Samantha Parker	22	Fred & Sophie Schrimsher
609	Spain Parker	8mos	Spain Parker & Malinda Parker
197	Bass Parks	75	Ann Parks
238	Laura Parks	32	Bart & Frances Thompson
467	Ada Parris	7	David & Amanda Parris
621	Aleck Parris	5	Anthony & Laura Parris
621	Anthony Parris	29	James & Serena Parris
467	Bertha Parris	3	David & Fannie Parris
647	Caleb Parris	56	Anthony & Mary Parris
621	Cora Parris	2	Anthony & Laura Parris
467	David Parris	29	Wat & Margarite Parris
467	David Jr. Parris	1	David & Fannie Parris
621	Earl Parris	4	Anthony & Laura Parris
467	Fannie Parris	19	Andy & Charlotte Brewer
385	Felix Parris	6	Robert & Nellie Parris
401	James Parris	50	Robert & Sarah Parris
467	Jane Parris	9	David & Amanda Parris
385	John Parris	7	Robert & Nellie Parris
621	Laura Parris	24	Will Musgrove & Maria Keys
467	Lillie Parris	3wks	David & Fannie Parris
621	Madie Parris	5mos	Anthony & Laura Parris
385	Mertie Parris	18mos	Robert & Nellie Parris
385	Patsy Parris	9	Robert & Nellie Parris

385	Robert Parris	31	Watt & Margaret Parris
401	Sarina Parris	54	Alex Benge & Maria Bark
401	Thomas Parris	20	James & Sarina Parris
440	William Parris	21	James & Serena Parris
621	William Parris	4	Anthony & Laura Parris
836	Arthur Patterson	19	York & Frances Patterson
836	Frances Patterson	60	George Lovett & Judy Williams
836	York Patterson	13	York & Frances Patterson
1180	James Payne	2	Wallace & Lou Payne
612	Wallace Payne	60	Charles & Easter Riley
1480	Susan Pee	75	
332	Anna Penn	3	Anderson & Sarah Penn
332	Lila Penn	6	Anderson & Sarah Penn
332	Sarah Penn	28	John & Cairsby Bean
1034	Mahala Pennington	8	George & Rachel Pennington
1034	Melissa Pennington	3	George & Rachel Pennington
1034	Rachel Pennington	39	George & Mahala Brown
1034	Rachel Pennington	2	George & Rachel Pennington
288	Ann Perry	48	Jack & Martha Pack
499	Patsie Perryman	40	Squire Sanders & Judie Taylor
120	Samuel Petit	25	George & Lizzie Petit
102	Annie Petitt	11	George & Philis Petitt
102	George Petitt	54	George & Dinah Petitt
102	Henry Petitt	5	George & Philis Petitt
102	Philis Petitt	49	Riley & Lutitia Harnage
102	Sophie Petitt	16	George & Philis Petitt
136	Ibby Pettit	20	Willis Pettit & Maria Ross
1171	Daniel Pinder	17	Daniel & Katie Pinder
1451	Lewis Pool	5	Charlie & Nancy Pool
333	Belle Poorboy	15	Josiah Poorboy & Sarah Ross
639	Ellen Porlar	1	Richard & Emma Porlar
639	Richard Porlar	32	Pollard & Katie Drew
564	Douglas Porter	10	John & Nan Porter
564	Edna Porter	6	John & Nan Porter
564	Ernest Porter	12	John & Nan Porter
564	Maudy Porter	5	John & Nan Porter
503	Nan Porter	32	Andy & Seenie Brewer
564	Willie Porter	1	John & Nan Porter
785	Alexander Powell	38	Rosanna Hardrick
179	Luvanda Powell	7	Jerry & Frances Powers

1134	Rilda Powell	27	Ellis & Eliza Jones
359	Emma Price	35	John Hall & Louisa Thompson
502	Jennie Price	5	Wesley & Ella Price
359	John Price	2	Jacob & Emma Price
359	Louisa Price	9	Jacob & Emma Price
502	Louvenia Price	11	Wesley & Ella Price
359	Matilda Price	5	Jacob & Emma Price
359	Minerva Price	7	Jacob & Emma Price
359	Perry Price	3mos	Jacob & Emma Price
502	Savannah Price	9	Wesley & Ella Price
1586	Emma Purtle	46	Riley & Maria McNair
779	Annie Ragsdale	47	Warren Adams & Ibby Vann
779	Jonas Ragsdale	60	Sophia Ragsdale
943	Willie Ragsdale	19	Lons Manley & Frances Ragsdale
1123	Myrtle Ratcliff	19	John & Ruth Ratcliff
940	Edith Ratliff	42	Tobe Schrimsher & Seemie Brewer
940	Enda Ratliff	4	Isaac & Edith Ratliff
940	Henry Ratliff	11	Isaac & Edith Ratliff
241	Jane Ray	23	Mose & Mary Johnson
241	Lewis Ray	4mos	William & Jane Ray
433	Bethel Reed	3mos	Dave & Sarah Reed
159	Frank Reed	22	Rachel Gunter
886	George Jr Reed	7	George & Harriet Reed
886	Harriet Reed	31	Simon & Sarah Sanders
886	Henry Reed	9	George & Harriet Reed
886	Lee Reed	3	George & Harriet Reed
886	Mabel Reed	3wks	George & Harriet Reed
967	Millie Reed	24	Lewis & Betsy Whitmire
433	Sarah Reed	31	Wallace & Marsha Payne
982	Sylvester Reed	12	Major Reed & Matilda Lynch
708	Amanda Reese	18	Jack & Nancy Baldridge
707	Anderson Reese	5	James & Savannah Reese
708	Beatrice Reese	4	Tom Downing & Amanda Reese
708	Ben Reese	24	Jesse & Betsy Reese
705	Betsy Reese	60	Sallie Walker
707	James Reese	23	Jesse & Betsy Reese
705	Jesse Reese	60	Eliowa
899	Sarah Reese	30	Ed Ross & Dinah Johnson
1340	Winnie Reeves	43	Dred & Caroline Foreman
1278	Daniel Reid	1mo	Frank & Molly Reid

1278	Mollie Reid	17	Dan & Mary Walker
57	Bessie Reynolds	4	Wash & Nancy Reynolds
154	Columbus Reynolds	6	James & Martha Reynolds
173	Harrison Reynolds	21	James & Martha Reynolds
154	Henry Reynolds	18	James & Martha Reynolds
57	Henry Reynolds	5	Wash & Nancy Reynolds
57	Laura Reynolds	8	Wash & Nancy Reynolds
57	Lilburn Reynolds	6	Wash & Nancy Reynolds
154	Maggie Reynolds	16	James & Martha Reynolds
154	Martha Reynolds	46	Jordan Thompson & Rachel
57	Mary Reynolds	12	Wash & Nancy Reynolds
57	Nancy Reynolds	34	Butler & Sarah Vann
57	Nellie Reynolds	10	Wash & Nancy Reynolds
154	Sheridan Reynolds	13	James & Martha Reynolds
134	Chaney Richardson	41	Joe & Ruth Tucker
1552	Lizzie Richardson	2	Will & Laura Richardson
624	Angeline Rider	2	James & Sallie Rider
585	Annie Rider	42	Ruben Klein & Betsie Leek
1137	Bertha Rider	14	Tom & Mary Rider
585	Betsie Rider	16	Jerry & Annie Rider
1459	Buck Rider	60	Lewis & Lizzie Starr
1565	Carlos Rider	13	Henry & Martha Rider
1032	Charlie Rider	21	Henry & Polly Rider
624	Clem Rider	11	James & Sallie Rider
670	Edie Rider	41	Peter & Fannie Lourey
585	Ella Rider	14	Jerry & Annie Rider
624	Ellen Rider	2mos	James & Sallie Rider
1565	Flora Rider	12	Henry & Martha Rider
620	Frank Rider	22	Jerry & Ann Rider
1563	George Rider	40	Henry & Elizabeth Rider
843	Georgia Rider	14	Andrew & Sarah Rider
1565	Henry Rider	39	Henry & Elizabeth Ride
624	James Rider	54	George Ross & Lucy Rider
585	Jerry Rider	43	Elijah & Lucy Rider
429	Jess Rider	50	Elijah & Lucy Rider
624	Jesse Rider	7	James & Sallie Rider
614	John Rider	27	James Rider & Catherine Durant
624	Leonard Rider	4	James & Sallie Rider
718	Lige Rider	74	Jack & Rachel Ratcliffe
1167	Lovely Rider	22	Jess & Nancy Rider

1565	Luellen Rider	11	Henry & Martha Rider
624	Luther Rider	9	James & Sallie Rider
1031	Mariah Rider	63	Charles & Fannie Lowrey
428	Reed Rider	24	Jesse & Nancy Rider
793	Robert Rider	27	William & Edie Rider
585	Rose Rider	20	Jerry & Annie Rider
588	Sam Rider	31	James & Catherine Rider
585	Sarah Rider	12	Jerry & Annie Rider
843	Sarah Rider	33	William & Malinda Madden
619	Thomas Rider	25	James & Catherine Rider
670	William Rider	57	Elijah & Lucy Rider
1572	Ada Riley	4	Jerry & Hannah Riley
270	Alex Riley	5	Robin & Emma Riley
1572	Amanda Riley	15	Jerry & Hannah Riley
1569	Andrew Riley	53	Riley & Maria McNair
412	Andy Riley	10	Solomon & Mary Riley
1556	Annie Riley	8mos	Ed & Mary Riley
1571	Arizona Riley	8	Frank & Mary Riley
1580	Arthur Riley	24	Jerry & Hannah Riley
1572	Bertha Riley	7	Jerry & Hannah Riley
1572	Calvin Riley	9	Jerry & Hannah Riley
412	Carrie Riley	12	Solomon & Mary Riley
1571	Clarence Riley	5mos	Pearl Wagoner & Lottie Riley
1571	Earl Riley	6mos	Frank & Mary Riley
1556	Ed Riley	33	Joseph & Mary Riley
1570	Elnora Riley	5	Jesse & Rutha Riley
303	Emiline Riley	55	Solomon & Malinda Foreman
270	Emma Riley	35	Jake & Lucy Crapo
290	Esther Riley	90	
1571	Fannie Riley	14	Frank & Mary Riley
775	Florence Riley	7mos	Frank Riley & Mamie Davis
1571	Frank Riley	35	Riley & Maria McNair
270	Frank Riley	12	Robin & Emma Riley
1559	Fred Riley	24	Joseph & Mary Riley
1592	Fred Riley	24	Joseph & Mary Riley
412	Georgia Riley	6	Solomon & Mary Riley
1424	Henry Riley	11	Moses McNair & Emma Bean
1556	Howard Riley	3	Ed & Mary Riley
1570	Ideller Riley	3	Jesse & Rutha Riley
1571	Inola Riley	6	Frank & Mary Riley

1572	James Riley	18	Jerry & Hannah Riley
1571	James Riley	12	Frank & Mary Riley
207	Jefferson Riley	21	Solomon & Lucinda Riley
1572	Jerry Riley	47	Riley & Maria McNair
1570	Jesse Riley	44	Riley & Maria McNair
1556	Jessie Riley	7	Ed & Mary Riley
1588	John Riley	5mos	William & Maud Riley
1570	Joseph Riley	13	Jesse & Rutha Riley
1576	Lenora Riley	5mos	Jesse & Ruth Riley
1572	Leona Riley	2	Jerry & Hannah Riley
1568	Lilly Riley	16	Moses & Jane Riley
1571	Lottie Riley	16	Frank & Mary Riley
1570	Luther Rilty	1	Jesse & Rutha Riley
1570	Mabel Riley	7	Jesse & Rutha Riley
1572	Maggie Riley	11	Jerry & Hannah Riley
1572	Mariah Riley	13	Jerry & Hannah Riley
1558	Mary Riley	8	Richard & Sarah Riley
1556	Matt Riley	9	Ed & Mary Riley
270	McKinley Riley	4	Robin & Emma Riley
1568	Moses Riley	51	Riley & Maria McNair
412	Moses Riley	15	Solomon & Mary Riley
270	Nannie Riley	15	Robin & Emma Riley
1569	Nathaniel Riley	5	Andrew & Jeanette Riley
1570	Ollie Riley	11	Jesse & Rutha Riley
1571	Ralph Riley	10	Frank & Mary Riley
1558	Richard Riley	31	Joseph & Mary Riley
270	Robin Riley	40	Charles & Hester Riley
412	Sallie Riley	18	Solomon & Mary Riley
1572	Samuel Riley	20	Jerry & Hannah Riley
270	Sarah Riley	2	Robin & Emma Riley
303	Stephen Riley	65	Henry & Rachel Riley
1570	Viola Riley	9	Jesse & Rutha Riley
1577	William Riley	23	Mose & Jane Riley
1558	Willie Riley	10	Richard & Sarah Riley
477	Bertha Roach	2mos	Tuxie & Ella Roach
365	Conway Roach	2mos	Henry & Rebecca Roach
40	Daniel Roach	75	Charles & Hannah Drew
976	Denis Roach	3mos	Jess & Lucy Roach
976	Earnest Roach	3	Jess & Lucy Roach
477	Ella Roach	26	Nelson & Rose Webber

365	Elmira Roach	2	Henry & Rebecca Roach
476	Fannie Roach	36	Rose Webber
476	Florence Roach	6	Joseph & Fannie Roach
365	Henry Roach	35	Daniel & Rose Roach
40	Jesse Roach	21	Daniel & Rose Roach
476	Joseph Roach	42	Daniel & Patsy Roach
365	Joseph Roach	4	Henry & Rebecca Roach
232	Joseph Roach	1mo	Jane Crossley
311	Julia Roach	26	Daniel Roach & Rose Gunter
478	Laura Roach	17	Alfred & Alice Wright
476	Leroy Roach	9	Joseph & Fannie Roach
476	Lillie Roach	3	Joseph & Fannie Roach
312	Lovely Roach	13	Henry Roach & Emma Lewis
976	Lucy Roach	26	Dennis & Lucy Whitmire
476	Maggie Roach	12	Joseph & Fannie Roach
312	Maud Roach	11	Henry Roach & Emma Lewis
477	Muggie Roach	2	Tuxie & Ella Roach
996	Maggie Roach	29	Dennis & Sarah Merrell
40	Nancy Roach	18	Daniel & Rose Roach
478	Ollie Roach	10mos	Samuel & Laura Roach
477	Oscar Roach	4	Tuxie & Ella Roach
476	Patsie Roach	15	Joseph & Fannie Roach
365	Patsie Roach	7	Henry & Belle Roach
365	Rebecca Roach	25	Butler & Sarah Vann
329	Robert Roach	35	Daniel & Patsy Roach
309	Samuel Roach	23	Daniel Roach & Rose Gunter
477	Stella Roach	7	Tuxie & Ella Roach
477	Tuxie Roach	27	Daniel & Patsy Roach
389	Mary Robbins	50	Jennie Roack
117	Amanda Roberson	12	Calvin Roberson & Tilda Vann
117	Arthur Roberson	9	Calvin Roberson & Tilda Vann
117	Belle Roberson	48	Caleb & Sallie Vann
117	Bertha Roberson	16	Calvin Roberson & Tilda Vann
117	Calvin Roberson	48	Watie & Philis Roberson
117	Watie Roberson	14	Calvin Roberson & Tilda Vann
115	Anna Robertson	7mos	Asbury & Lucinda Robertson
115	Fayette Robertson	3mos	Asbury & Lucinda Robertson
115	Lucinda Robertson	31	Isaac & Louisa Nivens
107	Jemima Robertson	100	Peter Ross
1036	Annie Robinson	1	Charlie Robinson & Julia Dickson

1147	Arthur Robinson	21	Tobe & Lizzie Robinson
435	Belle Robinson	19	Buster Vann & Rachel Gunter
1366	Bettie Robinson	42	Jake & Sarah Martin
977	Della Robinson	6	Tobe & Lizzie Robinson
977	Frederick Robinson	18	Tobe & Lizzie Robinson
977	George Robinson	14	Tobe & Lizzie Robinson
977	Hannah Robinson	3	Tobe & Lizzie Robinson
435	Katie Robinson	8mos	Sherman & Belle Robinson
977	Lizzie Robinson	39	George & Mahala Brown
977	Lola Robinson	10	Tobe & Lizzie Robinson
1370	Melly Robinson	1	Lucky & Rosa Robinson
1370	Nody Robinson	5	Lucky & Rosa Robinson
977	Nora Robinson	15	Tobe & Lizzie Robinson
977	Parine Robinson	7mos	Tobe & Lizzie Robinson
435	Roberta Robinson	2mos	Sherman & Belle Robinson
1370	Rosa Robinson	23	Jake & Sarah Martin
977	Tolly Robinson	5	Tobe & Lizzie Robinson
1546	Willie Rodgers	6	Nick & Neatie Rodgers
531	Cassie Roe	6	Perry Roe & Susan Vann
1062	Aggie Rogers	41	Pompey & Lucinda Wright
397	Albert Rogers	23	Tassie Rogers & Mary Robbins
1041	Allen Rogers	39	Nick Rogers & Sarah Murrell
955	Anderson Rogers	18	Houston & Sidney Rogers
1508	Augustus Rogers	22	Joe Rogers & Sarah Whitmire
615	Betsy Rogers	17	Nig Rogers & Esther Schrimsher
955	Bud Rogers	20	Houston & Sidney Rogers
1149	Charley Rogers	24	Houston & Sidney Rogers
1106	Clem Rogers	26	Rab & Rhoda Rogers
854	Cooey Rogers	20	Isaac Rogers & Sallie Vann
544	Daniel Rogers	21	George & Rose Rogers
389	Dollie Rogers	15	Charlie Atkins & Fannie Rogers
1115	Eli Rogers	23	Houston & Sidney Rogers
816	Eliza Rogers	19	Jack & Nancy Baldridge
1520	Eliza Rogers	28	Charles Chambers & Sidney West
615	Ella Rogers	14	Nig Rogers & Esther Schrimsher
1509	Ellis Rogers	39	Columbus & Mary Rogers
852	Ethel Rogers	15	Isaac Rogers & Sarah Whitmire
942	Florence Rogers	21	Lons Manley & Frances Ragsdale
615	Fred Rogers	10	Nig Rogers & Esther Schrimsher
236	Gabe Rogers	18	Joseph & Maggie Rogers

537	George Rogers	53	Hayden & Silvy Rogers
1021	Grace Rogers	14	Rab & Rhoda Rogers
1041	Gratt Rogers	8	Allen & Ruth Rogers
585	Henrietta Rogers	3mos	Willie Rogers & Rose Rider
955	Houston Sr Rogers	62	Shoo-cow & Lucy Rogers
1022	Houston Jr Rogers	29	Rab & Rhoda Rogers
1021	Isaac Rogers	16	Rab & Rhoda Rogers
1173	Jack Rogers	30	Rab & Rhoda Rogers
1108	Jasper Rogers	24	Rab & Rhoda Rogers
537	Jesse Rogers	19	George & Rose Rogers
236	Joseph Rogers	55	Will & Louisa Rogers
1062	Leonard Rogers	14	Sim & Aggie Rogers
1021	Lucy Rogers	18	Rab & Rhoda Rogers
240	Malinda Rogers	28	Joe & Caroline Rogers
1021	Margaret Rogers	11	Rab & Rhoda Rogers
1505	Mary Rogers	32	Joseph Rogers & Sarah Whitmire
942	Nellie Rogers	5	Gus & Florence Rogers
853	Nelson Rogers	23	Isaac & Sallie Rogers
543	Pompey Rogers	31	George & Rose Rogers
1224	Pompey Rogers	21	Nig Rogers & Esther Schrimsher
1021	Rab Rogers	66	Jesse Rowe & Lucy Rogers
852	Ray Rogers	13	Isaac Rogers & Sarah Whitmire
795	Reuben Rogers	23	Cephas Rogers & Ann Rider
1021	Rhoda Rogers	55	Sam & Amanda Perry
1062	Rosa Rogers	12	Sim & Aggie Rogers
537	Rose Rogers	57	Pompey & Lucinda Wright
1105	Rosie Rogers	20	Rab & Rhoda Rogers
852	Roy Rogers	5	Isaac Rogers & Sarah Whitmire
1073	Rufus Rogers	28	Houston & Sidney Rogers
1062	Sallie Rogers	17	Sim & Aggie Rogers
1150	Sam Rogers	30	Houston & Sidney Rogers
1506	Sam Rogers	36	Joe Rogers & Sarah Whitmire
1044	Sarah Rogers	40	Armstead Nave & Dinah Vann
1062	Sharp Rogers	8	Sim & Aggie Rogers
955	Sidney Rogers	42	John Brown
1062	Sim Rogers	42	Nick & Sarah Rogers
236	Sylvia Rogers	37	James & Jennie Beck
942	Walter Rogers	3	Gus & Florence Rogers
584	William Rogers	25	Nig & Esther Rogers
1505	William Rogers	26	Joseph Rogers & Sarah Whitmire

585	Willie Rogers	2	Willie Rogers & Rose Rider
1044	Willis Rogers	50	Alec & Mandy Rogers
677	Sarah Roland	44	Wash & Maria Nave
1026	Eliza Rose	24	Wash Marshall & Mittie Smith
1026	Frank Rose	7	Charlie & Eliza Rose
1026	George Rose	4	Charlie & Eliza Rose
1026	John Rose	2	Charlie & Eliza Rose
577	Aaron Ross	28	Benjamin & Edith Ross
644	Ada Ross	8	Joshua & Caroline Ross
362	Addie Ross	13	Nelson & Martha Ross
132	Alberty Ross	4	Robert & Sarah Ross
451	Alexander Ross	19	Joseph & Laura Ross
338	Amanda Ross	12	Stick & Nancy Ross
463	Austin Ross	30	Stick & Lou Ross
132	Bessie Ross	12	Robert & Sarah Ross
644	Caroline Ross	27	Simon & Sarah Sanders
335	Carrie Ross	33	Fred & Sophia Schrimscher
451	Clarence Ross	13	Joseph & Laura Ross
338	Clem Ross	7	Stick & Nancy Ross
1109	Edmond Ross	34	Moses & Betsy Ross
23	Edward Ross	27	Henry & Polly Ross
367	Edward Ross	11	Ned & Ann Ross
1	Elnora Ross	9	John & Peggy Ross
1272	Elnora Ross	11	John Ross & Dora Rogers
28	Ethel Ross	1	Joseph & Rhoda Ross
414	Etta Ross	5	Ed Ross & Melinda Baker
1109	Etta Ross	11	Edmond & Hannah Ross
367	Fannie Ross	18	Ned & Ann Ross
882	Frank Ross	53	William & Judy Ross
882	Frank Jr Ross	20	Frank & Susan Ross
814	George Ross	18	Hector Ross & Eliza Dixon
1095	George Ross	53	Charles & Sophia Lowrey
53	Hannah Ross	19	Johnson & Amy Ross
888	Henrietta Ross	8	James Martin & Aggie Muldrow
47	Henry Ross	50	George & Becky Ross
414	Henry Jr. Ross	7	Ed Ross & Melinda Baker
136	Ishmael Ross	14	Moses Ross & Mary Bird
367	Isaac Ross	19	Ned & Ann Ross
256	Jack Ross	50	Jack Ridge & Chaney Ross
679	Jack Ross	33	Mose & Becky Ross

362	Jackson Ross	20	Nelson & Martha Ross
451	James Ross	17	Joseph & Laura Ross
644	James Ross	10	Joshua & Caroline Ross
28	Jane Ross	22	Fred & Sophia Schrimpher
1083	Jesse Ross	25	Perry & Mariah Ross
28	Jessie Ross	5	Joseph & Rhoda Ross
644	Jessie Ross	2mos	Henry Funghauser & Caroline Ross
883	Jessie Ross	7	Lewis Peterson & Josie Ross
450	Jodie Ross	21	Joseph & Laura Ross
1524	Joe Ross	50	Dave & Louisa Ross
1	John Ross	34	Stephen Ross & Emily Humphry
1	John Jr. Ross.	6	John Ross
818	John Ross	31	Sandy Ross & Arilda Vann
1560	John Jr. Ross	15	John Ross & Rhodi Ford
28	Joseph Ross	47	Stephen Ross & Emily Vann
451	Joseph Ross	44	Isaac & Rosanna Ross
883	Josie Ross	26	Lewis & Betsy Whitmire
338	Julia Ross	17	Stick & Nancy Ross
362	Kate Ross	18	Nelson & Martha Ross
366	Lawrence Ross	18	Jack Ross & Harriett Johnson
446	Lawrence Ross	44	Edmund & Harriett Ross
672	Lee Ross	14	William Ross & Darcus Harlin
259	Lena Ross	11	William Ross & Darcas Harlin
462	Lewis Ross	22	Ned & Nan Ross
451	Lizzie Ross	11	Joseph & Laura Ross
136	Louis Ross	12	Moses & Maria Ross
644	Louis Ross	7	Joshua & Caroline Ross
888	Lovetta Ross	9	Manuel Davis & Aggie Muldrow
453	Lula Ross	13	Moses & Mary Ross
648	Maggie Ross	22	Henry & Polly Ross
338	Malcolm Ross	20	Stick & Nancy Ross
28	Mamie Ross	3	Joseph & Rhoda Ross
136	Maria Ross	36	Joshua & Nancy Sheppard
1080	Mariah Ross	49	Lige & Lucy Rider
362	Martha Ross	36	Simon & Katie Fields
777	Martha Ross	22	James & Rose Alberty
453	Mary Ross	32	Simon & Katie Fields
1253	Mary Ross	35	Richard & Rose Chambers
677	Minnie Ross	6	George & Jennie Ross
1311	Minnie Ross	9	Perry & Ella Ross

453	Moses Ross	42	Sam & Mary Ross
255	Moses Ross	67	Jack Ridge & Chaney Ross
136	Moses Ross	40	Isaac & Rosanna Ross
136	Moses Jr. Ross	3	Moses & Maria Ross
451	Motto Ross	7	Joseph & Laura Ross
338	Nancy Ross	44	Johnson & Edna Rowe
889	Nathan Ross	35	Frank & Susan Ross
367	Ned Ross	52	Lewis Pattlingburd & Fannie Ross
338	Patsie Ross	10	Stick & Nancy Ross
362	Peggie Ross	11	Nelson & Martha Ross
453	Percy Ross	12	Moses & Mary Ross
1088	Perry Ross	53	Sam & Rachel Ross
47	Polly Ross	57	Jack Thompson
206	Polly Ross	42	Prince & Rachel Mosely
1532	Rachel Ross	30	Frank & Jane Whitmire
1260	Rebecca Ross	50	Robert Banks & Martha Spencer
446	Rhoda Ross	38	Prince Mosely & Silva Gladney
132	Richard Ross	6	Robert & Sarah Ross
132	Robert Ross	10	Robert & Sarah Ross
451	Rosanna Ross	15	Joseph & Laura Ross
451	Samuel Ross	9	Joseph & Laura Ross
1169	Samuel Ross	49	William & Judy Ross
132	Sarah Ross	30	William & Phoebe Hudson
333	Sarah Ross	43	Moses & Philis Ross
414	Sarah Ross	9	Ed Ross & Melinda Baker
335	Stephen Ross	32	Isaac & Rosanna Ross
28	Stephen Ross	17	Joseph & Rhoda Ross
338	Stick Ross	52	Hecter & Sallie Ross
1136	Tom Ross	31	Sarah Ross
136	Tomy Ross	7mos	Moses & Maria Ross
777	Watie Ross	4	Robert & Martha Ross
1004	William Ross	5	John Ross & Clara Foster
824	Ada Rowe	14	Dave Jones & Martha Downing
1018	Aggie Rowe	1mo	Haywood & Lucinda Rowe
1018	Albert Rowe	8	Haywood & Lucinda Rowe
1484	Alexander Rowe	40	Jesse Rowe & Sylvia Grimmett
1018	Charles Rowe	18	Haywood & Lucinda Rowe
704	Daniel Rowe	9	Alex & Rosa Rowe
1018	Ella Rowe	17	Haywood & Lucinda Rowe
1018	Haywood Rowe	40	Daniel & Julia Rowe

824	Jennie Rowe	2mos	
704	Jesse Rowe	19	Alex & Rosa Rowe
830	Jesse Rowe	36	Lewis & Chaney Ross
1355	John Rowe	45	John & Emily Rowe
813	Laura Rowe	33	Lewis & Chaney Rowe
1018	Louis Rowe	10	Haywood & Lucinda Rowe
1018	Lucinda Rowe	34	Gracie Greenleaf
898	Luther Rowe	1	Luther Goldsby & Viola Rowe
704	Lutitia Rowe	13	Alex & Rosa Rowe
828	Perry Rowe	28	Alex & Rose Rowe
1018	Perry Rowe	13	Haywood & Lucinda Rowe
1018	Rachel Rowe	2	Haywood & Lucinda Rowe
704	Rosa Rowe	47	John Wildcat & Judy Williams
824	Viola Rowe	8	Nelson Carter & Martha Downing
824	Washington Rowe	9	Walter Mayfield & Martha Downing
1130	Annie Sales	11mos	Ira & Lille Sales
1130	Ira Sales	3	Ira & Lille Sales
1130	Lillie Sales	27	Reuben & Alice Sanders
1130	Peter Sales	8	Ira & Lille Sales
893	Pleas Sales	5	Hayes Sales & Mattie Meigs
1130	Robert Sales	4	Ira & Lille Sales
1130	Ulysses Sales	5	Ira & Lillie Sales
885	Aleck Sanders	9	Ben & Lizzie Sanders
413	Alexander Sanders	32	Andy & Patsy Sanders
892	Alice Sanders	46	Peter & Betsy Meigs
892	Alice Sanders	19	Reuben & Alice Sanders
247	Allen Sanders	19	Robert & Mary Sanders
354	Anderson Sanders	33	Simon & Sarah Sanders
25	Anderson Sanders	27	Tuxie Sanders & Dianah Walker
247	Andy Sanders	15	Robert & Mary Sanders
871	Ann Sanders	47	Charles Wofford & Jennie Sanders
871	Belle Sanders	16	Johnson Thompson & Ann Sanders
562	Ben Sanders	45	Charles Wofford & Jennie Sanders
885	Ben Sanders	37	Simon & Sarah Sanders
871	Benjamin Sanders	13	Loonie Glass & Ann Sanders
1120	Benjamin Sanders	33	Daniel & Malinda Sanders
892	Bessie Sanders	12	Reuben & Alice Sanders
25	Carrie Sanders	6	Anderson & Janie Sanders
891	Charley Sanders	4	Mason Sanders & Ellen Webber
891	Clyde Sanders	6	Mason Sanders & Ellen Webber

1048	Daniel Jr Sanders	21	Daniel & Melinda Sanders
1122	Daniel Sanders	58	Bob & Polly Perry
25	David Sanders	8	Anderson & Janie Sanders
1122	Ed Sanders	12	Daniel & Malinda Sanders
1122	Ellen Sanders	18	Daniel & Malinda Sanders
632	Elvie Sanders	16	Andy & Maria Sanders
380	Emma Sanders	7	George Sanders & Rosella Milam
1122	Ethel Sanders	15	Daniel & Malinda Sanders
25	Fannie Sanders	5mos	Anderson & Janie Sanders
413	Frances Sanders	30	John & Maria Gentry
885	George Sanders	5	Ben & Lizzie Sanders
1051	George Sanders	29	Andy & Betsy Sanders
892	James Sanders	8	Reuben & Alice Sanders
871	Jennette Sanders	10	Loonie Glass & Ann Sanders
885	Jesse Sanders	7	Ben & Lizzie Sanders
374	Joe Sanders	75	Jack & Rachel Sanders
1468	John Sanders	42	Burgess Williams & Fannie Cornish
247	John Sanders	12	Robert & Mary Sanders
937	Josephine Sanders	10days	Daniel & Malinda Sanders
655	Lewis Sanders	40	Andy & Patsy Sanders
885	Lizzie Sanders	26	George & Hannah Webber
1252	Louisa Sanders	18	Simon Sanders & Mary Ross
87	Lucy Sanders	25	Tuck Sanders & Dinah Walker
937	Malinda Sanders	18	Looney & Mary Whitmire
1122	Malinda Sanders	55	George & Katie Welch
645	Margaret Sanders	50	George Gentry & Silvia Irons
632	Maria Sanders	55	Robert Alberty & Elizabeth Leek
885	Mark Sanders	1	Ben & Lizzie Sanders
226	Matilda Sanders	44	Cynthia Harnage
247	Martha Sanders	8	Robert & Mary Sanders
1045	Michael Sanders	26	Reuben & Alice Sanders
892	Pearl Sanders	17	Reuben & Alice Sanders
892	Reuben Sanders	50	Mike & Polly Sanders
247	Robert Sanders	44	Andy & Patsy Sanders
1146	Rosa Sanders	34	Reuben & Maggie Sanders
1146	Rubetta Sanders	3	George Williams & Rosa Sanders
892	Rugartha Sanders	14	Reuben & Alice Sanders
616	Sam Sanders	22	Sam Sanders & Annie Franklin
355	Sarah Sanders	80	
25	Sarah Sanders	22	Sank & Fannie Vann

963	Tim Sanders	30	Andy Sanders
509	Tuxie Sanders	13	Tuxie & Elinor Sanders
655	Vina Sanders	15	Lewis & Mary Sanders
509	Willie Sanders	10	Tuxie & Elinor Sanders
1252	Willie Sanders	5mos	Aaron Council & Louisa Sanders
495	Alice Sango	30	Seymour Matthew & Nan Mackey
1144	Mary Scales	18	Mack & Alice Scales
887	Vinay Scales	69	Sam Saul & Judy Ross
472	Emma Scarborough	1	George & Laura Scarborough
472	Laura Scarborough	21	Cato & Rachel Vann
984	Myra Schaefer	30	George & Jane Lasley
67	Edward Schrimsher	8	Sam Landrum & Mary Grimmett
615	Esther Schrimsher	42	Charles Burgess & Betsy Rogers
67	Frank Schrimsher	4	John Ford & Mary Grimmett
1224	Henry Schrimsher	40	Seenie Brewer
615	John Schrimsher	5	Henry & Esther Schrimsher
1225	Lela Schrimsher	10	Henry Schrimsher & Mary Tucker
615	Ruth Schrimsher	7mos	Henry & Esther Schrimsher
615	Sadie Schrimsher	3	Henry & Esther Schrimsher
62	Sophie Schrimsher	60	Andy & Caroline Fields
335	Willie Schrimsher	13	Charlie Vann & Carrie Ross
1351	Bell Scott	2	James & Mary Scott
1573	Bessie Scott	5	Mack & Fannie Scott
900	Dutch Scott	14	Lewis & Rutha Scott
1573	Fannie Scott	44	Riley & Maria McNair
949	Henry Scott	6	John Scott & Jennetta Vann
949	James Scott	14	John Scott & Jennetta Vann
1573	Jimmie Scott	3	Mack & Fannie Scott
900	Lizzie Scott	8	Lewis & Rutha Scott
1595	Lucy Scott	10	James & Mary Scott
900	Martha Scott	3	Lewis & Rutha Scott
1351	Mary Scott	30	Thomas Harlin & Rachel LaFlore
901	Millie Scott	28	Dave Vann & Mary Campbell
900	Rutha Scott	40	Lucinda Wright
809	Cornelius Shankling	4	Henry Vann & Mary Shankling
809	Della Shankling	6	Henry Vann & Mary Shankling
809	Mary Shankling	21	William & Edie Rider
809	Nelson Shanklling	6mos	Richard & Mary Shankling
602	Roosevelt Shannon	7mos	Walter Shannon & Ella Duncan
360	Barney Shepard	15	Wash Sheppard & Lydia White

360	Elizabeth Shepard	18	Wash Sheppard & Lydia White
360	Siegel Shepard	20	Wash Sheppard & Lydia White
186	Annie Sheppard	14	Morris & Nancy Sheppard
186	Claud Sheppard	10	Morris & Nancy Sheppard
190	Clem Sheppard	21	Morris & Nancy Sheppard
509	Clementine Sheppard	21	Tuxie & Elinor Sanders
155	Coffee Sheppard	67	Sukey Sheppard
190	Delmer Sheppard	5mos	Clem & Lula Sheppard
37	Edna Sheppard	1	Thomas & Josephine Sheppard
186	Emma Sheppard	16	Morris & Nancy Sheppard
37	Etha Sheppard	3	Thomas & Josephine Sheppard
186	Fannie Sheppard	18	Morris & Nancy Sheppard
217	Gunter Sheppard	10	Joshua & Betsy Sheppard
190	Henry Sheppard	7	Clem Sheppard
37	Josephine Sheppard	29	Alex & Mary Nivins
190	Lula Sheppard	17	Alex Vann & Fanny Brown
527	Mary Sheppard	72	
547	Mary Sheppard	36	Coffee Sheppard & Mary Scales
560	Meuty Sheppard	15	Joshua & Betsy Sheppard
37	Morris Sheppard	5	Thomas & Josephine Sheppard
1254	Morris Sheppard	41	Caesar & Easter Sheppard
1273	Nancy Sheppard	54	Boston & Mila Lynch
186	Nancy Sheppard	48	Jesse & Hannah Hilderbrand
1208	Nathaniel Sheppard	19	Wash Sheppard & Addie Curtis
147	Simon Sheppard	23	Joshua & Betsy Sheppard
186	Thomas Sheppard	12	Morris & Nancy Sheppard
186	Willie Sheppard	9mos	Anderson Penn & Fannie Sheppard
1491	Mary Shields	24	Jordan Harper & Lydia Carter
245	Anderson Silk	28	Squire Silk & Josephine Thompson
245	Annie Silk	23	Roswell & Mary Mackey
442	John Silk	27	Squire Silk & Josephine Thompson
245	Josephine Silk	4	Anderson & Annie Silk
245	Lillie Silk	6	Anderson & Annie Silk
246	Squire Silk	26	Squire Silk & Josephine Thompson
1312	Janie Simmons	43	Jordan & Lela Thompson
82	Harriet Skates	37	Dred & Caroline Foreman
82	Henry Skates	13	Henry & Harriet Skates
82	John Skates	15	Henry & Harriet Skates
505	Elizabeth Slater	1mo	James & Lula Slater
505	Jethel Slater	2	James & Lula Slater

505	Lula Slater	23	Daniel Roach & Rose Gunter
229	Alice Smith	43	Mose & Nancy Ross
180	Annie Smith	70	Phil Mayes & Molly Pettit
566	Aurillia Smith	3mos	Joe & Sarah Smith
1163	Benjamin Smith	6mos	Sandy & Zora Smith
415	Bob Smith	65	Lizzie Smith
1458	Carrie Smith	2	Sonny & Hattie Smith
1159	Charley Smith	40	Robert & Delilah Smith
1428	Charley Smith	17	Henderson Smith & Lucy Daniels
613	Claude Smith	2	Dave Smith & Lula Mackey
225	David Smith	14	Sonney Smith & Sallie Brown
1458	David Smith	14	Sonny Smith & Sarah Smutt
229	Dora Smith	6	Andrew & Alice Smith
566	Ethel Smith	1	Joe & Sarah Smith
225	Flora Smith	16	Sonney Smith & Sallie Brown
1458	Flora Smith	16	Sonny Smith & Sarah Smutt
1458	Floyd Smith	2	Sonny & Hattie Smith
198	Gilbert Smith	17	July & Ibbie Smith
1458	Gladys Smith	3	Sonny & Hattie Smith
198	Henry Smith	19	July & Ibbie Smith
198	Ibbie Smith	46	Mayes & Theressia Thompson
191	James Smith	55	
504	Jimmie Smith	15	Alfred Thompson & Maria Smith
504	Joe Smith	12	James & Maria Smith
198	John Smith	13	July & Ibbie Smith
1229	Joseph Smith	22	Henry Smith & Eliza Watson
198	July Smith	5	July & Ibbie Smith
1184	Katie Smith	28	Eli Vann & Manerva Chouteau
566	Luther Smith	3	Joe & Sarah Smith
504	Luther Smith	10	James & Maria Smith
504	Maria Smith	39	Dred & Caroline Foreman
415	Melinda Smith	65	
1458	Neely Smith	6	Sonny & Hattie Smith
87	Ollie Smith	4mos	John Smith & Lucy Sanders
198	Pearl Smith	20	July & Ibbie Smith
274	Preston Smith	1	Hardy & Rosa Smith
2	Robert Jr. Smith	35	Robert & Malinda Smith
274	Rosa Smith	28	Robert & Nellie Mayfield
198	Ruth Smith	8	July & Ibbie Smith
198	Sarah Smith	11	July & Ibbie Smith

566	Sarah Smith	22	Isaac & Elmira Crossland
1458	Sonny Smith	45	Dave Smith & Flora Murrell
1458	Thomas Smith	7	Sonny & Hattie Smith
229	Thomas Smith	4	Andrew & Alice Smith
504	Wallie Smith	18	Thomas Hill & Maria Smith
415	Willie Smith	13	Robert & Jennett Smith
1163	Zora Smith	20	Wesley & Rose Warner
164	Daniel Snow	70	James & Jennie Snow
164	Jane Snow	13	Daniel & Ruth Snow
164	Ruth Snow	45	George Drew & Mary Scales
330	Delilah Spight	23	Jack & Katie Brown
330	Katie Spight	6mos	Daniel & Delilah Spight
330	Rachel Spight	4	Daniel & Delilah Spight
135	Emma Stanton	3mos	Calvin & Lucy Stanton
135	Lucy Stanton	28	Henry & Hannah Thomas
371	Amanda Starr	37	Anna Starr
371	Andy Starr	17	Roland Nave & Amanda Starr
105	Anise Starr	5	Harry & Martha Starr
1386	Annie Starr	19	Sam & Nancy Starr
1358	Arthur Starr	19	George & Malinda Starr
105	Caroline Starr	10	Harry & Martha Starr
105	Daniel Starr	18	Harry & Martha Starr
928	Earmy Starr	9	Jack & Georgia Starr
105	Emma Starr	4mos	Harry & Martha Starr
219	Florence Starr	30	Jack & Martha Pack
1358	George Starr	48	Mary Starr
1360	George Jr. Starr	26	George & Malinda Starr
1386	George Starr	16	Sam & Nancy Starr
928	Georgia Starr	40	Ben & Clarinda Grimmett
1477	Hannah Starr	29	Moses & Maria Whitmire
105	Harretora Starr	11	Harry & Martha Starr
105	Harry Starr	50	Ike & Sallie Starr
105	Harry Jr. Starr	9	Harry & Martha Starr
1387	Harry Starr	6mos	Henry & Peggie Starr
1387	Henrietta Starr	6	Henry & Peggie Starr
1387	Henry Starr	23	Samuel & Nancy Starr
928	Herbert Starr	13	Jack & Georgia Starr
1387	Jessie Starr	2	Henry & Peggie Starr
486	John Starr	23	Oliver & Eliza Starr
444	Julia Starr	36	Solomon & Lizzie Foster

219	Juliet Starr	7	Will & Florence Starr
1384	Leona Starr	15mos	Samuel & Sadie Starr
1477	Leone Starr	1mo	Charles & Hannah Starr
1477	Leota Starr	1mo	Charles & Hannah Starr
1384	Lillie Starr	3	Samuel & Sadie Starr
105	Linniebell Starr	16	Harry & Martha Starr
105	Luther Starr	2	Harry & Martha Starr
1477	Mabel Starr	2	Charles & Hannah Starr
928	Mark Starr	4	Jack & Georgia Starr
105	Martha Starr	37	Dred & Caroline Foreman
1477	Minerva Starr	7	Charles & Hannah Starr
1383	Nancy Starr	52	Henry West & Phoebe Mayfield
43	Oliver Starr	60	Dennis & Clarissa McDaniel
214	Pearl Starr	22	Columbus & Peggie Lasley
1384	Sallie Starr	5	Samuel & Sadie Starr
105	Sallie Starr	13	Harry & Martha Starr
1384	Samuel Starr	26	Samuel & Nancy Starr
165	Samuel Starr	20	Oliver Starr & Eliza Langston
275	Sarah Starr	9	Will & Sarah Starr
1477	Theodore Starr	4	Charles & Hannah Starr
1386	Turner Starr	13	Sam & Nancy Starr
1489	Viola Starr	1	Andy Vann & Emma Starr
928	Walter Starr	17	Jack & Georgia Starr
219	Willie Starr	5mos	Will & Florence Starr
214	Willie Starr	2wks	Willis & Pearl Starr
592	Charles Stidman	23	Sam & Dollie Stidman
267	Lizzie Stidman	5	Samuel Stidman & Sallie McConnell
617	Mary Stidman	19	Samuel & Dollie Stidman
617	Samuel Stidman	45	Buck Stidman & Mary Walker
1479	Della Still	31	Jonas & Jennie Ragsdale
876	Harry Still	50	Reuben Still & Maria Hayden
1340	Bennie Sumner	18	Ben Sumner & Winnie Reeves
1340	Charlie Sumner	16	Ben Sumner & Winnie Reeves
1340	Estella Sumner	13	Ben Sumner & Winnie Reeves
1341	Sylvester Sumner	22	Ben & Winnie Sumner
50	Mary Sumpter	38	Jack & Martha Pack
716	Joseph Sutton	18	Lewis & Kate Sutton
275	Peggie Swan	25	Silas & Elizabeth Holt
685	Jane Swepston	29	Turk & Clara Vann
685	Joanna Swepston	3	Perry & Jane Swepston

685	Lelia Swepston	8	Perry & Jane Swepston
685	Lena Swepston	6	Perry & Jane Swepston
685	Vann Swepston	2mos	Perry & Jane Swepston
1462	Della Sykes	14	Henry & Vina Sykes
318	Anderson Tatum	3mos	John Tatum & Gonie Youngblood
1303	Etta Taylor	6	Will Taylor & Allie McElroy
1357	Henry Taylor	37	Will Taylor & Octavia Evans
1465	James Taylor	51	Nancy Brewer
475	Judy Taylor	71	Amy
1142	Lewis Taylor	42	Judia Taylor
978	Nancy Taylor	60	Ben Vann & Patsy Martin
522	Osie Taylor	12	Henry & Fannie Taylor
950	William Taylor	24	Emanuel Taylor & Sophia Bird
522	Willie Taylor	10	Henry & Fannie Taylor
774	Corether Terry	2mos	Simon Terry & Eliza Bean
254	Edith Theodore	27	Lewis & Nellie Theodore
254	Idella Theodore	4	Andy Kirkham & Edith Theodore
6	Adelbert Thomas	12	Mattie Thomas
1188	Adelbert Thomas	13	James & Mattie Thomas
1478	Albert Thomas	9	Albert & Etta Thomas
227	Cynthia Thomas	36	Jack & Rose Campbell
6	Donald Thomas	6	Mattie Thomas
1188	Donald Thomas	6	James & Mattie Thomas
1478	Earl Thomas	7	Albert & Etta Thomas
1478	Etta Thomas	32	Jonas & Jennie Ragsdale
270	Fannie Thomas	15	Robin & Emma Riley
388	Florence Thomas	25	Henry Thomas & Rachel Penn
386	Freddie Thomas	20	Henry & Hannah Thomas
386	Gracie Thomas	7	Henry & Hannah Thomas
386	Hannah Thomas	44	George & Peggy Landrum
1046	John Thomas	15	Enoc Thomas & Rachel Walker
1046	Laura Thomas	7	Enoc Thomas & Rachel Walker
6	Leonard Thomas	4	Mattie Thomas
1188	Leonard Thomas	4	James & Mattie Thomas
6	Mattie Thomas	31	William & Mary Brown
665	Mattie Thomas	28	Lou Mosier & Jennie Vann
1188	Mattie Thomas	35	William & Mary Brown
665	Sammie Thomas	10mos	John Rider & Mattie Thomas
524	Willie Thomas	22	Henry & Hannah Thomas
593	Aaron Thompson	14	Bart & Lydia Thompson

1307	Ada Thompson	13	Blue & Jennie Thompson
681	Albert Thompson	9	William & Dolly Thompson
1113	Albert Thompson	15mos	Daniel & Eliza Thompson
603	Alex Thompson	13	Johnson & Flora Thompson
251	Alfred Thompson	47	William & Sarah Thompson
1584	Alpha Thompson	20	Sandy & Ophelia Thompson
720	Alsey Thompson	51	William & Jiney Cudjo
39	Annie Thompson	4	Junius & Cora Thompson
85	Annie Thompson	11	Jack & Sarah Thompson
1174	Annie Thompson	12	Alfred & Emma Thompson
593	Bart Thompson	60	Dave & Celia Thompson
1546	Bell Thompson	13	Nelson Thompson & Neatie Rodgers
1284	Berry Thompson	46	Dave Thompson & Mary Stover
561	Bertha Thompson	14	Robin & Jennie Thompson
302	Bessie Thompson	3	Edward & Susan Thompson
1113	Bessie Thompson	3	Daniel & Eliza Thompson
1174	Bessie Thompson	6	Alfred & Emma Thompson
1307	Blue Thompson	51	David & Viana Thompson
595	Carrie Thompson	22	Bart & Lydia Thompson
815	Cealy Thompson	39	George Johnson & Jincy Landrum
603	Charles Thompson	15	Johnson & Flora Thompson
281	Clarence Thompson	4	Henry & Lucinda Thompson
1174	Clarence Thompson	16	Isaac & Emma Thompson
1478	Clyde Thompson	16	Brandon Thompson & Etta Thomas
1584	Clyde Thompson	3	Sandy & Ophelia Thompson
203	Coleman Thompson	5	William & Victoria Thompson
144	Cora Thompson	29	Caleb & Belle Vann
203	Dora Thompson	3	William & Victoria Thompson
302	Edward Thompson	33	Thomas & Sarah Thompson
1307	Edward Thompson	8	Blue & Sallie Thompson
593	Egypt Thompson	19	Bart & Lydia Thompson
1113	Eliza Thompson	33	Eli & Jane Nave
203	Ellis Thompson	10	William & Victoria Thompson
1284	Elmer Thompson	14	Berry & Belle Thompson
815	Elyard Thompson	18	Nelson & Cealy Thompson
302	Emanuel Thompson	2	Edward & Susan Thompson
1441	Emily Thompson	51	John & Nancy Thornton
1174	Emma Thompson	40	John Hayes & Peggie Clay
85	Emmett Thompson	5	Jack & Sarah Thompson
637	Etha Thompson	13	William Thompson & Sarah Parris

742	Ethel Thompson	12	Nelson Thompson & Susan Johnson
646	Frank Thompson	23	Simon & Peggie Thompson
85	Grant Thompson	9	Jack & Sarah Thompson
1174	Grant Thompson	20	Isaac & Emma Thompson
85	Harrison Thompson	10	Jack & Sarah Thompson
603	Harry Thompson	9	Johnson & Flora Thompson
1584	Harvey Thompson	10	Sandy & Ophelia Thompson
85	Hayes Thompson	13	Jack & Sarah Thompson
422	Hayes Thompson	17	John & Sarah Thompson
441	Henrietta Thompson	14	Isaac Thompson & Katie Coody
281	Henry Thompson	31	Pompey & Sarah Thompson
63	Henry Thompson	20	John & Minnie Thompson
1584	Hirschel Thompson	15	Sandy & Ophelia Thompson
281	Houston Thompson	10mos	Henry & Lucinda Thompson
39	Ida Thompson	6	Junius & Cora Thompson
310	Jeff Thompson	27	Pompey & Sarah Thompson
302	Jeff Thompson	9	Edward & Susan Thompson
220	Jesse Thompson	18	Jeff & Josephine Thompson
203	Jesse Thompson	9	William & Victoria Thompson
422	Jeter Thompson	15	John & Sarah Thompson
422	John Thompson	45	William & Sarah Thompson
281	Johnanna Thompson	2	Henry & Lucinda Thompson
121	Johnnie Thompson	33	Bart & Frances Thompson
39	Jonas Thompson	34	Woody & Patsy Thompson
768	Jordan Thompson	26	Nelson Thompson & Sidney Johnson
203	Jordan Thompson	17	William & Victoria Thompson
144	Joseph Thompson	27	Robert & Emily Thompson
681	June Thompson	1	William & Dolly Thompson
681	Laura Thompson	8	William & Dolly Thompson
603	Laura Thompson	12	Johnson & Flora Thompson
589	Leander Thompson	4mos	Hayes Thompson & Eunice Webb
1284	Leo Thompson	13	Berry & Belle Thompson
139	Levi Thompson	23	John & Sarah Thompson
1174	Lewis Thompson	18	Isaac & Emma Thompson
1584	Libbie Thompson	17	Sandy & Ophelia Thompson
85	Lillie Thompson	14	Jack & Sarah Thompson
203	Lillie Thompson	13	William & Victoria Thompson
673	Louisa Thompson	50	Sarah Stop
281	Lucinda Thompson	26	John Hall & Louisa Thompson
1113	Luther Thompson	9	Daniel & Eliza Thompson

69	Lydia Thompson	21	Crow & Rose Vann
648	Malay Thompson	3	Levi Thompson & Maggie Ross
766	Martha Thompson	4	Jordan Thompson & Mary Hunter
1284	Morrison Thompson	10	Berry & Belle Thompson
523	Moses Thompson	39	Robin Thompson & Patsy Nevins
681	Nannie Thompson	4mos	William & Dolly Thompson
1195	Nelson Thompson	40	Jordan & Betsy Thompson
1113	Ollie Thompson	8	Daniel & Eliza Thompson
1584	Ophelia Thompson	38	Columbus Rogers & Millie McNair
1174	Peggie Thompson	10	Alfred & Emma Thompson
673	Pompey Thompson	62	Pompey Williams& Nellie Thompson
281	Pompey Thompson	9	Henry & Lucinda Thompson
815	Rachel Thompson	15	Nelson & Cealy Thompson
1174	Rebecca Thompson	8	Alfred & Emma Thompson
1113	Rena Thompson	4	Daniel & Eliza Thompson
298	Richard Thompson	29	Pompey & Sarah Thompson
603	Richard Thompson	7	Johnson & Flora Thompson
69	Robert Thompson	28	Robert & Emily Thompson
1269	Robin Thompson	38	Robin Thompson & Patsy Nivens
422	Sarah Thompson	55	Isaac Taplin & Melinda Smith
85	Sarah Thompson	36	Clark Riley & Josie Brown
1220	Simon Thompson	25	Bart & Lydia Thompson
1475	Stella Thompson	25	Joe Thompson & Polly Boyd
203	Steven Thompson	19	William & Victoria Thompson
302	Susan Thompson	24	Daniel & Rose Roach
302	Susie Thompson	5	Edward & Susan Thompson
561	Sylvia Thompson	40	John & Nancy Thornton
203	Turner Thompson	4	William & Victoria Thompson
766	Vicia Thompson	6	Jordan Thompson & Mary Hunter
203	Victoria Thompson	35	Cooser Hayes & Judy Taylor
742	Walker Thompson	14	Nelson Thompson & Susan Johnson
1474	William Thompson	28	Joe Thompson & Polly Boyd
203	William Thompson	35	Jordan & Lilah Thompson
637	William Thompson	35	Pompey & Sarah Thompson
681	William Thompson	28	Bart & Lydia Thompson
681	Willie Thompson	5	William & Dolly Thompson
768	Willis Thompson	4	Jordan & Nancy Thompson
156	Dollie Thornton	25	Daniel & Lottie Vann
1443	Georgann Thornton	70	John & Hannah Fields
600	Henrietta Thornton	25	Rosewell Mackey & Silva Thompson

1413	Rhoda Thornton	66	John & Dorcus Downing
1440	Robert Thornton	28	Seymour Thornton & Rachel Graves
156	Salina Thornton	7mos	Robert & Dollie Thornton
156	Thomas Thornton	6	Robert & Dollie Thornton
1218	John Towers	40	Jerry Towers & Winnie Landrum
1585	Arthur Townsend	4	William & Mollie Townsend
1585	Ethel Townsend	1	William & Mollie Townsend
1585	George Townsend	5	William & Mollie Townsend
1585	Mollie Townsend	22	Jesse Vann & Emma Purtle
1585	Rosa Townsend	7	William & Mollie Townsend
1069	Albert Tucker	27	Morris Tucker & Grace Vann
49	Cynthia Tucker	38	Crow Vann & Lydia Crockett
1123	Eliza Tucker	45	Lewis Scott & Winnie Ratcliff
1301	George Tucker	4	John & Harriett Tucker
1301	Harriett Tucker	32	Aaron & Queen Martin
1123	Lee Tucker	18	Dan & Eliza Tucker
590	Lewis Tucker	50	Joe & Ruth Tucker
1301	Lloyd Tucker	2	John & Harriett Tucker
1301	Sarah Tucker	8mos	John & Harriett Tucker
1166	William Tucker	2	Lewis Tucker & Lizzie Weaver
1549	William Tucker	65	Lucy Faught
48	Ada Tyner	13	John Tyner
68	Andrew Tyner	9	Andy & Emily Tyner
68	Charlotte Tyner	13	Andy & Emily Tyner
68	Daniel Tyner	8	Andy & Emily Tyner
86	Daniel Tyner	9	John & Sarah Tyner
86	Della Tyner	11	John & Sarah Tyner
68	Emily Tyner	41	Dan & Cynthia Pinder
130	John Tyner	16	John & Nancy Tyner
124	Martha Tyner	25	Moses & Mary Johnson
124	Prince Tyner	39	Andy Tyner & Maria Vann
86	Sarah Tyner	29	Charlotte Walker
68	Tessie Tyner	16	Andy & Emily Tyner
68	William Tyner	5	Andy & Emily Tyner
124	Willie Tyner	6	Prince & Nancy Tyner
394	Lillie Van Zant	4mos	Henry & Maggie Van Zant
394	Maggie Van Zant	25	Rockwell & Lydia Fields
394	Rockwell Van Zant	3	Henry & Maggie Van Zant
394	Sarah Van Zant	2mos	Henry & Maggie Van Zant
358	Albert Vann	2mos	Jesse & Mary Vann

519	Alex Vann	21	Alex Martin & Martha Vann
875	Alex Vann	18	Dave Vann & Patsy Daniels
737	Alexander Vann	12	Ben & Eliza Vann
410	Alexander Vann	30	Gilbert & Emily Vann
375	Alford Vann	3mos	Rufus & Sallie Vann
404	Alice Vann	25	Butler & Sarah Vann
794	Alice Vann	17	Ben & Lizzie Vann
945	Amanda Vann	30	Sam & Katie Vann
684	Andrew Vann	28	Turk & Clora Vann
631	Anna Vann	5	Sam & Lizzie Vann
1342	Annie Vann	17	William & Hannah Vann
175	Annie Vann	25	Thomas & Martha Vann
319	Annie Vann	7	Cato & Rachel Vann
119	Anois Vann	2	Napoleon & Maria Vann
375	Ardelia Vann	3	Rufus & Sallie Vann
96	Arie Vann	5	John Vann & Jennie Workman
737	Arreano Vann	9	Ben & Eliza Vann
40	Arthur Vann	14	Buster & Minnie Vann
1055	Arthur Vann	16	Eli & Patience Vann
657	Augustine Vann	14	William Jr & Sarah Vann
803	Ave Vann	22	Turk & Clora Vann
657	Beatrice Vann	16	William Jr & Sarah Vann
737	Ben Vann	44	Jesse & Katie Vann
794	Ben Vann	40	William & Hannah Vann
851	Ben Vann	26	Dunk & Chick Vann
870	Benjamin Vann	80	Jane Nivens
1047	Bert Vann	13	John Vann & Sarah Cox
991	Bessie Vann	9	Gilbert & Sarah Vann
625	Bertha Vann	18	Dave & Sarah Vann
847	Birt Vann	15	Steve & Mary Vann
581	Bishop Vann	18	Daniel & Lottie Vann
1105	Blue Vann	5mos	Joe Vann & Rosie Rogers
740	Bruce Vann	10	Samuel & Rachel Vann
1433	Buster Vann	5	James Vann & Georgia Eastric
970	Callie Vann	22	San & Cynthia Butler
692	Caroline Vann	25	Turk & Flora Vann
52	Carrey Vann	2	George & Cynthia Vann
321	Carrie Vann	3	Charles & Katie Vann
998	Carrie Vann	25	Dave & Ellen Nave
87	Catherine Vann	4	Jesse Vann & Lucy Sanders

319	Cato Vann	45	Jesse Foreman & Mary Vann
321	Charles Vann	33	Thomas & Martha Vann
1457	Charles Vann	36	Robert Vann & Flora Murrell
1047	Charlie Vann	10	John Vann & Sarah Cox
850	Chick Vann	50	Jesse & Katie Vann
96	Clara Vann	7	John Vann & Jennie Workman
158	Clark Vann	11	Reed & Mary Vann
666	Cleveland Vann	13	James & Nancy Vann
167	Clifton Vann	1	Clifton & Ruth Vann
682	Clora Vann	55	Richard & Nancy Shaw
737	Cooley Vann	16	Ben & Eliza Vann
46	Cora Vann	12	Butler & Sarah Vann
1480	Cull Vann	12	Josh & Mattie Vann
737	Cullis Vann	4	Ben & Eliza Vann
822	Cunnigan Vann	22	Johnson & Lila Vann
52	Cynthia Vann	31	Butler & Sarah Vann
745	Daisy Vann	19	Johnson & Delilah Vann
294	Dan Vann	10mos	Jim Vann & Rachel Ward
657	Daniel Vann	7	William Jr & Sarah Vann
185	Daniel Jr. Vann	37	Daniel & Fannie Vann
10	Daniel Vann	32	Marsha Vann
515	Dara Vann	13	Jack & Rachel Vann
625	Dave Vann	49	Joe & Maria Vann
608	David Vann	19	Samuel & Lydia Vann
1009	David Vann	28	Eli & Patience Vann
740	Dennis Vann	17	Samuel & Rachel Vann
1521	Dennis Vann	50	William & Caroline Vann
404	Della Vann	3	Alfred Smith & Alice Vann
847	Dewey Vann	3	Steve & Mary Vann
906	Dinah Vann	70	Peter Nave
850	Dunk Vann	51	James & Patsy Vann
172	Eddie Vann	27	Ned & Rhea Vann
212	Eddie Vann	17	Buster Vann & Sallie Crossland
625	Eddie Vann	8	Dave & Sarah Vann
634	Edmond Vann	29	Sank & Fannie Vann
906	Edmond Vann	58	Jim Foreman & Matilda Vann
847	Elder Vann	6mos	Steve & Mary Vann
27	Eli Vann	22	Butler & Sarah Vann
850	Eli Vann	18	Dunk & Chick Vann
941	Eli Vann	25	Dave Vann & Patsy Daniels

985	Eli Vann	7	William & Victoria Vann
1347	Eli Vann	5	Jackson & Mattie Vann
847	Elia Vann	10	Steve & Mary Vann
209	Ella Vann	17	Thomas & Martha Vann
319	Ella Vann	10	Cato & Rachel Vann
10	Ellen Vann	4mos	Daniel & Susie Vann
847	Ellen Vann	18	Steve & Mary Vann
29	Ellis Vann	27	Sank & Diana Vann
185	Ellis Vann	9	Daniel & Ida Vann
808	Ellis Vann	20	William & Rachel Vann
1160	Ellis Vann	61	William & Caroline Vann
1113	Elmer Vann	13	Eli Vann & Eliza Thompson
93	Emanuel Vann	36	Russell & Louisa Vann
381	Emma Vann	16	Joe & Rachel Vann
319	Estella Vann	3	Cato & Rachel Vann
358	Estella Vann	3	Jesse & Mary Vann
865	Esther Vann	11	Jim & Rosa Vann
1480	Eva Vann	11	Josh & Mattie Vann
22	Fannie Vann	50	Jesse & Lillie Ross
456	Floyd Vann	10	James & Ella Vann
8	Frank Vann	45	Caleb & Maria Vann
1587	Frank Vann	19	Jesse Vann & Emma Purtle
358	Frank Vann	7	Jesse & Mary Vann
1032	Frank Vann	9	Eli & Polly Vann
847	Fred Vann	19	Steve & Mary Vann
965	Fred Vann	7	Will Vann & Alice Durant
847	Fredonia Vann	11	Steve & Mary Vann
158	Garfield Vann	9	Reed & Mary Vann
1191	Garfield Vann	2	Samuel & Mollie Vann
699	George Vann	51	William & Caroline Vann
157	George Vann	36	Daniel & Lottie Vann
754	George Vann	27	Walker Johnson & Minta Vann
865	George Vann	7	Jim & Rosa Vann
998	George Vann	25	Jesse & Cynthia Vann
1050	George Vann	24	Morris Tinnon & Sarah Cox
320	George Vann	25	Cato & Rachel Vann
1480	George Vann	16	Josh & Mattie Vann
1434	George Vann	13	James Vann & Avis Watson
666	George Vann	17	James & Nancy Vann
209	George Vann	13	Thomas & Martha Vann

22	Gertrude Vann	5	Sank & Fannie Vann
1433	Gifton Vann	4	James Vann & Georgia Eastrick
991	Gilbert Vann	45	Tobe & Lettie Vann
1207	Gilbert Vann	52	William & Caroline Vann
870	Grace Vann	58	Loury Bowling & Lucy Rogers
1342	Hannah Vann	40	George Johnson & Nancy Watie
657	Harrison Vann	10	William Jr & Sarah Vann
1487	Harry Vann	9	Robert Wallace & Mary Vann
266	Henry Vann	20	Ed Wright & Hannah Vann
10	Henry Vann	5	Daniel & Susie Vann
185	Henry Vann	1mo	Daniel & Ida Vann
970	Henry Vann	27	Johnson & Delilah Vann
1336	Herbert Vann	1	Johnson & Mandy Vann
581	Hettie Vann	16	Daniel & Lottie Vann
185	Ida Vann	30	Wash & Amy Smith
1245	Isabell Vann	25	George & Martha McNair
515	Jack Vann	52	Jack & Londa Vann
171	Jacob Vann	35	Crow Vann & Delilah Smith
683	James Vann	30	Turk & Clora Vann
660	James Vann	38	Daniel & Lottie Vann
456	James Vann	29	Butler & Sarah Vann
466	James Vann	24	Thomas Vann & Martha Hicks
22	James Vann	16	Sank & Fannie Vann
1480	James Vann	14	Josh & Mattie Vann
666	James Vann	46	Neal & Jennie Vann
157	James Vann	6	George & Rosa Vann
794	James Vann	5	Ben & Sarah Vann
800	James Vann	17	Ben Vann & Eliza Folsom
1141	James Vann	30	James & Nancy Vann
1032	Jane Vann	15	Eli & Polly Vann
949	Jennetta Vann	25	Harry & Polly Rider
1347	Jennie Vann	6mos	Jackson & Mattie Vann
356	Jennie Vann	16	Jerry & Sallie Vann
356	Jerry Vann	47	James & Patsy Vann
358	Jerry Vann	6	Jesse & Mary Vann
970	Jess Vann	6mos	Henry & Callie Vann
358	Jesse Vann	25	James & Patsy Vann
358	Jesse Jr. Vann	4	Jesse & Mary Vann
421	Jesse Vann	29	Daniel & Lottie Vann
8	Jesse Vann	16	Frank & Julia Vann

22	Jesse Vann	8	Edmund & Lou Vann
158	Jesse Vann	6	Reed & Mary Vann
998	Jesse Vann	8	George & Virginia Vann
657	Jessie Vann	12	William Jr & Sarah Vann
356	Jessie Vann	8	Jerry & Sallie Vann
872	Jettie Vann	14	Joe & Katie Vann
865	Jim Vann	40	William & Hannah Vann
377	John Vann	31	Joseph Vann & Dinah Martin
456	John Vann	8	James & Ella Vann
171	John Vann	13	Jacob & Maggie Vann
210	John Vann	21	Thomas & Martha Vann
970	John Vann	16mos	Henry & Callie Vann
212	Johnnie Vann	10	Buster Vann & Sallie Crossland
356	Johnnie Vann	6	Jerry & Sallie Vann
1047	Johnnie Vann	15	John Vann & Sarah Cox
745	Johnson Vann	58	Henry & Tilda Vann
844	Johnson Jr Vann	35	Johnson & Delilah Vann
321	Joseph Vann	3mos	Charles & Katie Vann
953	Joseph Vann	23	Dave Vann & Patsy Daniels
1047	Joseph Vann	21	John Vann & Sarah Cox
1480	Josh Vann	45	Cull Vann & Susan Pee
745	Juanita Vann	3mos	Ben Harlin & Daisy Vann
1544	Julia Vann	2	Ben & Irene Vann
966	Julia Vann	22	Dave Vann & Mary Campbell
321	Katie Vann	23	Betsy Buffington
872	Katie Vann	56	Jesse & Malinda Rowe
872	Katie Vann	18	Joe & Katie Vann
794	Laura Vann	7	Ben & Sarah Vann
625	Lewis Vann	14	Dave & Sarah Vann
946	Lewis Vann	21	Dave Vann & Patsy Daniels
1348	Lieutenant Vann	15	Charley Vann & Susan Melton
158	Lila Vann	3	Reed & Mary Vann
1047	Lilah Vann	19	John Vann & Sarah Cox
22	Lillie Vann	9	Sank & Fannie Vann
158	Lillie Vann	12	Reed & Mary Vann
737	Lillie Vann	7	Ben & Eliza Vann
158	Lincoln Vann	5	Reed & Mary Vann
1389	Lindsey Vann	25	Dave & Mary Vann
8	Lonnie Vann	19	Frank & Julia Vann
10	LorenaVann	3	Daniel & Susie Vann

581	Lottie Vann	58	William Vann & Aggie Tally
160	Louis Vann	28	Thomas & Martha Vann
1587	Lovat Vann	11	Jesse Vann & Emma Purtle
515	Lovely Vann	14	Jack & Rachel Vann
981	Lucille Vann	7	Eli Vann & Martha Virgel
865	Lucinda Vann	6	Jim & Rosa Vann
320	Lucy Vann	6mos	George & Minerva Vann
356	Luella Vann	11	Jerry & Sallie Vann
594	Lula Vann	22	Eli & Patience Vann
1047	Lula Vann	17	John Vann & Sarah Cox
740	Lula Vann	15	Samuel & Rachel Vann
865	Luversa Vann	12	Jim & Rosa Vann
794	Lydia Vann	8	Ben & Sarah Vann
61	Mabel Vann	2wks	Moses & Lottie Vann
1050	Magdaline Vann	23	Henry & Polly Rider
625	Maggie Vann	5	Dave & Sarah Vann
13	Major Vann	27	Russell Vann
608	Mamie Vann	11	Samuel & Lydia Vann
119	Maria Vann	29	Wash & Lydia Sheppard
657	Marie Vann	3	William Jr & Sarah Vann
1487	Mary Vann	42	Bill Buffington & Mary Stover
991	Mary Vann	12	Gilbert & Sarah Vann
158	Mary Vann	31	John & Causby Bean
10	MarshaVann	9mos	Daniel & Susie Vann
64	Martha Vann	60	Little Jack & Londa Vann
209	Martha Vann	50	John Bean
96	Martha Vann	10	John Vann & Jennie Workman
657	Martha Vann	2	William Jr & Sarah Vann
358	Mary Vann	23	Lewis & Hester Johnson
22	Mary Vann	12	Sank & Fannie Vann
872	Mary Vann	20	Sam & Katie Vann
778	Matilda Vann	22	William & Sarah Vann
1347	Mattie Vann	21	Zack Foreman & Nan Franklin
625	Mattie Vann	2	Dave & Sarah Vann
1050	Maude Vann	2	George & Magdaline Vann
1191	McKinley Vann	5	Samuel & Mollie Vann
46	Melinda Vann	18	Butler & Sarah Vann
320	Minerva Vann	20	Fox & Lucy Glass
157	Minnie Vann	7	George & Rosa Vann
61	Moses Vann	28	Butler & Sarah Vann

212	Myrtle Vann	15	Buster Vann & Sallie Crossland
1140	Nancy Vann	55	Coon & Polly Vann
319	Nannie Vann	7	Cato & Rachel Vann
319	Narcissus Vann	13	Cato & Rachel Vann
875	Nealy Vann	14	Dave Vann & Patsy Daniels
740	Nolan Vann	7	Samuel & Rachel Vann
1481	Ollie Vann	15	Nick Vann & Lettie Brown
212	Oma Vann	13	Buster Vann & Sallie Crossland
1347	Ora Vann	3	Jackson & Mattie Vann
1336	Pansy Vann	2	Johnson & Mandy Vann
850	Patsie Vann	14	Dunk & Chicak Vann
970	Pearlie Vann	3	Henry & Callie Vann
991	Phillis Vann	14	Gilbert & Sarah Vann
631	Priscilla Vann	15mos	Sam & Lizzie Vann
22	Proctor Vann	14	Sank & Fannie Vann
22	Rachel Vann	7	Sank & Fannie Vann
319	Rebecca Vann	4	Cato & Rachel Vann
158	Reed Vann	32	Daniel & Lottie Vann
158	Reed Jr. Vann	2	Reed & Mary Vann
1047	Reed Vann	23	John Vann & Sarah Cox
1587	Riley Vann	15	Jesse Vann & Emma Purtle
319	Roand Vann	14	Cato & Rachel Vann
625	Robert Vann	20	Dave & Sarah Vann
1396	Rolla Vann	40	James & Patsy Vann
515 .	Rosa Vann	26	Daniel & Ruth Snow
1099	Rosa Vann	24	Sam & Katie Vann
228	Roswell Vann	14	Sam & Lydia Vann
1561	Rufus Vann	23	James & Nancy Vann
375	Rufus Vann	36	Walker & Mary Vann
167	Ruth Vann	27	Phill Vann & Lilly
375	Sallie Vann	22	Robert & Millie Mayfield
1496	Sallie Vann	47	
74	Samuel Vann	27	Sank & Fannie Vann
168	Samuel Vann	28	Jack Vann
608	Samuel Vann	38	Henry & Litha Vann
740	Samuel Vann	40	Rufus & Lucy Vann
22	Sank Vann	50	Caleb & Mariah Vann
46	Sarah Vann	57	Charles & Mintie Girty
625	Sarah Vann	41	Jack & Martha Pack
657	Sarah Vann	35	Isom & Martha Nave

794	Sarah Vann	30	Fred & Juliet Marcum
73	Simon Vann	27	Crow & Rose Vann
421	Sophia Vann	24	Joseph & Josephine Brown
434	Sophie Vann	14	Luster Vann & Rachel Gunter
185	Spiberry Vann	6	Daniel & Ida Vann
806	Stanford Vann	25	William & Rachel Vann
46	Stella Vann	1	Reed Wilson & Melinda Vann
1009	Sterling Vann	5mos	David & Bessie Vann
847	Steve Vann	42	Tobe & Charlott Vann
73	Susan Vann	27	George & Lucy Sheppard
531	Susan Vann	28	Joe Vann & Dinah Crapo
157	Susan Vann	9	George & Rosa Vann
157	Sylvester Vann	11	George & Rosa Vann
662	Thomas Vann	14	Lincoln & Saphronia Vann
657	Thomas Vann	5	William Jr & Sarah Vann
321	Thomas Vann	4mos	Charles & Katie Vann
319	Thursday Vann	11	Cato & Rachel Vann
991	Tollie Vann	4	Gilbert & Chaney Vann
358	Tressie Vann	1	Jesse & Mary Vann
740	Ulysses Vann	12	Samuel & Rachel Vann
985	Victoria Vann	30	Eli & Patience Vann
320	Viola Vann	1	George & Minerva Vann
865	Virgil Vann	8	Jim & Rosa Vann
657	Walter Vann	18	William Jr & Sarah Vann
847	Walter Vann	13	Steve & Mary Vann
1590	Walter Vann	22	Jesse Vann & Emma Purtle
1590	Waneta Vann	1	Walter & Elnora Vann
850	Watt Vann	6	Dunk & Chick Vann
1009	Wiley Vann	1	David & Bessie Vann
46	William Vann	16	Butler & Sarah Vann
666	William Vann	19	James & Nancy Vann
657	William Jr Vann	48	William & Hannah Vann
944	William Vann	28	Sam & Katie Vann
985	William Vann	38	James Vann & Rosanna Melton
73	Willie Vann	4mos	Simon & Susan Vann
1457	Willie Vann	10	Charles & Kizzy Vann
625	Willie Vann	10	Dave & Sarah Vann
608	Willie Vann	17	Samuel & Lydia Vann
375	Willis Vann	18mos	Rufus & Sallie Vann
594	Willie Vann	4	Wiley Morris & Lula Vann

171	Zeb Vann	14	Jacob & Maggie Vann
1461	Rodia Wade	25	Andy Tyner & Rachel Payne
1579	Cora Wagoner	22	Jerry & Hannah Riley
1579	Oval Wagoner	5wks	Sam & Cora Wagoner
1091	Aggie Walker	38	Harry Vann & Sidney Rogers
642	Alice Walker	24	Jack Walker & Polly Ross
116	Ambrose Walker	7	Charlie Walker & Sallie Mayfield
26	Charlotte Walker	10	Thomas & Dinah Walker
1093	Charlotte Walker	28	Daniel & Aggie Walker
1046	Clarence Walker	3mos	Wesley & Rachel Walker
131	Clark Walker	18	Thomas Walker & Rachel Payne
1091	Daniel Walker	50	Coosie & Charlott Walker
1274	David Walker	19	Daniel & Mary Walker
1091	Della Walker	15	Daniel & Aggie Walker
26	Dinah Walker	47	Louisa Crapo
1091	Eddie Walker	3	Daniel & Aggie Walker
26	Edward Walker	12	Thomas & Dinah Walker
1091	Effie Walker	11	Daniel & Aggie Walker
196	Elizabeth Walker	22	Boon Walker & Betsy Mayfield
1046	Elnora Walker	5	Wesley & Rachel Walker
510	Fannie Walker	65	George & Diana Drew
1274	Frances Walker	29	Isaac James & Nancy Sheppard
26	Frank Walker	15	Thomas & Dinah Walker
193	Isaac Walker	19	Boon Walker & Betsy Mayfield
1091	Jesse Walker	4	Daniel & Aggie Walker
296	Lewis Walker	8mos	Charles & Susan Walker
490	Lizzie Walker	5	William Walker & Julia Cravens
1091	Lonie Walker	6wks	Daniel & Aggie Walker
1093	Luther Walker	4	George Murrell & Charlotte Walker
1091	Mack Walker	17	Daniel & Aggie Walker
529	Mary Walker	50	Mose & Phillis Ross
642	May Walker	3	George Ferguson & Alice Walker
1091	May Walker	9	Daniel & Aggie Walker
19	Moses Walker	39	Mose & Charlotte Walker
423	Nancy Walker	31	Johnson Meigs & Charlott Walker
196	Paul Walker	5	Bud Mayfield & Elizabeth Walker
296	Pearl Walker	7	Charles & Susan Walker
1046	Rachel Walker	27	Joe Martin & Eliza Alberty
196	Rosabella Walker	3	Bud Mayfield & Elizabeth Walker
296	Rowena Walker	2	Charles & Susan Walker

296	Susan Walker	26	Amos & Rachel Aldrich
26	Thomas Walker	48	Moses & Charlotte Walker
196	Violet Walker	8mos	Houston Mayfield&Elizabeth Walker
1046	Walter Walker	3	Wesley & Rachel Walker
296	William Walker	4	Charles & Susan Walker
1046	William Walker	1	Wesley & Rachel Walker
1274	Willis Walker	16	Daniel & Mary Walker
1231	Dora Wallace	21	Reuben & Amanda Johnson
752	Elma Wallace	8	John & Mary Wallace
752	Oliver Wallace	10	John & Mary Wallace
1334	Clarence Ward	11	Ben & Sarah Ward
294	Cora Ward	4	Nelson & Rachel Ward
908	Elmira Ward	15	George & Nancy Ward
908	Hattie Ward	8mos	James Powell & Elmira Ward
908	Henry Ward	7	George & Nancy Ward
859	Iva Ward	9	George Ward & Helen Whitmire
1335	Lena Ward	21	Ben Ward & Sarah Hudson
908	Luther Ward	9	George & Nancy Ward
1334	Martha Ward	13	Ben & Sarah Ward
1334	Myrtle Ward	7	Ben & Sarah Ward
908	Nancy Ward	33	Henry & Minta Ward
1334	Neal Ward	10	Ben & Sarah Ward
294	Rachel Ward	38	James & Lottie Beck
1334	Sarah Ward	42	Peter & Charity Hudson
248	Sylvester Ward	16	Richard Ward & Lena Crawford
1334	Vannie Ward	15	Ben & Sarah Ward
973	Maggie Warren	22	Looney & Mary Whitmire
1462	Matilda Warren	70	William & Judy Ross
840	Nancy Washington	44	James Webber & Frances Patterson
1265	Ritta Washington	55	Henry & Hannah Melton
51	Leona Watkins	11days	Lee & Nannie Watkins
51	Nannie Watkins	22	Lage Meadows & Mary Sumpter
195	Amanda Watie	23	Jacob Wilson & Frances McNack
195	David Watie	25	Joseph & Martha Watie
78	Everett Watie	18	Thomas & Minta Watie
304	Joseph Watie	50	Thomas & Mary Watie
78	Leona Watie	12	Thomas & Minta Watie
304	Martha Watie	37	Robert & Sylva Smith
78	Mary Watie	14	Thomas & Minta Watie
78	Minta Watie	46	William & Nicie West

78	Nannie Watie	13	Thomas & Minta Watie
78	Thomas Watie	45	Mary Watie
129	Walter Watie	21	Tom & Minty Watie
1229	David Watson	2	George & Eliza Watson
1229	Eliza Watson	41	Allen & Elizabeth Latta
449	Maggie Watson	38	Ary Pack
449	Minnie Watson	13	E.A. & Maggie Watson
373	Sarah Watson	40	Charlie & Elmira Nave
242	Conway Wear	11	Bruster & Dora Ware
242	Dora Wear	28	Jesse & Ary McClure
242	Edward Wear	3mos	Bruster & Dora Ware
242	Mamie Wear	14	Bruster & Dora Ware
242	McKinley Wear	4	Bruster & Dora Ware
242	William Wear	9	Bruster & Dora Ware
242	Zandora Wear	3	Bruster & Dora Ware
1553	Emily Weaver	60	Lewis Crittenden & Nellie Cole
1227	Lewis Weaver	49	Joe & Emily Weaver
1282	Jane Webb	51	Edmond Vann & Mary Stover
1058	Aaron Webber	25	Sam & Sarah Webber
1527	Aaron Webber	36	Sam & Nancy Webber
269	Alice Webber	5	Samuel & Judy Webber
1427	Andrew Webber	50	Robbin & Cinda Webber
1428	Andy Webber	5	Hayes Sales & Mary Webber
1547	Andy Webber	25	Johnson & Frances Webber
1058	Annie Webber	25	Daniel & Malinda Sanders
891	Boyd Webber	9mos	Moses & Ellen Webber
834	Clarence Webber	10	John Webber & Susan Lane
1127	David Webber	22	Sam & Sarah Webber
12	Dugald Webber	76	Wallace & Winnie Webber
1132	Eliza Webber	14	Samuel & Sarah Webber
891	Ellen Webber	23	William & Susan Hudson
271	Frank Webber	21	Sam & Julia Webber
269	George Webber	12	Samuel & Judy Webber
1133	George Webber	24	George Webber & Hannah Johnson
891	Helia Webber	4mos	Moses & Ellen Webber
1058	Johnie Webber	3mos	Aaron & Annie Webber
269	Johnson Webber	16	Samuel & Judy Webber
1513	Josh Webber	33	Robert & Margaret Webber
269	Judy Webber	58	Frank & Sylva McCoy
1519	Julia Webber	3	Frank Webber & Susie Whitmire

1428	Katie Webber	7mos	Stephenson & Mary Webber
12	Katie Webber	45	Jesse & Tena Roach
1528	Levi Webber	29	Samuel & Judy Webber
1428	Mary Webber	26	Andy Webber & Rachel Lasley
1058	Minnie Webber	2	Aaron & Annie Webber
1058	Nora Webber	6mos	Aaron & Annie Webber
1058	Ola Webber	5	Aaron & Annie Webber
1428	Rachel Webber	6	Hayes Sales & Mary Webber
1511	Robert Webber	65	Carr & Winnie Webber
1512	Sam Webber	30	Robert & Margaret Webber
269	Samuel Webber	58	Robert & Betsy Webber
1132	Samuel Webber	58	Samuel West & Nancy Webber
1519	Samuel Webber	1	Frank Webber & Susie Whitmire
1132	Sarah Webber	46	Thomas & Manerva Hill
1132	Thomas Webber	2	Samuel & Sarah Webber
1353	William Webber	51	Robert Webber & Lucinda French
420	Daniel Welch	11	Isaac & Sadie Welch
589	Eunice Welch	21	Ike Welch & Silva Thompson
1014	Frank Welch	12	Sam Welch & Lucy Hill
99	Henry Welch	15	Jos Welch & Lizzie Vann
561	Lone Welch	13	Isaac Welch & Sylvia Thompson
1014	Louis Welch	18	Sam Welch & Lucy Hill
420	Lula Welch	7	Isaac & Sadie Welch
420	Sadie Welch	24	Seymour & Nan Mathis
420	Walter Welch	9	Isaac & Sadie Welch
1203	Amanda Welcome	50	John Wildcat & Judy Williams
1415	Alberta West	2	George West
1494	Callis Jr. West	16	Callis & Carrie West
1494	Carrie West	12	Callis & Carrie West
1494	Charlie West	14	Callis & Carrie West
1416	Collis West	49	Henry & Phoebe West
1417	Collis West	21	Houston & Lizzie West
1494	Cornelius West	15	Callis & Carrie West
1494	Ella West	11	Callis & Carrie West
1414	Fannie West	15	Houston & Lizzie West
1134	Garfield West	9	Garfield West & Rilda Powell
1415	George West	34	Henry & Phoebe West
1415	George Jr West	8	George West
1414	Georgia West	13	Houston & Phoebe West
1494	Henry West	17	Callis & Carrie West

1414	Houston West	47	Henry & Phoebe West
1414	Ida West	19	Houston & Lizzie West
1134	Jesse West	6	Garfield West & Rilda Powell
1415	Jessie West	6	George West
1494	Martha West	4	Callis & Carrie West
1414	Nancy West	17	Houston & Lizzie West
1494	Sadie West	6	Callis & Carrie West
1516	Sidney West	56	Lowen Vann & Nancy West
1494	Vinita West	1	Callis & Carrie West
1494	Walter West	7	Callis & Carrie West
1494	Watie West	9	Callis & Carrie West
1414	William West	9	Houston & Lizzie West
907	Alice White	18	William & Fannie White
907	Clayborn White	8	William & Fannie White
907	Clora White	16	William & Fannie White
757	Della White	6	Thomas & Louisa White
907	Fannie White	46	Mike Whitmire & Dinah Kliens
757	Frank White	13	Thomas & Louisa White
757	Louisa White	35	Jerry & Ruth Alberty
360	Lydia White	50	Toss & Susie Rogers
907	Melissa White	12	William & Fannie White
948	Nathaniel White	21	William & Fannie White
907	Rachel White	11	William & Fannie White
757	Ray White	9	Thomas & Louisa White
907	Serena White	6	William & Fannie White
757	Stella White	11	Thomas & Louisa White
757	Willie White	7	Thomas & Louisa White
907	Winona White	14	William & Fannie White
903	Aaron Jr Whitmire	22	Lewis & Betsy Whitmire
918	Aaron Whitmire	67	Major Wright & Peggie Whitmire
1534	Ada Whitmire	16	Frank & Martha Whitmire
758	Albert Whitmire	18	Martin & Lucy Whitmire
879	Aleck Whitmire	20	Lewis & Betsy Whitmire
964	Angeline Whitmire	30	Robert & Lizzie Glass
1189	Ann Whitmire	60	Malinda Coody
1542	Annie Whitmire	26	Frank & Martha Whitmire
1535	Arthur Whitmire	6	Austin & Josie Whitmire
1535	Austin Whitmire	26	Frank & Martha Whitmire
352	Austin Whitmire	2	Charles & Maggie Whitmire
1379	Benjamin Whitmire	8	Samuel & Lydia Whitmire

1534	Bessie Whitmire	10	Frank & Martha Whitmire
879	Betsy Whitmire	56	Jennie Sanders
1117	Blanche Whitmire	7	Nathan & Patsy Whitmire
1379	Blanche Whitmire	2	Samuel & Lydia Whitmire
1379	Booker Whitmire	2mos	Samuel & Lydia Whitmire
352	Charles Whitmire	32	Joshua & Frances Whitmire
922	Charles Whitmire	18	Dick & Hannah Whitmire
922	Charles Whitmire	4	Daniel & Louisa Whitmire
1535	Cora Whitmire	3	Austin & Josie Whitmire
937	Crawford Whitmire	6	Looney & Mary Whitmire
1060	Daniel Whitmire	5	Dick & Jane Whitmire
1085	Dave Whitmire	23	Ed & Mary Wright
975	Dennis Whitmire	55	Major Wright & Peggy Whitmire
1060	Dick Whitmire	50	Dick Whitmire & Julia Markum
922	Dora Whitmire	9	Daniel & Louisa Whitmire
1379	Earnest Whitmire	16	Samuel & Lydia Whitmire
863	Edward Whitmire	3	Zeke & Lucinda Whitmire
902	Eliza Whitmire	67	Jennie Sanders
937	Ella Whitmire	10	Looney & Mary Whitmire
1514	Ella Whitmire	25	Robert & Margaret Webber
857	Elmer Whitmire	11	John Lasley & Maria Whitmire
922	Emma Whitmire	15	Dick & Hannah Whitmire
922	Eva Whitmire	17	Daniel & Louisa Whitmire
852	Fannie Whitmire	9mos	Joe & Sarah Whitmire
352	Frances Whitmire	7	Charles & Maggie Whitmire
1534	Frank Whitmire	56	Mose Alberty & Hannah Whitmire
918	George Whitmire	14	Nelson & Rachel Whitmire
1534	George Whitmire	12	Frank & Martha Whitmire
937	Georgia Whitmire	5	Gus Parker & Maggie Warren
910	Gertie Whitmire	21	Dennis & Sallie Whitmire
1082	Gettie Whitmire	23	Mose Whitmire & Mariah Vander
1379	Harvey Whitmire	5	Samuel & Lydia Whitmire
922	Hattie Whitmire	16	Daniel & Louisa Whitmire
937	Hattie Whitmire	3	Looney & Mary Whitmire
859	Helen Whitmire	25	Mose & Maria Whitmire
937	Hubbard Whitmire	12	Looney & Mary Whitmire
1063	Ida Whitmire	5	Walter Whitmire & Susie Musgrove
980	Isaac Whitmire	21	Looney & Mary Whitmire
758	Jacob Whitmire	20	Martin & Lucy Whitmire
407	James Whitmire	17	Jesse & Mary Whitmire

905	James Whitmire	29	Lewis & Betsy Whitmire
1378	Jane Whitmire	36	Joe & Nancy Wolfe
1060	Jeff Whitmire	13	Dick & Jane Whitmire
1534	Jesse Whitmire	14	Frank & Martha Whitmire
852	Joe Whitmire	28	Dennis & Sallie Whitmire
968	Joe Whitmire	20	Cealey Wofford
937	Johney Whitmire	4mos	Looney & Mary Whitmire
1060	Joseph Whitmire	15	Dick & Jane Whitmire
1535	Josephine Whitmire	5	Austin & Josie Whitmire
1530	Lela Whitmire	9mos	William Whitmire & Elsie Adair
937	Lena Whitmire	17	Looney & Mary Whitmire
352	Leroy Whitmire	10	Charles & Maggie Whitmire
863	Lettie Whitmire	8	Zeke & Lucinda Whitmire
1379	Levi Whitmire	12	Samuel & Lydia Whitmire
879	Lewis Whitmire	62	Major Wright & Peggie Whitmire
937	Looney Whitmire	45	Ike Glass & Betsy Whitmire
937	Looney Jr Whitmire	15	Looney & Mary Whitmire
922	Louisa Whitmire	47	Melissa Foster
352	Lucy Whitmire	16mos	Charles & Maggie Whitmire
352	Maggie Whitmire	28	Isaac & Roseanna Ross
1082	Mamie Whitmire	2mos	Gettie & Ruth Whitmire
857	Maria Whitmire	51	George & Peggy Landrum
170	Mary Whitmire	42	Henry & Phoebe West
879	Mary Whitmire	16	Lewis & Betsy Whitmire
937	Mary Whitmire	43	Lewis Rogers & Amanda Brown
975	Mary Whitmire	6	Joe & Lucy Whitmire
305	Mattison Whitmire	14	Jess Whitmire & Mary Alberty
857	Maudie Whitmire	14	Mose & Maria Whitmire
1535	Minnie Whitmire	1	Austin & Josie Whitmire
863	Mose Whitmire	4	Zeke & Lucinda Whitmire
972	Moses Sr Whitmire	70	Peggy Whitmire
1117	Nancy Whitmire	10	Nathan & Patsy Whitmire
1117	Nathan Whitmire	37	Lewis & Betsy Whitmire
918	Needham Whitmire	17	Nelson & Rachel Whitmire
1536	Nelson Whitmire	22	Frank & Martha Whitmire
1507	Patsy Whitmire	31	Joe Rogers & Sarah Whitmire
1232	Rosa Whitmire	22	Reuben & Amanda Johnson
1060	Rosella Whitmire	10	Dick & Jane Whitmire
879	Ruth Whitmire	18	Lewis & Betsy Whitmire
352	Sam Whitmire	4	Charles & Maggie Whitmire

1379	Samuel Whitmire	55	Hannah Whitmire
1060	Sanford Whitmire	2	Dick & Jane Whitmire
852	Sarah Whitmire	33	Andy & Millie Frye
1505	Sarah Whitmire	52	James Vann & Patsy Wright
863	Sequoyah Whitmire	1	Zeke & Lucinda Whitmire
1519	Susie Whitmire	21	Henry Smith & Sidney West
974	Thomas Whitmire	35	George Sanders & Eliza Whitmire
920	Walter Whitmire	33	Aaron & Sarah Whitmire
861	William Whitmire	21	Mose & Maria Whitmire
863	William Whitmire	10	Zeke & Lucinda Whitmire
863	Zeke Whitmire	33	Mose & Amanda Whitmire
1430	Cynthia Wickliff	21	George & Eliza Daniels
1430	George Wickliff	3mos	Jackson & Cynthia Wickliff
1430	William Wickliff	1	Jackson & Cynthia Wickliff
150	Peggy Wiggins	38	Peter & Gracie Crapo
694	Alexander Williams	14	Arthur & Eliza Williams
1181	Alf Williams	22	Williams & Ruth Williams
694	Arthur Williams	20	Arthur & Eliza Williams
694	Augustus Williams	18	Arthur & Eliza Williams
94	Belle Williams	16	Sam & Matilda Williams
635	Carrie Williams	26	James & Jennie Beck
303	David Williams	18	David Williams & Louisa Riley
925	Easter Williams	50	Jack Ratcliff & Sylva Grimmett
1350	Elizabeth Williams	37	Henry Grayson & Betsy Whitmire
694	Ellis Williams	14	Arthur & Eliza Williams
395	Evaline Williams	8mos	Riley & Fannie Williams
395	Fannie Williams	27	Rockwell & Lydia Fields
751	Flossie Williams	1	Gus Williams & Carrie Martin
909	George Williams	24	York Patterson & Frances Williams
155	Henry Williams	12	James & Edna Williams
416	Lewis Williams	21	Sam & Matilda Williams
694	Martha Williams	16	Arthur & Eliza Williams
1216	Martha Williams	21	James & Nancy Vann
694	Mary Williams	12	Arthur & Eliza Williams
94	Matilda Williams	54	Jack & Margaret Lipe
1492	Melvina Williams	36	John Smith & Susan Rider
880	Peggy Williams	30	Lewis & Betsy Whitmire
703	Peter Williams	77	Ruth Williams
540	Sarah Williams	23	George & Rose Rogers
925	Sylvia Williams	20	Dan & Easter Williams

98	Eva Willis	14	Glendon Willis & Alice Jones
530	Frank Willis	4mos	Moses Willis & Fannie Evans
178	Ada Wilson	7mos	Sam Stidmon & Rebecca Wilson
60	Allie Wilson	13	Oliver & Sarah Wilson
45	Amanda Wilson	17	Isaac & Rachel Wilson
663	Anna Wilson	2	Henry & Lizzie Wilson
231	Barto Wilson	9	JB & Katie Wilson
60	Bertha Wilson	16	Oliver & Sarah Wilson
1455	Blanche Wilson	14	Dud Wyly & Eliza Wilcox
1253	Clarence Wilson	12	Nick Wilson & Mary Ross
231	Cora Wilson	19	JB & Katie Wilson
231	Elizabeth Wilson	17	JB & Katie Wilson
1455	Emma Wilson	5	George & Eliza Wilson
1386	Ernest Wilson	2	Arena Wilson
178	Fannie Wilson	7	Dock Bean & Rebecca Wilson
45	Florence Wilson	12	Isaac & Rachel Wilson
663	Florence Wilson	2mos	Henry & Lizzie Wilson
192	Frances Wilson	26	Joe & Martha Watie
1386	Frances Wilson	7	Arena Wilson
45	Frederick Wilson	19	Isaac & Rachel Wilson
192	Griggs Wilson	1	Manuel & Frances Wilson
663	Henry Wilson	34	Isaac & Glassie Wilson
45	Isaac Wilson	14	Isaac & Rachel Wilson
663	John Wilson	8	Henry & Lizzie Wilson
231	Katie Wilson	48	Gilbert & Jane Vann
231	Kittie Wilson	12	JB & Katie Wilson
60	Lelia Wilson	20	Oliver & Sarah Wilson
663	Lizzie Wilson	38	Thomas Hicks & Mary Funghauser
192	Manuel Wilson	26	Jacob Wilson & Frances McNack
231	Myrtle Wilson	14	JB & Katie Wilson
45	Rachel Wilson	53	Jack Lipe & Sylvia Baldridge
178	Rebecca Wilson	23	Isaac & Rachel Wilson
127	Reed Wilson	22	Oliver & Sarah Wilson
60	Robert Wilson	10	Oliver & Sarah Wilson
60	Sarah Wilson	43	Ned & Adaline Johnson
60	Thomas Wilson	18	Oliver & Sarah Wilson
192	Thomas Wilson	7	Manuel & Frances Wilson
1386	William Wilson	4	Arena Wilson
1455	Winnie Wilson	11	George & Eliza Wilson
610	Fannie Winters	3	Charlie & Rachel Winters

610	Hannah Winters	5mos	Charlie & Rachel Winters
610	Rachel Winters	25	Ed & Fannie Drew
250	Alice Wofford	10	Sam & Josephine Wofford
470	Alma Wofford	30	Samuel & Josephine Wofford
470	Amanda Wofford	30	John & Mariah Gentry
470	Cooly Wofford	7mos	Alma & Amanda Wofford
250	Ellis Wofford	12	Sam & Josephine Wofford
250	Lizzie Wofford	14	Sam & Josephine Wofford
250	Napoleon Wofford	34	Sam & Josephine Wofford
250	Sherley Wofford	19	Sam & Josephine Wofford
250	Wallace Wofford	16	Sam & Josephine Wofford
376	Walter Wofford	24	Samuel & Josephine Wofford
1327	Charles Wolfe	30	Joe & Nancy Wolfe
1377	Charlie Wolfe	3	Grant & Paulina Wolfe
1377	Elnora Wolfe	4mos	Grant & Paulina Wolfe
1377	Grant Wolfe	33	Joe & Nancy Wolfe
1377	Jesse Wolfe	8	Grant & Paulina Wolfe
1377	Lilah Wolfe	10	Grant & Paulina Wolfe
1328	Ola Wolfe	9mos	Solomon & Leanna Wolfe
1377	Robert Wolfe	12	Grant & Paulina Wolfe
1328	Solomon Wolfe	27	Joe & Nancy Wolfe
1226	Chess Woodall	50	Joe Wright & Cynthia Woodall
1259	Rachel Woodall	27	George Woodall & Emily Weaver
913	Charles Woodard	36	Susie Woodard
914	Ella Woodard	14	James Woodard & Lou Peters
914	John Woodard	12	James Woodard & Lou Peters
1134	Annie Woods	2mos	Israel Woods & Rilda Powell
96	Henry Workman	15mos	Alfred & Jennie Workman
96	Jennie Workman	26	Sam & Matilda Williams
96	Rosa Workman	5mos	Alfred & Jennie Workman
479	Charles Wright	22	Alfred & Alice Wright
478	Edward Wright	16	Alfred & Alice Wright
478	Frank Wright	13	Alfred & Alice Wright
939	George Wright	23	Lewis & Ellen Wright
277	Hannah Wright	40	Roswell & Mattie Mackey
478	John Wright	12	Alfred & Alice Wright
264	Richard Wright	21	Ed & Hannah Wright
517	Robert Wright	5	Henry Drew & Maggie Mackey
277	Rosetta Wright	2	Will & Hannah Wright
917	Rosevelt Wright	4mos	Thomas & Laura Wright

733	Sallie Wright	23	William Davis & Amy Bean
917	Thomas Wright	19	Lewis & Ellen Wright
399	Bethel Young	22	Jake & Polly Young
323	Ella Young	8mos	John & Lucinda Young
907	Fannie Young	3	
11	Frank Young	11	Jacob & Polly Young
72	Jacob Young	27	Jacob & Polly Young
323	Lucinda Young	24	William & Fannie White
1211	Nellie Young	39	Andrew Daugherty&Nancy Campbell
11	Peggy Young	19	Jacob & Polly Young
11	Polly Young	46	Caleb & Sallie Vann
11	Rosa Young,	12	Jacob & Polly Young
318	Clayton Youngblood	10	Haywood & Savina Youngblood
318	Gonie Youngblood	16	Haywood & Savina Youngblood
331	Oakley Youngblood	5	Reedy Youngblood
331	Reedy Youngblood	32	Savina Youngblood
318	Savina Youngblood	59	Washington & Betsy Melton

INDEX TWO

REJECTED ENROLLEES

.

NATIONAL ARCHIVES PUBLICATION
MICROFILM
M1186 Rolls 36, 37, 38

CARD #	NAME	AGE	PARENTS
R1174	Betsey	62	
R1178	Cynthia	57	
R1180	Fige-lum-ma	82	
R1185	Lucy	25	
R891	Aleck Adair	20	George Adair & Celia Thompson
R106	Amos Adair	66	Becky Adair
R894	Benjamin Adair	33	George Adair & Celia Chamber
R891	Elsie May Adair	16	George Adair & Celia Thompson
R891	Goldie Adair	18	George Adair & Celia Thompson
R855	Henry Adair	77	Jack & Lucy Dailey
R99	Ida Adair	38	Robert & Matilda Love
R106	Katie Adair	40	Dick Sims & Ann Lewis
R106	Lillian Adair	7	Amos & Katie Adair
R106	Louis Adair	16	Amos & Katie Adair
R106	Oatie Adair	12	Amos & Katie Adair
R924	Peter Adair	24	George Adair & Celia Chambers
R106	Remus Adair	18	Amos & Katie Adair
R106	Thomas Adair	19	Amos & Katie Adair
R1001	Willie Adair	36	Henry & Dicey Adair
R1067	Amanda Adams	42	Jesse Wright & Martha Richardson
R980	Ben Adams	38	Warren & Ibbie Adams
R1013	Blanche Adams	15	Perry & Sadie Adams
R1013	George Adams	10	Perry & Sadie Adams
R82	George Adams	48	Arthur Martin & Paulina Adams
R1013	Perry Adams	40	Rector & Polly Landrum
R1013	Sadie Adams	40	Charlotte Berry
R93	Samuel Adams	34	Harvey & Fannie Adams
R418	Elijah Albert	19	Colly & Martha Albert
R421	Harry Albert	3	Henry & Florence Albert
R421	Henry Albert	29	Collie & Martha Albert
R418	Ida Albert	10	Colly & Martha Albert
R423	Jerry Albert	28	Collie & Martha Albert
R421	Lowey Albert	5mos	Henry & Florence Albert
R418	Martha Albert	55	Charles Bolin & Nancy Whitmire
R1069	Paralee Albert	32	George Mason & Joan Taylor
R421	Raymond Albert	1	Henry & Florence Albert
R707	Alex Alberty	27	Jim & Charity Alberty
R32	Annie Alberty	40	Oliver Harnage

R340	Clyde Alberty	6	Joe & Lettie Alberty
R567	Cora Alberty	17	Anderson & Melvina Alberty
R567	Daisy Alberty	15	Anderson & Melvina Alberty
R766	Daniel Alberty	52	Burgess Williams & Hannah Alberty
R1117	Edward Alberty	49	
R766	Ellis Alberty	11	Daniel & Martha Alberty
R350	George Alberty	37	William & Lila Alberty
R157	Hannah Alberty	75	Mike Sanders & Jennie Wright
R766	Hannah Alberty	16	Daniel & Martha Alberty
R157	Henry Alberty	70	Stephen Ross
R567	Jim Alberty	70+	Dick Gates & Millie Alberty
R578	James Jr. Alberty	29	Jim & Millie Alberty
R176	Joe Alberty	25	Henry & Hannah Alberty
R340	Joe Alberty	32	William & Lila Alberty
R766	Joseph Alberty	20	Daniel & Martha Alberty
R340	Lettie Alberty	32	Oliver & Nancy Harnage
R163	Lila Alberty	60	Phil Mayes & Mollie Petitt
R126	Lizzie Alberty	19	Dave & Mattie Fuller
R1234	Lucy Alberty	41	
R567	Melvina Alberty	57	Jordan & Martha Dial
R340	Mima Alberty	7mos	Joe & Lettie Alberty
R340	Nancy Alberty	4	Joe & Lettie Alberty
R340	Robert Alberty	2	Joe & Lettie Alberty
R766	Willie Alberty	13	Daniel & Martha Alberty
R164	William Alberty	66	George Adair & Sallie Alberty
R619	Alice Alexander	30	Becky Cunningham
R619	Elizabeth Alexander	9	Albert & Alice Alexander
R661	Ermer Alexander	17mos	Pleas & Phillis Alexander
R661	Ezra Alexander	3	Pleas & Phillis Alexander
R619	Floyd Alexander	10	Albert & Alice Alexander
R619	Joseph Alexander	9mo	Albert & Alice Alexander
R661	Luther Alexander	6	Pleas & Phillis Alexander
R661	Phillis Alexander	27	Joe & Sarah Ross
R661	Vessie Alexander	5	Pleas & Phillis Alexander
R619	Walter Alexander	7	Albert & Alice Alexander
R269	Anna Allen	32	William & Louvisia Buffington
R1033	Clara Allen	14	John & Clara Allen
R103	Claude Allen	21	Sarah Starr
R269	Flossie Allen	15	James & Anna Allen
R979	Frank Allen	7	Will & Lizzie Allen

R269	Gracie Allen	12	James & Anna Allen
R269	James Allen	8	James & Anna Allen
R979	Lizzie Allen	27	Jim & Margaret Landrum
R920	Sarah Allen	30	Jacob & Mariah Ross
R610	Thomas Allen	58	Alfred & Mary Allen
R269	Wilma Allen	9	James & Anna Allen
R1019	Eva Anderson	26	William & Willie Robinson
R949	Frances Anderson	56	Joe Curry & Polly Adair
R1075	Lucinda Anderson	28	Boson & Jane Loondy
R240	Birdie Archer	24	Lewis Gunter & Rachel Rector
R240	Christina Archer	2	Eli & Birdie Archer
R1051	Eli Archer	25	Thomas & Dilsa Archer
R1024	Georgeann Archer	35	Stephen & Virginia Little
R1024	Thomas Archer	50	Bigbend & Delilah Vann
R551	Claudie Arkle	9	Fred & Cora Arkle
R551	Cora Arkle	30	Charles & Mariah Lewis
R591	Ibbie Armstrong	13	John Armstrong & Nicey Vann
R592	John Armstrong	21	John Armstrong & Nicey Vann
R485	Eliza Arnold	35	Nancy Rider
R57	Lizzie Baker	16	George & Rachel Baker
R495	Nat Baker	26	Bill & Wren Rankin
R57	Rachel Baker	65	
R1236	Ellen Baldridge	21	
R307	Bertha Baldridge	23	William & Viney Farris
R802	Abraham Ballard	78	Charlie Loyd & Judy Thurman
R976	Earl Banks	7	Will & Frances Banks
R976	Frances Banks	30	James & Margaret Landrum
R976	Hortense Banks	1mo	Will & Frances Banks
R553	Irene Banks	15	William & Mary Banks
R976	McKinley Banks	4	Will & Frances Banks
R229	Tenney Banks	14	Abe & Ann Shaw
R553	Virdie Banks	10	William & Mary Banks
R553	William Banks	20	William & Mary Banks
R175	Azzie Barker	13	Tom & Lucy Barker
R175	Lucy Barker	25	Henry & Hannah Alberty
R422	Gussie Barnes	1	John & Ruth Barnes
R422	John Barnes	24	Samuel & Jennie Barnes
R422	John Barnes	2mos	John & Ruth Barnes
R576	John Barnes	30	Moses Barnes & Jennie Willie
R427	Joshua Barnes	21	Samuel & Jennie Barnes

R429	Minnie Barnes	14	Samuel & Jennie Barnes
R419	Robert Barnes	33	Samuel & Jennie Barnes
R1265	Catch Barnett	6mos	Catch & Mary Barnett
R1265	Emma Barnett	3	Catch & Mary Barnett
R1265	Joseph Barnett	10	Catch & Mary Barnett
R1265	Leroy Barnett	4	Catch & Mary Barnett
R1265	Monday Barnett	9	Catch & Mary Barnett
R1265	Susie Barnett	4	Catch & Mary Barnett
R1074	Ella Baxter	37	Ed & Sarah London
R884	Bertha Bean	15	Jacob & Julia Bean
R344	Della Bean	18	Henry & Irene Bean
R674	Ellen Bean	23	Jess Vann & Emma Purtle
R98	Henry Bean	52	Jack & Mary Bean
R344	Henry Bean	48	Jacob & Mary Bean
R884	Jacob Bean	50	Sandy & Rachel Bean
R545	Jane Bean	50	Jim & Tillie Randolph
R266	Lucy Bean	23	George & Bettie Bean
R987	Mannie Bean	26	Ben Bean & Sallie Whitmire
R344	Manotee Bean	15	Henry & Irene Bean
R1115	Margaret Bean		
R77	Mary Bean	108	Harry & Nancy Martin
R267	Mary Bean	27	George & Bettie Bean
R1237	Mary Bean	19	
R344	Pearlie Bean	6	Henry & Irene Bean
R1114	Pola Bean		
R267	Samuel Bean	6	Fred LaFlore & Mary Bean
R543	Sarah Bean	27	Mose & Patient Hardrick
R267	William Bean	11	Fred LaFlore & Mary Bean
R134	Abbie Beardon	60	Mose & Darcus Nave
R1123	Angeline Beck	52	
R682	Bettie Beck	55	George Carter
R756	Charlotte Beck	24	Henry Sidney & Mina Beck
R1125	Louis Beck		
R812	Mary Beck	40	Peter & Betsy Meigs
R999	Mina Beck	41	George & Millie Bryant
R1175	Walter Beck	31	
R1271	Christy Beeson	2	Jesse & Mary Beeson
R1271	Clifton Beeson	5	Jesse & Mary Beeson
R959	Ella Beeson	13	Beeson & Jane Holt
R732	Jesse Beeson	27	Mary Hudson

R1037	John Beeson	32	William Beeson & Mary Hudson
R959	Laura Beeson	19	Beeson & Jane Holt
R1271	Mary Beeson	23	Jeff Rowe
R1271	Mercy Beeson	4	Jesse & Mary Beeson
R1271	Sanford Beeson	7	Jesse & Mary Beeson
R278	William Beeson	20	John Beeson & Mary Hudson
R338	Alfred Bell	47	
R436	Alfred Bell	51	Sam Jackson & Hannah Cunningham
R331	Annie Bell	32	Amos & Emily Bell
R188	Arthur Bell	20	Thomas & Tensie Bell
R761	Beatrice Bell	7	George & Margaret Bell
R761	Beulah Bell	5mos	George & Margaret Bell
R436	Cena Bell	12	Alfred & Missouri Bell
R436	Earl Bell	18	Alfred & Missouri Bell
R436	Eddie Bell	14	Alfred & Missouri Bell
R192	Effie Bell	10	George Bell & Sallie Chandler
R900	Ellen Bell	40	Jackson & Julia Davis
R338	Geneva Bell	8	Alfred & Marinda Bell
R192	George Bell	34	Thomas & Tensie Bell
R415	George Bell	41	Amica Bell
R761	George Bell	3	George & Margaret Bell
R431	George Bell	2mos	George & Maggie Bell
R777	Granville Bell	28	Elijah & Mary Watie
R436	James Bell	20	Alfred & Missouri Bell
R211	John Bell	23	Spencer & Elizabeth Bell
R416	July Bell	43	A. Phillips & Annie Cunningham
R784	Leslie Bell	29	Elijah Watie & Mary Bell
R436	Lucian Bell	16	Alfred & Missouri Bell
R431	Maggie Bell	27	Samuel & Jennie Barnes
R761	Margaret Bell	27	Harry & Adaline Daniels
R761	Ord Bell	5	George & Margaret Bell
R212	Rector Bell	27	Spencer & Elizabeth Bell
R331	Rector Bell	15	Andy Fulson & Annie Bell
R439	Robert Bell	24	Alfred & Missouri Bell
R436	Russia Bell	16	Alfred & Missouri Bell
R338	Teddy R. Bell	1	Alfred & Marinda Bell
R188	Tensie Bell	52	Gracie Starr
R188	Thomas Bell	68	Archilla Smith & Nancy Bell
R437	William Bell	28	Alfred & Missouri Bell
R1229	George Benton	12	

R883	Stella Benton	2wks	Dave & Vina Benton
R883	Vina Benton	20	Joe & Sophia Lynch
R955	Bonnie Beson	8	John Beson & Rosetta Whitmire
R955	Essie Beson	9	John Beson & Rosetta Whitmire
R1239	Venia R. Bird	6	
R1221	Robert Bishop	12	Alex Bishop & Ellen Payne
R900	Bud Blackburn	13	Charlie Blackburn & Ellen Bell
R900	Carrie Blackburn	15	Charlie Blackburn & Ellen Bell
R900	Charley Blackburn	17	Charlie Blackburn & Ellen Bell
R1119	Frank Blackburn	26	
R900	John Blackburn	20	Charlie Blackburn & Ellen Bell
R900	Julia Blackburn	9	Charlie Blackburn & Ellen Bell
R650	Mary Blackburn	23	John Rose & Emily Nolen
R900	Nora Blackburn	19	Charlie Blackburn & Ellen Bell
R900	Sarah Blackburn	11	Charlie Blackburn & Ellen Bell
R1118	Willie Blackburn	29	
R577	Katie Blackwell	55	John Fox & Martha Knight
R581	Lucinda Blackwell	25	Albert Thompson & Katie Blackwell
R581	Margery Blackwell	2mos	Frank & Lucinda Blackwell
R581	Pearlee Blackwell	4	Frank & Lucinda Blackwell
R216	Charley Blagburne	48	Thos Blagburne & Martha Downing
R62	Calvin Blue	13	King Blue & Susan Harlin
R62	Elizabeth Blue	16	King Blue & Susan Harlin
R590	Emma Blue	23	Charles & Maggie Mayfield
R43	Tony Blue	48	Jack & Louisa Blue
R854	Abbie Blythe	60	Mahala Blythe
R854	Calis Blythe	12	Calvin Hilderbrand & Abbie Blythe
R859	Edmond Blythe	28	Abbie Blythe
R854	Minnie Blythe	16	Calvin Hilderbrand & Abbie Blythe
R1238	Tomie Bollen	48	
R42	Mary Boone	40	George Benge & Lydia Coody
R425	Annie Borkum	15	Dutch & Nancy Borkum
R425	Nancy Borkum	31	Collie & Martha Albert
R425	Walter Borkum	9	Dutch & Nancy Borkum
R335	Ben Bowland	14	Charley & Sarah Bowland
R335	Charley Bowland	46	Charles Bowland & Nancy Whitmire
R335	Charley Jr. Bowland	9	Charley & Sarah Bowland
R335	Eddie Bowland	12	Charley & Sarah Bowland
R335	James Bowland	6	Charley & Sarah Bowland
R335	Mattie Bowland	16	Charley & Sarah Bowland

R733	Leonard Bowles	70	
R614	John Bowlin	51	Alex & Sophia Bowlin
R518	Jack Brady	38	Barney Brady & Eliza Thompson
R500	Mary Brady	40	Mose & Charlotte Vann
R737	Florence Bratcher	25	Isaac & Caroline Rogers
R1235	Jennie Brewer	22	
R33	Leah Brewer	30	Caleb & Martha Brown
R378	Hannah Briggins	21	Fred & Emily Walker
R378	Lottie Briggins	8	Oscar & Hannah Briggins
R1124	George Brooks	30	
R54	Henry Brooks	13	Henry & Sallie Brooks
R54	Sallie Brooks	31	Andrew & Mary Counsel
R628	Alfred Brown	4	Lucinda Brown
R259	Amanda Brown	60	Charley & Mary Rogers
R1040	Amelia Brown	24	Steward Neeley & Winnie Mackey
R893	Bessie Brown	7	Robert & Josie Brown
R628	Cag Brown	9	Jeff & Isabella Brown
R893	Cela Brown	3mos	Robert & Josie Brown
R400	Charles Brown	79	Joe & Debbie Brown
R401	Charles Jr. Brown	32	Charles & Sarah Brown
R893	Claudy Brown	2	Robert & Josie Brown
R459	Debbie Brown	1	John & Serina Brown
R459	Della Brown	3	John & Serina Brown
R628	Dovie Brown	15	Jeff & Isabella Brown
R529	Edna Brown	3	Mack & Mary Brown
R193	Emily Brown	28	Thomas. & Tensie Bell
R22	Emma Brown	24	Richard & Laura Gross
R491	Emma Brown	27	Richard & Laura Gross
R755	Emma Brown	26	John Willis & Chaney Ross
R630	Essie Brown	3	Richard & Lillie Brown
R569	George Brown	21	Jeff & Isabella Brown
R771	George Brown	2	Alexander & Mary Brown
R893	Gracie Brown	5	Robert & Josie Brown
R404	Hannah Brown	17	Charlie Green & Rachel Brown
R604	Henry Brown	6	John Brown & Johnnie Tucker
R630	Isabel Brown	1	Richard & Lillie Brown
R628	Isabella Brown	40	Nelson & Henny Martin
R724	Jane Brown	30	
R193	Jessie May Brown	5	Floyd & Emily Brown
R261	John Brown	30	George & Amanda Brown

R402	John Brown	36	Charles Sr & Sarah Brown
R400	Joseph Brown	18	Charles & Sarah Brown
R893	Josie Brown	31	George Adair & Celia Chamber
R765	Lewis Brown	26	Samuel Brown & Amanda Richie
R193	Loretta Brown	8	Floyd & Emily Brown
R628	Lucinda Brown	17	Jeff & Isabella Brown
R529	Mack Brown	16mos	Mack & Mary Brown
R529	Mary Brown	26	Charlie & Eliza Robinson
R771	Mary Brown	19	George & Mary Hazelrig
R630	Mary Brown	8mos	Richard & Lillie Brown
R404	Myrtle Brown	14	John & Rachel Brown
R529	Oma Brown	6	Mack & Mary Brown
R1201	Otha Brown	17	
R630	Richard Brown	24	Jeff & Isabell Brown
R100	Robert Brown	44	
R771	Robert Brown	3	Alexander & Mary Brown
R1040	Robert Brown	7	Wilson & Amelia Brown
R585	Samuel Brown	48	Peter Brown
R428	Sarah Brown	30	Samuel & Jennie Barnes
R459	Serina Brown	19	James & Queenie Smith
R763	Susan Brown	44	Thomas & Ibby Brown
R893	Turner Brown	10	Robert & Josie Brown
R628	Warren Brown	19	Jeff & Isabella Brown
R403	Washington Brown	27	Charles Sr & Sarah Brown
R262	William Brown	23	George & Amanda Brown
R795	Annie Bruner	9	Joseph Bruner & Mary Carter
R795	Joseph Bruner	65	Joe & Betsy Bruner
R795	Mary Bruner	11	Joseph Bruner & Mary Carter
R795	Priscilla Bruner	7	Joseph Bruner & Annie Nelson
R795	Susie Bruner	15	Joseph Bruner & Mary Carter
R1121	Jack Bruwer	39	
R228	Charles Bryant	5	Ephriam & Eliza Bryant
R228	Eliza Bryant	26	Jerry Martin & Julia Scott
R580	George Bryant	65	Ben Vann & Mina Bryant
R228	Homer Bryant	3	Ephriam & Eliza Bryant
R228	Lewis Bryant	9	Ephriam & Eliza Bryant
R298	Sherman Bryant	23	Ephriam & Flora Bryant
R199	Arthur Buckner	20	George & Sarah Buckner
R199	Bessie Buckner	16	George & Sarah Buckner
R199	George Buckner	54	Thomas & Elizabeth Buckner

R199	George W. Buckner	13	George & Sarah Buckner
R730	John Buckner	50	
R199	Sarah Buckner	45	Mariah Hayden
R875	Ab Buffington	26	William & Liz Buffington
R274	Bessie Buffington	21	William & Louvisia Buffington
R1112	James Buffington	25	
R271	John Buffington	23	William & Louvisia Buffington
R268	Lewis Buffington	13	William & Louvisia Buffington
R886	Lula Buffington	12	John Buffington & Nancy Curls
R268	Mariah Buffington	80+	Reuben & Ann Ridge
R268	Rector Buffington	11	William & Louvisia Buffington
R275	Reuben Buffington	25	William & Louvisia Buffington
R273	Rosa Buffington	26	William & Louvisia Buffington
R268	Roy Buffington	14	William & Louvisia Buffington
R268	Solomon Buffington	9	William & Louvisia Buffington
R268	William Buffington	52	Rector & Mariah Buffington
R1113	Willie Buffington	22	
R876	William Buffington	34	William & Liz Buffington
R270	Wm Jr Buffington	30	William & Louvisia Buffington
R336	Estella Burdine	17	Charlotte Potts
R1086	Minty Burgess	38	
R1085	William Burgess	28	
R1200	Jane Burgis	28	
R1042	Howard Bushyhead	24	Buck Bushyhead & Sallie Miller
R1122	Samuel Buster	47	
R1041	Anna Butler	30	Buck Bushyhead & Sallie Miller
R114	Condon Calahan	7	Fred Calahan & Chaney Ross
R114	Willie Calahan	14	Fred Calahan & Chaney Ross
R498	Annie Campbell	45	Dave & Celia Thompson
R60	Edmond Campbell	79	Isaac & Rachel Bush
R498	Elizabeth Campbell	16	Elias & Annie Campbell
R521	Joseph Campbell	46	Edmond & Sophia Campbell
R498	Madaline Campbell	7	Shermon Davis & Lottie Vann
R1202	Mame Campbell	28	
R564	Mary Campbell	27	David & Susan Morris
R498	Nathaniel Campbell	10	Sherman Davis & Lottie Vann
R525	Reuben Campbell	63	Robert & Catherine Campbell
R498	Susie Campbell	18	Elias & Annie Campbell
R998	David Canard	22	Hope & Polly Canard
R997	Delia Canard	18	Hope & Polly Canard

R997	Polly Canard	57	Major & Peggy Wright
R27	Rhoda Canard	65	Harry & Judie Grimmett
R368	Rhoda Canard	63	Judy Grimmett
R942	Eliza Cannon	31	John & Margaret Fuman
R85	Aleck Carbin	15	Felix & Malzy Carbin
R85	Ervin Carbin	12	Felix & Malzy Carbin
R120	Frank Carbin	5	Wesley Robinson & Nettie Carbin
R116	James Carbin	25	Felix & Malzy Carbin
R85	Lee Carbin	19	Felix & Malzy Carbin
R120	Lonie Carbin	3	Charlie Martin & Nettie Carbin
R85	Malzy Carbin	53	Reuben & Jennie Downing
R120	Nettie Carbin	28	Felix & Malzy Carbin
R123	Sanford Carbin	23	Felix & Malzy Carbin
R120	Teenie Carbin	2 mos	Charlie Martin & Nettie Carbin
R118	William Carbin	30	Felix & Malzy Carbin
R819	Hattie Carell	21	Simon & Fannie Meigs
R1241	Calvin Carter	22	
R1177	Cora Carter	26	
R54	Ellis Carter	7	Andy Carter & Sallie Brooks
R1256	Ernest Carter	13	
R742	George Carter	22	Nelse & Mollie Carter
R54	James Carter	3	Andy Vann & Sallie Brooks
R670	Jerry Carter	16	John Carter & Amanda Sanders
R772	John Carter	43	Mose Carter & Sallie Ross
R743	John Carter	19	George Carter & Mariah Reynolds
R1176	Mary Carter	45	
R54	Mattie Carter	5	Andy Vann & Sallie Brooks
R1240	Richard Carter	25	
R1256	Sallie Carter	40	Willis Rider & Jennie Penn
R741	Tenah Carter	24	Nelse & Mollie Carter
R1256	Trudie Carter	11	
R773	Victoria Carter	45	Eddie Thompson
R743	Wiley Carter	23	George Carter & Mariah Reynolds
R549	Augustus Cash	17	Calvin & Gettie Cash
R549	Calvin Cash	6	Calvin & Gettie Cash
R549	Clarence Cash	18	Calvin & Gettie Cash
R549	Ethel Cash	13	Calvin & Gettie Cash
R549	Gettie Cash	37	July Lynch & Phillis Hayes
R549	Hester Cash	14	Calvin & Gettie Cash
R549	John Cash	8	Calvin & Gettie Cash

R549	Oce Cash	12	Calvin & Gettie Cash
R549	Toots Cash	4	Calvin & Gettie Cash
R549	William Cash	15	Calvin & Gettie Cash
R102	Allie Chambers	22	Jake & Samantha Renfroe
R828	Green Chambers	60	Henry Hurd & Minerva
R788	Judy Chambers	41+	Henry & Eliza Chambers
R101	Mary Chambers	21	Thomas & Addie Ross
R379	Mose Chambers	50	Peter Williams & Louisa Choteau
R231	Bessie Chapman	25	Tobe & Ellen Martin
R234	Clarence Childers	14 mos	Paul & Jiney Childers
R234	Paul Childers	24	Jim & Malinda Childers
R235	Jay Childers	32	Jim & Matilda Childers
R1163	Richard Childers	46	
R1008	Lillie Chinnett	6	George & Martha Chinnett
R1008	Martha Chinnett	10	George & Martha Chinnett
R466	Isaac Chism	51	Twohead Doublehead& Sarah Chism
R509	Edward Choate	40	Minerva Thompson
R672	Lucy Chouteau	31	Reuben & Emily Campbell
R1164	Cynthia Chukelate	47	
R571	Alex Claggett	70	Henson & Lydia Claggett
R735	Charles Claggett	35	Alex & Mariah Claggett
R776	John Claggett	48	Alex & Mariah Claggett
R108	Benjamin Clark	36	Lilburn & Nancy Clark
R1	Sophronie Coats	56	Spence Bell & Patsy Martin
R255	Andrew Colbert	9	Lewis & Sophrony Colbert
R570	Arthur Colbert	18	William & Sallie Colbert
R653	Ernisteen Colbert	2	James & Susie Colbert
R570	Fannie Colbert	10	William & Sallie Colbert
R653	James Colbert	40	Mose Starr & Matilda Dannenberg
R570	Jeff Colbert	16	William & Sallie Colbert
R653	Mable Colbert	10	James & Hattie Colbert
R255	Marie Colbert	5	Lewis & Sophrony Colbert
R570	Matilda Colbert	6	William & Sallie Colbert
R255	Millie Colbert	3	Lewis & Sophrony Colbert
R653	Minnie Colbert	8	James & Susie Colbert
R653	Myrtle Colbert	12	James & Hattie Colbert
R653	Pearl Colbert	5mos	James & Susie Colbert
R570	Roy Colbert	4	William & Sallie Colbert
R255	Sophrony Colbert	29	Lewis & Vicey Jackson
R653	Susie Colbert	25	Thomas & Mary Hill

R255	Vicey Colbert	7	Lewis & Sophrony Colbert
R653	Walter Colbert	4	James & Susie Colbert
R570	Warneetee Colbert	15	William & Sallie Colbert
R172	Catherine Collins	7 mos	Wesley & Catherine Collins
R406	John Collins	13	Abe Collins & Senie Dorgan
R406	Rebecca Collins	16	Abe Collins & Senie Dorgan
R172	Susie Collins	18	West & Mary Wyly
R768	Irene Connor	22	William Wallis & Lucy Brown
R1058	Jackson Coody	40	Lewis Coody & Mary Bell
R627	Jennetta Coody	21	George Drew & Becky Parlor
R708	Joanna Cook	22	Jim & Charity Alberty
R182	Annie Cooper	35	Thomas & Barbara Corker
R44	Annie Counsel	7	Andrew & Mary Counsel
R44	Beatrice Counsel	15	Andrew &Mary Counsel
R44	Jackson Counsel	5	Andrew & Mary Counsel
R53	Jenkins Counsel	23	Andrew & Mary Counsel
R44	Mary Counsel	50	Caleb & Sallie Alberty
R44	Mary Counsel	18	Andrew & Mary Counsel
R44	Rachel Counsel	20	Andrew & Mary Counsel
R174	Alfonso Counts	4	John & Amanda Counts
R174	Amanda Counts	19	George & Rachel Baker
R731	Willis Cox	53	Wilson & Louisa Cox
R1127	Joseph Crapo	44	
R501	Mark Crawford	56	Jack Bedford & Maria Crawford
R1165	Usurga Cricket	48	
R809	Jane Crittenden		
R253	Arthur Cross	15	John & Jennie Cross
R253	Gertie Cross	13	John & Jennie Cross
R253	Jennie Cross	35	Allen & Angeline Wilson
R253	Kitty Cross	2	John & Jennie Cross
R253	Lula Cross	7	John & Jennie Cross
R253	Maud Cross	9	John & Jennie Cross
R253	Ozella Cross	11	John & Jennie Cross
R253	Viola Cross	5	John & Jennie Cross
R1217	Ella Crossland	10	
R1217	Martha Crossland	8	
R1126	Morris Crossland	29	
R370	Sally Crossland	39	Martha Battes
R927	Modale Crump	1mo	Walter & Sallie Crump
R927	Sallie Crump	21+	Moses & Nancy Smith

R1230	Corenia Culwell	11	
R1230	Mary Culwell	16	
R1230	Nancy Culwell	55	
R1230	Sallie Culwell	9	
R997	Bennie Cunningham	8	Andrew & Susie Cunningham
R997	Edward Cunningham	4	Andrew & Susie Cunningham
R997	Louis Cunningham	2	Andrew & Susie Cunningham
R414	Herbert Curls	7	Julius Curls & Lottie Lynch
R411	Maggie Curls	36	Henry & Katie Thornton
R886	Nancy Curls	30	Joe & Sophie Lynch
R1027	Eli Curry	21	Soney Curry & Rebecca Webber
R1270	Harrison Curry	25	John Curry & Charlotte Vann
R1268	Joseph Curry	30	John Curry & Charlotte Vann
R258	Leah Cushingberry	50	Nelson Martin & Siney McCoy
R258	Winnie Cushingberry	18	Samuel & Leah Cushingberry
R1179	Eli Daniel	24	
R1083	Sally Daniel	36	
R249	Andrew Daniels	71	Charles & Nancy Daniels
R395	Andrew Daniels	37	Burrell & Mevinda Daniels
R395	Burley Daniels	7	Andrew & Dora Daniels
R40	Burrell Daniels	70	Lewis & Susie Taylor
R390	Burrell Daniels	30	Burrell Sr & Mary Daniels
R566	Caroline Daniels	26	Wesley & Manerva Haines
R395	Essie Daniels	9	Andrew & Dora Daniels
R616	Ethel Daniels	11	Thomas Daniels & Celia Kirkpatrick
R618	George Daniels	34	Thomas Daniels & Celia Kirkpatrick
R225	Harriet Daniels	55	Betsy Daniels
R746	Harry Daniels	17	Harry & Caroline Daniels
R792	Jane Daniels	28	Joe & Lucinda Smith
R746	Joseph Daniels	19	Harry & Caroline Daniels
R391	Julia Daniels	2	Garfield Dixon & Mary Daniels
R1272	Laura Daniels	19	Cornelius & Laura Ridge
R395	Lewis Daniels	16	Andrew & Dora Daniels
R391	Louella Daniels	16	Thomas & Silla Daniels
R621	Luther Daniels	1	Thomas Daniels & Martha Hill
R392	Mack Daniels	25	Burrell Sr & Mary Daniels
R392	Mady Daniels	6	Mack & Ella Daniels
R746	Maggie Daniels	20	Harry & Caroline Daniels
R391	Mary Daniels	18	Thomas & Silla Daniels
R40	Meranda Daniels	71	Charles & Nancy Daniels

R395	Minnie Daniels	5	Andrew & Dora Daniels
R395	Miranda Daniels	2	Andrew & Dora Daniels
R746	Ransome Daniels	23	Harry & Caroline Daniels
R40	Robert Daniels	20	Burell & Meranda Daniels
R395	Ruth Daniels	1	Andrew & Dora Daniels
R146	Susan Daniels	50	Susan Johnson
R395	Susie Daniels	13	Andrew & Dora Daniels
R395	Thomas Daniels	10	Andrew & Dora Daniels
R391	Thomas Daniels	43	Burrell Sr & Mary Daniels
R395	Willie Daniels	18	Andrew & Dora Daniels
R798	Clark Dannenberg	22	Henry Dannenbery & Judy Chambers
R798	Essie Dannenberg	2	Clark & Easter Dannenberg
R803	Equilla David	6	King & Laura David
R803	King David	36	King David & Joanna Taylor
R803	Laura David	27	James Rosson & Hannah Rosson
R803	Mary David	9	King & Laura David
R803	Matthew David	18	King & Laura David
R803	Mattie David	3	King & Laura David
R803	Paralie David	7mos	King & Laura David
R803	Robert David	13	King & Laura David
R583	Belle Davis	39	
R657	Beulah Davis	10	Zack & Maggie Davis
R657	Blanche Davis	15	Zack & Maggie Davis
R896	Caroline Davis	53	John Hood & Betsy Whitmire
R183	Clarence Davis	11	Edmund & Cliander Davis
R183	Cliander Davis	49	Cass & Silla Davis
R657	Frances Davis	6	Zack & Maggie Davis
R90	George Davis	60	Dave Landrum & Hannah Vann
R90	George Jr Davis	16	George Davis & Mary Smith
R310	Henry Davis	59	Henry & Anna Davis
R896	Jackson Davis	74	
R898	John Davis	50	Julia Davis
R634	Katie Davis	41	Henry & Frances George
R1034	Katie Davis	22	Douglas Putman & Nettie Downing
R657	Maggie Davis	41	John McNair & Betsy Martin
R183	Marquette Davis	14	Edmund & Cliander Davis
R657	Maude Davis	12	Zack & Maggie Davis
R309	Paul Davis	10	Henry & Anna Davis
R309	Pearl Davis	16	Henry & Anna Davis
R309	Robert Davis	17	Henry & Anna Davis

R657	Sherman Davis	8	Zack & Maggie Davis
R499	William Davis	52	Samuel & Malaiah Carter
R899	William Davis	46	Jackson & Julia Davis
R703	Stepney Dawn	75	Brum Dawn
R47	Andrew Day	15	William Day & Laura Garlington
R47	Clarence Day	5	William Day & Laura Garlington
R47	Ella Day	11	William Day & Laura Garlington
R47	Lena Day	8	William Day & Laura Garlington
R830	Anna Dean	29	Ephram & Nancy Humphries
R829	Gentry Dean	13	Jack & Mary Dean
R829	Mary Dean	29	Ephram & Nancy Humphries
R829	Samuel Dean	8mos	Jack & Mary Dean
R191	Edward Derrick	50	
R815	Edward Derrick	52	John Derrick & Katie Whitmire
R438	Nannie Derrick	22	Alfred & Missouri Bell
R1128	Blossom Dick	22	
R1073	John Dickman	39	John & Pauline Dickman
R650	Jeff Dickson	6	James Dickson & Mary Blackburn
R496	Birdie Dixon	23	Wren Rankin
R406	Senie Dorgan	40	Robert Foster & Betsy Reed
R513	John Dotson	35	Isaac & Hannah Dotson
R1231	Johnie Dotson	7	
R1231	Nora Dotson	6	
R530	Lillie Doty	21	Charles & Eliza Robinson
R1044	Maggie Doty	21	Steward Neely & Winnie Mackey
R79	Alex Downing	38	Alex & Phoebe Downing
R684	Alex Downing	32	Alex & Edie Downing
R687	Andrew Downing	23	Alex & Edie Downing
R849	Elias Downing	60	Reuben & Jennie Downing
R324	Frederic Downing	70	Harris & Charlott Downing
R686	John Downing	27	Alex & Edie Downing
R860	Johnson Downing	25	Elias & Phoebe Downing
R887	Rachel Downing	21	Joe & Sophie Lynch
R688	Solomon Downing	21	Alex & Edie Downing
R685	Thomas Downing	25	Alex & Edie Downing
R457	Becky Drew	45	Rowland & Martha Battise
R227	Frederick Drew	10	Sam & Louisa Drew
R1198	Gus Drew	17	
R1198	Jennie Drew	12	
R227	Jesse Drew	12	Sam & Louisa Drew

R227	Odessa Drew	6	Sam & Louisa Drew
R1198	Ola Drew	14	
R227	Savanah Drew	8	Sam & Louisa Drew
R240	Mahala Driver	7	Will Driver & Birdie Archer
R109	Frank Duffin	17	Joshua Duffin & Annie Johnson
R909	George Duffin	50	Nathan & Frances Duffin
R912	Joshua Duffin	50	Nathan & Frances Duffin
R759	Benjamin Duncan	12	Joseph & Elizabeth Duncan
R759	Elizabeth Duncan	47	Benjamin & Polly Spence
R759	Harry Duncan	16	Joseph & Elizabeth Duncan
R351	Henry Duncan	4	Charley Duncan & Ida Johnson
R351	Jennie Duncan	11	Charley Duncan & Ida Johnson
R759	Jewell Duncan	14	Joseph & Elizabeth Duncan
R351	Mary Duncan	8	Charley Duncan & Ida Johnson
R147	Minnie Duncan	33+	Jerry & Savannah Taylor
R264	Pompey Duncan	45	Ann Duncan
R759	Robert Duncan	18	Joseph & Elizabeth Duncan
R351	Walter Duncan	7	Charley Duncan & Ida Johnson
R351	Willie Duncan	9	Charley Duncan & Ida Johnson
R673	Alice Durant	28	
R938	Edmond Durant	34	Jobe & Peggy Durant
R1072	Eva Durant	9	Ed Durant & Bertha Glass
R938	Nelson Durant	3	Ed & Alice Durant
R938	William Durant	6wks	Ed & Alice Durant
R873	Lovely Eaton	14	Thomas Eaton & Alice Lynch
R1158	Lucy Eaton	24	
R535	Nettie Eaton	35	Steve & Peggy Lynch
R339	Ella Edmondson	16	Elijah & Sudie Edmondson
R339	Eugene Edmondson	14	Elijah & Sudie Edmondson
R339	Lucille Edmondson	9	Elijah & Sudie Edmondson
R339	Lula Edmondson	19	Elijah & Sudie Edmondson
R339	Sarah Edmondson	10	Elijah & Sudie Edmondson
R339	Sudie Edmondson	49	Jess & Lydia Lowery
R339	Tommie Edmondson	12	Elijah & Sudie Edmondson
R339	Tyman Edmondson	16	Elijah & Sudie Edmondson
R1132	CharlesEll	23	
R1129	Creek Ell	26	
R1131	I-Yah-sky Ell	34	
R1130	Lila Ell	32	
R758	Annie Elms	34	Ellis & Amanda Warren

R758	Byron Elms	5	Dock & Annie Elms
R758	Virgie Elms	15	Dock & Annie Elms
R562	Johnson Escoe	3	Charley & Dora Escoe
R562	Luther Escoe	9mos	Charley & Dora Escoe
R313	Laurena Ezell	21	Joseph & Charlotte Smith
R326	Fannie Fairchild	17	John & Nancy Fairchild
R326	John Fairchild	20	John & Nancy Fiarchild
R326	Nancy Fairchild	56	
R304	Elijah Farris	18	William & Melvina Farris
R306	Frederic Farris	21	William & Viney Farris
R304	Leroy Farris	10	William & Viney Farris
R304	Lula Farris	13	William & Viney Farris
R304	Luther Farris	7	William & Viney Farris
R304	Mattie Farris	15	William & Viney Farris
R304	Melvina Farris	46	Andy Frye & Sophia Ross
R305	Solomon Farris	25	William & Viney Farris
R304	Watt Farris	4	William & Viney Farris
R452	Alexander Fields	6	Jackson & Lucretia Fields
R454	Elias Fields	20	William & Lou Fields
R452	Eliza Fields	14	Jackson & Lucretia Feilds
R452	Hester Fields	10	Jackson & Lucretia Fields
R452	Jackson Fields	46	Andy & Chaney Ross Fields
R452	James Fields	15	Jackson & Lucretia Fields
R1243	Katie Fields	21	
R534	Nellie Fields	29	Ellis & Sylvia Bolin
R452	Oby Fields	4mos	Jackson & Lucretia Fields
R1242	Simon Jr. Fields	22	
R452	Sisley Fields	8	Jackson & Lucretia Fields
R452	Wesley Fields	2	Jackson & Lucretia Fields
R452	William Fields	4	Jackson & Lucretia Fields
R454	William Fields	43	Abram & Sally Fields
R617	Eva Finley	27	Thomas Daniels & Celia Kirkpatrick
R617	Frank Finley	3days	Tyre & Eva Finley
R617	Haydee Finley	2	Tyre & Eva Finldy
R1133	Nannie Fish	40	
R1134	Reader Fish	22	
R433	Katie Fishtail	90	Millie Alberty
R258	Samuel Flack	19	Wesley Flack & Leah Cushingberry
R171	Alice Foot	13	Arthur & Annie Foot
R171	Annie Foot	32	West & Mary J. Wyly

R171	Dibrel Foot	11	Arthur & Annie Foot
R171	Josie Foot	13	Arthur & Annie Foot
R254	Ethel Ford	4	Thomas & Rhodie Ford
R254	Frank Ford	10	Thomas & Rhodie Ford
R69	Jackson Ford	1	William & Nona Ford
R254	James Ford	6	Thomas & Rhodie Ford
R254	Joseph Ford	11	Thomas & Rhodie Ford
R69	Nona Ford	30	Harrison Foreman & Liz Hornback
R254	Rhodie Ford	32	Allen & Angeline Wilson
R254	Wilson Ford	8	Thomas & Rhodie Ford
R95	Dennis Foreman	6	Robert Foreman & Fan Goldsby
R52	Etha Foreman	1	Benjamin Foreman & Maggie Harris
R46	Mattie Foreman	7	John Foreman & Maggie Haynes
R1205	Mattie Foreman	22	
R1232	Mattie Foreman	18	
R1057	Ned Foreman	44	Ben & Nancy Ross
R52	Silvester Foreman	5	Benjamin Foreman & Maggie Harris
R706	Annie Foster	40	
R1204	Annie Foster	13	
R879	Arthur Foster	7mos	Robert & Hester Foster
R879	Ethel Foster	2	Robert & Hester Foster
R879	Hester Foster	32	Joe & Sophia Lynch
R879	James Foster	7	Robert & Hester Foster
R879	Josephine Foster	5mos	Robert & Hester Foster
R1203	Lizzie Foster	33	
R1050	Luvina Foster	50	Hagar Kernel
R1088	Malinda Foster	28	
R775	Nellie Foster	23	Soney Curry & Becky Webber
R879	Pearlie Foster	3	Robert & Hester Foster
R484	Phillis Foster	21	Randal & Luvina Foster
R914	Robert Foster	52	Robert & Eliza Foster
R1087	Susie Foster	31	
R643	Arthur Fox	11	Esau & Nancy Fox
R189	Carrie Fox	23	Ellis & Mandy Warren
R643	Esaw Fox	74	Sam Melton & Lettie Stinnet
R308	Ethel Fox	6	Jim & Carrie Fox
R643	Hattie Fox	9	Esau & Nancy Fox
R643	Joe Fox	14	Esau & Nancy Fox
R643	Mary Fox	2	Esau & Nancy Fox
R643	Nancy Fox	43	Thomas Ross & Winnie Murrell

R643	Ruthis Fox	4	Esau & Nancy Fox
R189	Sadie Fox	2	Jim & Carrie Fox
R327	Susan Franklin	50	Johnson & Vinie Ratliff
R902	Annie Freeman	9	George & Carrie Freeman
R901	Arizona Freeman	2	John & Nettie Freeman
R902	Carrie Freeman	28	John & Emma Rose
R901	Charlie Freeman	16	John & Nettie Freeman
R901	Elnora Freeman	18	John & Nettie Freeman
R902	George Freeman	36	John & Margaret Freeman
R957	Gertie Freeman	22	George Calender & Edie Harlin
R903	Isa Freeman	24	John & Nettie Freeman
R901	Jesse Freeman	14	John & Nettie Freeman
R901	John Freeman	20	John & Nettie Freeman
R901	John Freeman	65	Jennie Evans
R901	Luther Freeman	6	John & Nettie Freeman
R901	Nettie Freeman	45	Margaret Dannenberg
R901	Ora Freeman	2mos	John & Nettie Freeman
R901	Walter Freeman	9	John & Nettie Freeman
R8	Ben French	49	John White & Maria French
R1030	Ben French	51	Mariah French
R1054	Charlotte French	43	Fred Markham & Rhoda Alberty
R787	Mariah French	48	Stephen & Mary Littles
R420	Sarah French	8	Austin French & Lula Knalls
R561	Mary Frye	20	John & Hannah Kimbo
R346	Bud Fuller	16	Dave & Malt Fuller
R346	Cynthia Fuller	9	Dave & Malt Fuller
R346	Dick Fuller	8	Dave & Malt Fuller
R346	Myra Fuller	17	Dave & Malt Fuller
R346	Nettie Fuller	18	Dave & Malt Fuller
R346	Peter Fuller	5	Dave & Malt Fuller
R762	Martha Gales	55	Charlie Thompson & Ibby Brown
R430	Frank Gardner	22	Lewis Gardner & Lula Knalls
R258	Jerome Gardner	10	Rufian & Clara Gardner
R258	Odeal Gardner	6	Rufian & Clara Gardner
R258	Ovie Gardner	7	Rufian & Clara Gardner
R47	Laura Garlington	30	Samuel Meigs & Amanda Meads
R1048	Amanda Gaskin	30	Ben Alberty & Mary Joe
R563	Bernice Gentry	8	Eddie & Susie Gentry
R563	Eddie Gentry	35	Eli & Caroline Gentry
R643	Leever Gibson	6mos	Posey & Ollie Gibson

R220	Lewis Gibson	59	Posy Gibson & Caroline Childers
R1206	Luther Gibson	18	Flora Nave
R219	Napoleon Gibson	35	Lewis & Mary Gibson
R643	Ollie Gibson	18	Esau & Nancy Fox
R221	Posey Gibson	23	Lewis & Mary Gibson
R222	William Gibson	28	Lewis & Mary Gibson
R1072	Bertha Glass	26	Sauney Curry & Rebecca Webber
R462	Ora Glover	3	Al Glover & Grace Sheppard
R179	Alberta Goins	10	Calvin & Elvira Goins
R179	Calvin Goins	60	Lucy Goins
R179	Hattie Goins	14	Calvin & Elvira Goins
R179	James Goins	18	Calvin & Elvira Goins
R179	Margarett Goins	12	Calvin & Elvira Goins
R179	Narcissa Goins	16	Calvin & Elvira Goins
R144	Fannie Goldsby	25	Andrew Mack & Katie Vann
R400	Louvena Gorham	20	Charles & Sarah Brown
R861	Edna Graves	18	Charles & Eliza Martin
R1082	Rachel Graves	50	John & Cosby Bean
R603	Elizabeth Gray	32	Rollie Roach & Annie Prince
R603	Golie Gray	13	Charley & Elizabeth Gray
R603	Gussie Gray	6	Charley & Elizabeth Gray
R603	Josephine Gray	11	Charley & Elizabeth Gray
R603	Julius Gray	9	Charley & Elizabeth Gray
R936	Louisa Gray	59	Stephen & Edie Davis
R603	Samuel Gray	18	Charley & Elizabeth Gray
R811	Chlora Grayson	52	Dave & Louisa Ross
R1273	Gertrude Grayson	9	Armstead Foster & Louisa Grayson
R405	Cora Green	16	Charlie Green & Sarah Hines
R405	Eva Green	18	Charlie Green & Sarah Hines
R405	Jesse Green	20	Charlie Green & Sarah Hines
R1181	Manda Griffin	23	
R1089	Melton Grimmet	34	
R24	Adalissa Grimmett	15	William & Lulu Grimmett
R24	Eddie Grimmett	19	William & Lulu Grimmett
R558	Franke Grimmett	12	William Grimmett & Hattie Adair
R24	George Grimmett	9	William & Lulu Grimmett
R24	Henry Grimmett	17	William & Lulu Grimmett
R142	Joe Grimmett	18	William Grimmett & Willie Brown
R1029	Peggie Grimmett	35	Jack & Charlotte Starr
R24	William Grimmett	39	Ben Grimmett & Melissa Duncan

R613	William Grimmett	40	Ben Grimmett & Malissa Duncan
R233	Eliza Grooms	26	Henry Nash & Eliza Gaines
R233	Ennis Grooms	1	Guss & Eliza Grooms
R490	Chlora Gross	20	Squire & Katie Sanders
R21	Chloria Gross	18	Squire & Katie Sanders
R7	Ed Gross	6	William & Letty Gross
R21	Fink Gross	2	Lee & Chloria Gross
R4	Kay Gross	16	Richard & Laura Gross
R4	Laura Gross	49	Savanna Thompson
R559	Laura Gross	49	Savanah Thompson
R6	Lee Gross	23	Richard & Laura Gross
R490	Lee Gross	25	Richard & Laura Gross
R4	Mary Gross	18	Richard & Laura Gross
R7	Matttie Gross	7	William & Letty Gross
R7	Richard Gross	5	William & Letty Gross
R4	Sallie Gross	12	Richard & Laura Gross
R7	William Gross	31	Richard & Laura Gross
R489	WilliamGross	32	Richard & Laura Gross
R112	John Groves	45	Sallie Musgroves
R105	Alice Gunter	18	Nancy Best
R166	Elizabeth Gunter	1	William & Mary Gunter
R1135	Esther Gunter	82	
R237	Forest Gunter	10	Lewis & Rachel Gunter
R166	James Gunter	4	William & Mary Gunter
R166	Joseph Gunter	3	William & Mary Gunter
R239	Lewis Gunter	25	Lewis Gunter & Rachel Rector
R166	Mary Gunter	28	William French & Elvira Gillis
R241	Michell Gunter	21	Lewis Gunter & Rachel Rector
R637	Phyllis Gunter	51	Mariah Starr
R237	Rachel Gunter	16	Lewis Gunter & Rachel Rector
R166	William Gunter	6	William & Mary Gunter
R348	Sandy Hall	67	
R492	Adeline Hampton	43	Bark & Mollie Rankin
R824	Flemon Hanks	11mos	Steve & Irene Hanks
R824	George Hanks	3	Steve & Irene Hanks
R824	Irene Hanks	21	George & Lucinda Meigs
R679	Adeline Hardman	19	Andy Rider & Mary Riley
R631	Eliza Hardrick	44	Moses & Patient Hardrick
R599	Leona Hardrick	1mo	William & Anna Hardrick
R557	Leroy Hardrick	7	Nelson & Minnie Hardrick

R599	Mabel Hardrick	7	William & Anna Hardrick
R557	Malinda Hardrick	8	Nelson & Minnie Hardrick
R579	Mary Hardrick	38	Moses & Patience Hardrick
R574	Moses Hardrick	71	Silas & Winnie Hardrick
R557	Nelson Hardrick	37	Moses & Patient Hardrick
R536	Silas Hardrick	31	Moses & Patient Hardrick
R599	William Hardrick	32	Moses & Patience Hardrick
R329	Frank Harlan	30	Henry & Emma Harlan
R329	William Harlan	10	Frank & Epsy Harlan
R138	Cordelia Harlin	10	Henry & Melvina Harlin
R1183	Darkey Harlin	32	Tom & Lucy Harlin
R138	David Harlin	3	Henry & Melvina Harlin
R138	Edwin Harlin	17mos	Henry & Melvina Harlin
R138	Elijah Harlin	12	Henry & Melvina Harlin
R138	Elisha Harlin	14	Henry & Melvina Harlin
R138	Henry Harlin	65	Henry & Lucinda Harlin
R138	Lenora Harlin	7	Henry & Melvina Harlin
R527	Mary Harlin	35	
R352	Susan Harlin	49	Sam & Sallie Brewer
R180	Chester Harnage	13	Peter & Gilam Harnage
R178	Frank Harnage	68	Aggie Harnage
R180	Katie Harnage	15	Peter & Gilam Harnage
R180	Lula Harnage	17	Peter & Gilam Harnage
R180	Peter Harnage	53	Ceasar & Lucinda Sheppard
R626	Anna Harris	37	John Collins & Mary Riley
R1267	Irene Harris	12	Nelson & Mary Harris
R794	Janie Harris	5	
R794	Lugenia Harris	21	
R1267	Mary Harris	33	John Curry & Charlotte Vann
R1267	Olive Harris	10	Nelson & Mary Harris
R1267	Rheta Harris	6	Nelson & Mary Harris
R404	Mamie Harris	16	Charlie & Aggie Harris
R404	Mima Harris	13	Charlie & Aggie Harris
R404	Silas Harris	18	Charlie & Aggie Harris
R1207	Minnie Harrison	46	
R15	Coodie Harrison	9	John & Susie Harrison
R15	Dewey Harrison	1	John & Susie Harrison
R15	Ella Harrison	13	John & Susie Harrison
R15	Freeman Harrison	7	John & Susie Harrison
R15	Hetty Harrison	18	John & Susie Harrison

R15	Laura Harrison	16	John & Susie Harrison
R15	Nettie Harrison	6	John & Susie Harrison
R15	Phoenix Harrison	11	John & Susie Harrison
R15	Susie Harrison	35	Rose Archie
R15	Sylvia Harrison	15	John & Susie Harrison
R15	Washington Harrison	3	John & Susie Harrison
R29	Letha Harvey	39	Dred Foreman & Lenora Rankins
R869	Eliza Hawkins	22	Dennis & Mary Hicks
R177	Henry Hawkins	72	Albert & Jane Hawkins
R1084	Jerry Hawkins	72	
R177	Mary Hawkins	40	Zeke & Mariah Bowling
R869	Tyndle Hawkins	2mos	Arthur & Eliza Hawkins
R198	Henry Hayden	60	Reason & America Hayden
R198	Maria Hayden	71	Peggie Whitmire
R257	Eli Hayes	8	Monroe & Elmira Hayes
R257	Elmira Hayes	30	Rolly Poach & Ann Prince
R257	Evie Elizabeth Hayes	3	Monroe & Elmira Hayes
R257	Frank Hayes	5mos	Monroe & Elmira Hayes
R786	Lewis Hayes	24	Brady & Phillis Hayes
R774	Phillis Hayes	50	Peter & Sophia Rogers
R257	Rosa Allie Hayes	5	Monroe & Elmira Hayes
R1258	Allen Haynes	23	Ben Patton & Martha Haynes
R393	Amos Haynes	4mos	Tanker & Lizzie Haynes
R393	Edward Haynes	1	Tanker & Lizzie Haynes
R393	Lizzie Haynes	26+	Burrell Sr & Mary Daniels
R1258	Martha Haynes	53	Ben Grimmett & Liza Blair
R167	Mabel Haywood	20	Horace & Nora Haywood
R167	Nora Haywood	48	Armstead & Jane Ray
R770	Alexander Hazelrig	10	George & Mary Hazelrig
R770	Fred Hazelrig	1	George & Mary Hazelrig
R770	George Hazelrig	50	Mary Hazelrig
R770	Jacob Hazelrig	3	George & Mary Hazelrig
R770	James Hazelrig	6	George & Mary Hazelrig
R770	Jesse Hazelrig	19	George & Mary Hazelrig
R770	Joseph Hazelrig	8	George & Mary Hazelrig
R770	Lucy Hazelrig	15	Geroge & Mary Hazelrig
R770	Mary Hazelrig	44	Thomas Watie & Mary Riley
R770	William Hazelrig	21	George & Mary Hazelrig
R728	Nellie Hazlevig	19	David & Nancy Ross
R833	Mary Hemitte	29	William & Lizzie Buffington

R1064	Anna Henry	35	Willis Owens & Abbie Blythe
R1182	Henry Henson	52	
R866	Bettie Hicks	56	Jess Hicks & Esther Holt
R500	Cicero Hicks	18	Mose Hicks & Mary Brady
R866	Dennis Sr. Hicks	52	William Hazelnut & Eliza Hicks
R866	Dennis Jr. Hicks	17	Dennis & Mary Hicks
R866	Dilana Hicks	14	Dennis & Mary Hicks
R866	Elmer Hicks	9	Dennis & Mary Hicks
R872	James Hicks	26	Dennis & Mary Hicks
R417	Jesse Hicks	74	Jack & Amy Hicks
R870	Joseph Hicks	28	Dennis & Mary Hicks
R871	Katie Hicks	24	Dennis & Mary Hicks
R866	Leroy Hicks	19	Dennis & Mary Hicks
R500	Lula Hicks	15	Mose Hicks & Mary Brady
R866	Mabel Hicks	12	Dennis & Mary Hicks
R1055	Matilda Hicks	22	Jess & Nancy Hicks
R870	Otto Hicks	2	Joseph & Susie Hicks
R1244	Simon Hicks	6	
R870	Susie Hicks	26	George & Martha Blackwell
R417	William Hicks	19	Jesse & Nancy Hicks
R394	Adran Hill	2mos	Andy & Mary Hill
R394	Alice Hill	2	Andy & Mary Hill
R1274	Amanda Hill	20	Watis & Angeline Hill
R678	Amanda Hill	29	Johnson Webber & Margaret Ward
R764	Bessie Hill	3	Stephen & Ella Hill
R840	Cornelia Hill	22	Bailam Hill & Mary Youngblood
R678	Della Hill	12	George & Amanda Hill
R764	Ella Hill	28	Samuel Brown & Amanda Richie
R442	Ethel Hill	1mo	Hayes & Elsie Hill
R678	Flossie Hill	9	George & Amanda Hill
R442	Hayes Hill	22	Milton Hill & Mary Robinson
R764	Herbert Hill	11mos	Stephen & Ella Hill
R440	James Hill	27	Milton Hill & Mary Robinson
R441	John Hill	20	Milton Hill & Mary Robinson
R621	Martha Hill	38	Mumford & Annie Robinson
R394	Mary Hill	22	John Newton & Nancy Daniels
R839	Pearly Hill	18	Bailum Hill & Mary Youngblood
R678	Sadie Hill	8	George & Amanda Hill
R621	Savannah Hill	11	Reuben & Martha Hill
R1274	Thaddeus Hill	23	Watis & Angeline Hill

R441	William Hill	33	Milton Hill & Mary Robinson
R405	Clifton Hines	2	Thomas & Sarah Hines
R405	Clinton Hines	4	Thomas & Sarah Hines
R405	Sarah Hines	43	Robert Foster & Betsy Reed
R681	Annie Hoard	11	Henry & Cynthia Hoard
R681	Clifton Hoard	7	Henry & Cynthia Hoard
R681	Cynthia Hoard	43	Edmund Campbell & Fannie Walker
R681	Edmund Hoard	5	Henry & Cynthia Hoard
R681	Robert Hoard	17	Henry & Cynthia Hoard
R681	Tecumseh Hoard	3	Henry & Cynthia Hoard
R681	Zella Hoard	15	Henry & Cynthia Hoard
R959	Clifford Holt	6	Joshua & Jane Holt
R443	Esther Holt	85	Nellie Holt
R959	Jane Holt	32	Anderson & Dinah Johnson
R959	Jessie Holt	10	Joshua & Jane Holt
R959	Joshua Holt	52	Jonas Pack & Esther Holt
R959	Marcelia Holt	3mos	Joshua & Jane Holt
R185	Moses Holt	56	Sip Pack & Esther Holt
R399	Tecumseh Holt	50	Fox & Esther Holt
R959	Willard Holt	9	Joshua & Jane Holt
R398	William Holt	25	Tecumseh & Sarah Holt
R666	Alfred Hopkins	43	William & Lucinda Hopkins
R353	Hartwell Houston	67	Almon & Leanna Joyner
R71	Narcissa Houston	58	Jerry & Rebecca Flemmins
R303	Bent Howell	20	Bent & Mary Howell
R56	George Howell	34	Nelson & Mary Howell
R303	Mary Howell	36	Rose Vann
R839	Sarah Howell	20	Bailum Hill & Mary Youngblood
R201	Ella Huddleston	27	George & Sarah Buckner
R201	Ora L. Huddleston	5mos	Lewis & Ella Huddleston
R281	Eliza Hudson	31	Abraham & Caroline Ward
R279	Mary Hudson	50	James Beck & Rachel Eaton
R800	William Hudson	56	William & Sarah Hudson
R1208	Bertie Hughs	8	
R463	Rachel Humphrey	43	Coos & Charlotte Walker
R14	Julia Humphries	25	Dick & Louise Humphries
R542	Nancy Humphries	50	Mary Riley
R542	Thomas Humphries	20	Eph & Nancy Humphries
R542	William Humphries	15	Eph & Nancy Humphries
R31	Bias Hunegan	20	Rufus & Mary Hunegan

R31	Burk Hunegan	15	Rufus & Mary Hunegan
R31	Dennis Hunegan	12	Rufus & Mary Hunegan
R31	Ida Hunegan	6	Rufus & Mary Hunegan
R31	Ivory Hunegan	9	Rufus & Mary Hunegan
R31	Lilly Hunegan	4	Rufus & Mary Hunegan
R31	Mary Hunegan	43	Sam Sanders & Louise Launge
R31	Rufus Hunegan	7	Rufus & Mary Hunegan
R31	William Hunegan	18	Rufus & Mary Hunegan
R533	Alexander Irons	46	Nero Irons & Rachel Vann
R36	Bertha Irons	16	George & Winnie Irons
R36	Bettie Irons	13	George & Winnie Irons
R36	George Irons	37	Naro Irons & Rachel Wright
R738	Samuel Irven	27	Williard & Julia Irven
R58	Letitia Irving	12	Jeff & Patsie Irving
R58	Olivia Irving	16	Jeff & Patsie Irving
R58	Patsie Irving	40	Riley & Tisha Harnage
R1275	Addie Ives	15	Tom Eaton & Sadie Ives
R1275	Sadie Ives	34	Watis & Angeline Hill
R255	Annie Jackson	11	Lewis & Vicey Jackson
R256	Felix Jackson	23	Lewis & Vicey Jackson
R256	George Jackson	18	Lewis & Vicey Jackson
R782	Jack Jackson	41	Andrew & Betsy Jackson
R255	Jennie Jackson	13	Lewis & Vicey Jackson
R1136	Jennie Jim	42	
R1136	Lewis Jim	42	
R1137	Nancy Jim	26	
R1138	Patsy Jim	24	
R1140	Dewy John	30	
R1141	Tub-kah John	62	
R1116	John Johnaon	22	
R136	Ada Johnson	11	Isaac & Mamie Johnson
R835	Adam Johnson	8	Isom & Matilda Johnson
R326	Admiral Johnson	2	Seymour Johnson & Fannie Fairchild
R210	Aleck Jr. Johnson	6	Aleck & Mariah Johnson
R640	Alex Johnson	53	
R205	Ann Johnson	45	Caesar & Judy Merrell
R788	Annie Johnson	13	Albert Johnson & Judy Chambers
R205	Bessie Johnson	2	Blake & Ann Johnson
R136	Charles Johnson	19	Isaac & Jane Johnson
R970	Clarence Johnson	12	Addison & Frances Johnson

R1167	Cornelius Johnson	24	
R956	Ellen Johnson	33	Boson & Jane Looney
R205	Elmira Johnson	16	Blake & Ann Johnson
R515	Frances Johnson	50	Isaac & Catherine Gunter
R970	Frances Johnson	36	Bettie Hicks
R705	Frances Johnson	24	
R1011	Frank Johnson	28	Anderson Johnson&Rebecca Webber
R232	George Johnson	5mos	Lewis & Melinda Johnson
R1246	George Johnson	6	
R210	George Johnson	8	Aleck & Mariah Johnson
R1184	Grace Johnson	48	
R210	Gracie Johnson	7	Aleck & Mariah Johnson
R1166	Hanner Johnson	44	
R210	Herman Johnson	9	Aleck & Mariah Johnson
R351	Ida Johnson	41	Jim Grayson & Betty Whitmire
R835	Ida Johnson	3	Isom & Matilda Johnson
R835	Isaac Johnson	18	Isom & Lucy Johnson
R835	Isom Johnson	66	Turner & Sookie Johnson
R136	Jane Johnson	52	Melissa Foster
R210	Johnanna Johnson	4	Aleck & Mariah Johnson
R205	Judy Johnson	13	Blake & Ann Johnson
R970	Katie Johnson	14	Addison & Frances Johnson
R205	Laura Johnson	18	Blake & Ann Johnson
R319	Lizzie Johnson	55	D. Marin & Ann Pack Rogers
R136	Luella Johnson	15	Isaac & Jane Johnson
R1011	Luella Johnson	2	Frank & Charlotte Johnson
R835	Lulu Johnson	17	Isom & Lucy Johnson
R210	Luther Johnson	2	Aleck & Mariah Johnson
R464	Mamie Johnson	24	John & Annie Armstrong
R210	Mariah Johnson	31	Spencer & Elizabeth Bell
R793	Mary Johnson	43	Mattie Hasting
R1007	Mary Johnson	24	Anderson & Dinah Johnson
R1233	Mary Johnson	18	
R835	Matilda Johnson	28	Bose & Millie West
R1245	Maude Johnson	8	
R136	Minnie Johnson	18	Isaac & Jane Johnson
R970	Nettie Johnson	16	Addison & Frances Johnson
R835	Paul Johnson	20	Isom & Lucy Johnson
R932	Phoebe Johnson	46	Henry & Katie Ridge
R547	Sallie Johnson	24	William & Needy Martin

R1247	Samuel Johnson	13	
R205	Sherman Johnson	7	Blake & Ann Johnson
R663	Susie Johnson	37	Whitson Lowe & Catherine Brooks
R835	Turner Johnson	6	Isom & Matilda Johnson
R867	Walker Johnson	57	Reuben & Mary Johnson
R970	Wilda Johnson	2	Addison & Frances Johnson
R705	Frances Johnson	24	
R51	Aggie Jones	55	Nero & Winnie Irons
R621	Annie Jones	8	William Jones & Martha Hill
R850	Arrilous Jones	6wks	William & Elizabeth Jones
R260	Carrie Jones	33	George & Amanda Brown
R960	Cornelias Jones	3wks	Thomas & Ida Jones
R850	Elizabeth Jones	24	Elias & Phebe Downing
R850	Flora Jones	5	William & Elizabeth Jones
R260	George Jones	7	Alfonso & Carrie Jones
R830	George Jones	11	Sam Jones & Anna Dean
R173	Henderson Jones	53	Sol & Lucinda Jones
R960	Ida Jones	25	Cornuelius & Laura Ridge
R830	Ida May Jones	5	Sam Jones & Anna Dean
R104	Isom Jones	40	
R1261	Jeanette Jones	4	Sam & Mary Jones
R263	Julia Jones	25	Bose & Millie West
R263	Laura Jones	2	Sam & Julia Jones
R263	Lillie Jones	8	Sam & Julia Jones
R260	Luella Jones	10	Alfonso & Carrie Jones
R830	Nancy Jones	13	Sam Jones & Anna Dean
R830	Rosetha Jones	2	William & Elizabeth Jones
R260	Roy Jones	4	Alfonso & Carrie Jones
R1262	Sherman Jones	8mos	William Jones & Mary Robbins
R1068	Thella Jones	10	Lycurgus & Mattie Jones
R260	Theodore Jones	9	Alfonso & Carrie Jones
R229	Vergie Jones	19	Abe & Ann Shaw
R263	Watie Jones	3	Sam & Julia Jones
R263	Wenona Jones	11	Sam & Julia Jones
R1261	Wilburn Jones	7	Sam & Mary Jones
R1142	Daniel Josh	23	
R1139	Alcy Josiah	36	
R316	Ida Kahler	28	Joseph & Charlotte Smith
R190	Lillie Kenty	26	Lewis & Jane Daniels
R190	Maud Kenty	6	Smith & Lillie Kenty

R227	Charles Keys	18	Jim Stephens & Louisa Drew
R911	Eliza Keys	40+	Nathan & Frances Duffin
R837	Fatima Keys	70	Israel Block
R227	Samuel Keys	14	Sam & Louisa Drew
R539	John Kimbo	54	John & Lettie Kimbo
R552	Buster King	11	Ed & Mary King
R552	Frances King	18	Ed & Mary King
R197	John King	?	
R552	Mary King	37	Charles McIntosh & Mariah Lewis
R990	Emory Kirk	72	Jim Kirk & Sarah Alberty
R990	Evaline Kirk	74	David Brown & Charlotte Vann
R616	Celia Kirkpatrick	50	George & Cassie Landrum
R420	Fred Knalls	2mos	John & Lula Knalls
R420	Lula Knalls	39	Jerry Whitmire & Jennie Barnes
R609	Kender Lampton	78	Tom & Delapha Lampton
R223	Albert Landrum	10	Sam & Fearbey Landrum
R223	Annie Landrum	8	Sam & Fearbey Landrum
R969	Barbara Landrum	10	Jim & Margaret Landrum
R977	Belle Landrum	24	Jim & Margaret Landrum
R1053	Bessie Landrum	9	Nicholas & Florence Landrum
R482	Carrie Landrum	37	
R939	Charles Landrum	33	Ben Landrum & Jane Riley
R1053	Clellie Landrum	7	Nicholas & Florence Landrum
R620	Clydie Landrum	14	Sam & Laura Landrum
R1077	Ed Landrum	33	James & Margaret Landrum
R979	Emma Landrum	12	James Landford & Lizzie Allen
R223	Eva Landrum	1	Sam & Fearbey Landrum
R223	Fearbey Landrum	31	Rachel Martin
R1053	Florence Landrum	30	Eli & Amelia Wilson
R620	Fravius Landrum	11	Sam & Laura Landrum
R223	Jane Landrum	12	Sam & Fearbey Landrum
R969	Jessie Landrum	20	Jim & Margaret Landrum
R969	Jim Sr. Landrum	54	George & Peggy Landrum
R969	Jim Jr. Landrum	13	Jim & Margaret Landrum
R969	John Landrum	15	Jim & Margaret Landrum
R481	Joseph Landrum	37	George Grayson & Kate Landrum
R1053	Lela Landrum	1	Nicholas & Florence Landrum
R874	Lucy Landrum	19	Thomas Eaton & Alice Lynch
R969	Margaret Landrum	51	Jeff Ross & Hannah Rowe
R203	Martha Landrum	28	Gilbert Vann & Susan Pee

R223	Nannie Landrum	6	Sam & Fearbey Landrum
R969	Nelson Landrum	8	Jim & Margaret Landrum
R1053	Nicholas Landrum	45	Gilbert Vann & Ellen Landrum
R1053	Ora Landrum	5	Nicholas & Florence Landrum
R381	Polly Landrum	75	Jack & Patty Martin
R852	Rachel Landrum	27	Jeff & Mahala Lyons
R223	Rachel Landrum	14	Sam & Fearbey Landrum
R223	Sam Landrum	23	Dan & Jane Landrum
R977	Velma Landrum	2	John Wesson & Belle Landrum
R979	Viola Landrum	9	William Tinch & Lizzie Allen
R1053	Viola Landrum	3	Nicholas & Florence Landrum
R223	Woody Landrum	3	Sam & Fearbey Landrum
R600	Chaney Lane	15	Jerry & Rachel Lane
R155	David Lane	44	Charlie & Nancy Lane
R598	Emma Lane	20	Jerry & Rachel Lane
R598	Fannie Lane	3	Charley Martin & Emma Lane
R723	George Lane	48	John Lane & Malinda Moore
R597	Ira Lane	28	Jerry & Rachel Lane
R598	Laura Lane	18	Jerry & Rachel Lane
R1061	Mitchell Lane	23	Jerry & Rachel Lane
R601	Reuben Lane	30	Jerry & Rachel Lane
R600	William Lane	32	Jerry &Rachel Lane
R598	Willis Lane	7wks	Charlie Martin & Emma Lane
R1071	Leroy Lang	4	Will Lang & Neatie Rodgers
R469	Charlotte Lasley	30	Vongie Lasley & Clarissa Johnson
R938	Leroy Lasley	17	John Lasley & Peggy Durant
R34	Lula Lasley	22	Reuben & Carrie Nave
R2	Arthur Laster	17	Nancy Laster
R2	Nancy Laster	35	Crow & Rachel Sutton
R602	Buck Ledman	46	George & Nancy Ledman
R444	Mary Leek	38	David & Jane Martin
R125	Nelson Lett	23	Mose & Mary Lett
R194	Georgeanna Lewis	9	Joe & Nancy Lewis
R550	Hattie Lewis	12	Charles & Mariah Lewis
R550	Henry Lewis	19	Charles & Mariah Lewis
R503	Lucinda Lewis	16	Charley & Alice Richardson
R550	Mariah Lewis	60	Jesse Foreman & Millie Vann
R194	Nancy Lewis	25	Thomas & Tensie Bell
R550	Rosa Lewis	11	Charles & Mariah Lewis
R194	Tennessee Lewis	8	Joe & Nancy Lewis

R333	Janie Lindsey	50	James & Eliza Crutchfield
R669	Aggie Little	55	Houston & Malinda Martin
R184	Albert Little	18	William & Katie Little
R669	James Little	13	Granson & Aggie Little
R669	John Little	7	Granson & Aggie Little
R184	Katie Little	47	Nathan & Pinky Davis
R669	Mary Little	5	Granson & Aggie Little
R669	Samuel Little	10	Granson & Aggie Little
R184	Victor Little	20	William & Katie Little
R669	Virginia Little	17	Granson & Aggie Little
R669	Willie Little	14	Granson & Aggie Little
R48	Lawson Logan	60	
R1120	Sarah Logan	24	
R14	Louise Loines	8	Catch Loines & Julia Humphries
R14	Simpson Loines	10	Catch Loines & Julia Humphries
R19	Ham London	19	Ed & Sarah London
R19	Irene London	20	Ed & Sarah London
R19	Levi London	18	Ed & Sarah London
R962	Miner London	26	Ed & Sarah London
R19	Sarah London	57	Peter & Sophie Rogers
R929	Sarah London	65	Peter & Sophia Rogers
R964	William London	28	Ed & Sarah London
R1145	Charlotte Lonely	44	
R579	Amos Lonien	18	Mose Lonien & Mary Hardrick
R579	Jackson Lonien	16	Mose Lonien & Mary Hardrick
R667	Alice Looney	18	Allen & Eliza Looney
R667	Allen Looney	48	Tobe & Mary Looney
R667	Bert Looney	17	Allen & Eliza Looney
R446	Clarence Looney	13	Al & Josie Looney
R446	Coral Looney	10	Al & Josie Looney
R658	Eliza Looney	20	Esau & Nancy Fox
R235	Elmer Looney	2	Frank Looney & Joy Childers
R110	Emily Looney	55	Robert Long & Amy Albright
R659	Frank Looney	25	Tobe & Mary Looney
R671	Freddie Looney	33	Willie & Addie Cox
R953	George Looney	22	Boson & Jane Looney
R446	Georgia Looney	3	Al & Josie Looney
R958	Henry Looney	37	Boson & Jane Looney
R660	Irving Looney	13	Allen & Eliza Looney
R671	Jake Looney	37	Tobe & Mary Looney

R935	Jane Looney	57	Rosa Might
R446	Jettie Looney	6mos	Al & Josie Looney
R950	John Looney	31	Boson & Jane Looney
R654	John Looney	5	Frank Looney & Geneva Lynch
R446	Josie Looney	31	David & Jane Martin
R446	Julia Looney	7	Al & Josie Looney
R652	Peggy Looney	68	John Harper & Rachel Ross
R652	Steve Looney	58	Squalldaie & Judy Rattinggourd
R645	Tobe Looney	80	
R446	Wayne Looney	2	Al & Josie Looney
R446	William Looney	8	Al & Josie Looney
R1143	Creek Louisa	40	
R1144	Wuttie Louisa	24	
R159	Charlie Love	25	Robert & Mollie Love
R1012	Frank Love	22	Robert Love & Emma Powell
R160	Lloyd Love	21	Robert & Mollie Love
R137	Maude Love	16	Robert & Mollie Love
R137	Mollie Love	44	Ben Grimmett & Betsy Candy
R137	Uliau Love	19	Robert & Mollie Love
R907	William Love	23	Robert Lewis & Emma Powell
R1264	Bertha Lowe	5mos	William & Lillie Lowe
R1264	Evalina Lowe	11mos	William & Lillie Lowe
R748	Frank Lowe	6mos	John & Susie Lowe
R1264	Lillie Lowe	26	Tassie Rogers & Mary Robbins
R748	Needa Lowe	2	John & Susie Lowe
R1264	Ransom Lowe	2	William & Lillie Lowe
R748	Susie Lowe	23	George Carter & Mariah Reynold
R514	Thomas Lowe	32	Woodson Lowe & Katie Westbrook
R555	William Lowe	37	Red Lowe
R810	Thomas Lowrey	47	Marksman & Judy Lowrey
R458	Fannie Lowry	80	
R524	Vann Luther	48	George & Rebecca Luther
R873	Alice Lynch	30	George Walker & Abbie Blythe
R978	Alice Lynch	34	Jim & Margaret Landrum
R70	Amanda Lynch	6mos	Charles & Ary Lynch
R880	Arthur Lynch	22	Joe & Sophia Lynch
R631	Arthur Lynch	20	Charlie Lynch & Eliza Hardrick
R301	Arthur Lynch	4	Daniel & Mary Lynch
R70	Ary Lynch	45	Lou Hall
R1260	Casdona Lynch	10	

R631	Claud Lynch	7	Charlie Lynch & Eliza Hardrick
R877	Cynthia Lynch	16	Joe & Sophia Lynch
R881	Cyrus Lynch	26	Joe & Sophia Lynch
R301	Daniel Lynch	29	Steven & Peggy Lynch
R873	Eddie Lynch	5mos	William & Alice Lynch
R877	Eliza Lynch	18	Joe & Sophia Lynch
R985	Eliza Lynch	16	George & Lutetia Brown
R97	Elmer Lynch	9	George Lynch & Caroline Frances
R128	Elmer Lynch	9	George Lynch & Caroline Frances
R70	Emily Lynch	8	Charles & Ary Lynch
R631	Ethel Lynch	14	John Ross & Eliza Hardrick
R654	Geneva Lynch	21	John Rose & Emily Nolen
R985	George Lynch	48	Tobias & Mahala Lynch
R1259	George Lynch	4	William Lynch & Tib Chock
R877	Jackson Lynch	11	Joe & Sophia Lynch
R1065	Jessie May Lynch	10	Watson Hicks & Martha Lynch
R882	John Lynch	24	Joe & Sophia Lynch
R242	Joseph Lynch	45	George & Rachel Johnson
R877	Joseph Lynch	60	Viney Lynch
R242	Josie Lynch	7	Joseph & Nettie Lynch
R1215	Kate Lynch	23	
R978	Laura Lynch	11	Ed & Alice Lynch
R1065	Leo Bennett Lynch	7	Watson Hicks & Martha Lynch
R414	Lottie Lynch	20	Albert Webb & Maggie Curls
R301	Lucine Lynch	10mos	Daniel & Mary Lynch
R1065	Martha Lynch	26	Joe & Sophie Lynch
R301	Mary Lynch	25	Nancy Ross
R1260	Mary Lynch	23	
R631	Mattie Lynch	10	Charlie Lynch & Eliza Hardrick
R1216	Nancy Lynch	17	
R1276	Nettie Lynch	33	Watis & Angeline Hill
R654	Prue Lynch	2	Will & Geneva Lynch
R877	Randolph Lynch	15	Joe & Sophia Lynch
R985	Rosetta Lynch	17	George & Lutetia Brown
R877	Ruth Lynch	13	Joe & Sophia Lynch
R877	Sophia Lynch	50+	Chaney Ross
R243	William Lynch	22	Joseph Lynch & Caroline Sanders
R853	Elias Lyons	35	Jeff & Mahala Lyons
R363	Martha Lyons	24	Jess & Permelia Rowe
R851	Ned Lyons	31	Jeff & Mahala Lyons

R853	Nelson Lyons	4	Elias & Martha Lyons
R1022	Winnie Mackey	50	Robert & Margaret Davis
R480	Floyd MacKey	9	John & Minnie MacKey
R480	Leroy MacKey	11	John & Minnie MacKey
R480	Neasty MacKey	7	John & Minnie MacKey
R612	Mattie Madden	29	Morris Sorrel & Dicey Tinnon
R540	William Madden	53	James & Clarinda Madden
R1209	Amanda Maddin	26	
R865	Alonza Manley	13	Alonzo & Maud Manley
R74	Charlotte Manley	10	Allen & Jessie Manley
R865	Etta Manley	15	Alonzo & Maude Manley
R865	Freddie Manley	10	Alonzo & Maud Manley
R865	Hamey Manley	11	Alonzo & Maud Manley
R865	Howard Manley	7	Alonzo & Maud Manley
R74	Jessie Manley	35	Rector & Polly Landrum
R805	Joseph Sr Manley	35	Alonzo & Eliza Manley
R73	Lloyd Manley	6	Andrew Landrum & Martha Manley
R865	Maynard Manley	8	Alonzo & Maud Manley
R73	Martha Manley	38	Rector & Polly Landrum
R589	Maude Manley	33	Kit Bullock & Millie Bennett
R865	Tessie Manley	3	Alonzo & Maud Manley
R1076	Irene Mann	22	Ed & Sarah London
R447	Eliza Manuel	26	
R838	Charlotte Markham	37	Joe & Maria Vann
R346	Jackie Markham	20	Dave & Matt Fuller
R1091	Johnson Markham	41	
R511	Mary Markham	26	Henry & Fannie Davis
R274	Viola Marrill	2	John Marrill & Bessie Buffington
R1221	Henry Marshall	11	Budkin Marshall & Ellen Payne
R1186	Jeff Marshall	48	
R204	Alice Martin	8	Payton & Amanda Martin
R622	Allen Martin	3wks	Samuel & Melvina Martin
R967	Allie Martin	21	Lewis & Sarah Martin
R572	Amanda Martin	47	Ann Bradley
R448	Amanda Martin	3	William & Carrie Martin
R204	Anna Martin	16	Payton & Amanda Martin
R565	Arthur Martin	33+	Nelson & Henny Martin
R1032	Australia Martin	9	William & Jennette Martin
R1032	Bendina Martin	12	William & Jennette Martin
R448	Bunk Roscoe Martin	4mos	William & Carrie Martin

R448	Captola Martin	5	William & Carrie Martin
R107	Carrie Martin	25	Sol & Fannie Washington
R861	Charles Martin	59	Charles & Mary Martin
R697	Charlie Martin	21	Otto & Frances Martin
R448	Charles Martin	1	William & Carrie Martin
R916	Cornelia Martin	29	John & Charlotte Curry
R584	Corrail Martin	5	Fred & Venita Martin
R826	Cy Martin	11	Joe Martin
R445	David Martin	64	Henry & Mary Martin
R204	Deota C. Martin	2mos	Payton & Amanda Martin
R857	Earnest Martin	12	Lewis & Sarah Martin
R960	Eddie Martin	9	James Martin & Ida Jones
R827	Edna Martin	6	Joe & Laura Martin
R3	Eliza Martin	28	David & Jane Martin
R575	Eliza Martin	48	Gillie Collins
R691	Eliza Martin	12	Otto & Frances Martin
R848	Ella Martin	23	Charles & Eliza Martin
R1032	Eulah Martin	4mos	William & Jennette Martin
R204	Eva Martin	12	Payton & Amanda Martin
R691	Frances Martin	52	Elijah & Margaret Thomas
R966	Fred Martin	26	Lewis & Sarah Martin
R691	Fred Martin	15	Otto & Frances Martin
R856	Galatha Martin	1	Harvey & Gurtie Martin
R1028	George Martin	30	Lewis & Sarah Martin
R1032	Goldburn Martin	7	William & Jennette Martin
R856	Grover Martin	3wks	Harvey & Gurtie Martin
R856	Gurtie Martin	26	Penn & Phillis Majors
R691	Guy Martin	16	Otto & Frances Martin
R81	Harvey Martin	12	Arthur Martin & Ary Hall
R856	Harvey Martin	29	Nelson & Henny Martin
R780	Helena Martin	3mos	William & Sarah Martin
R594	Houston Martin	26	William & Neatie Martin
R862	James Martin	42	Joshua & Harriett Martin
R861	James Martin	16	Charles & Eliza Martin
R638	Jane Martin	62	William & Margaret Haskey
R538	Jennie Martin	44	Nelson & Hennie Martin
R861	Jennie Martin	10	Charles & Eliza Martin
R622	Jesse Martin	14	Samuel & Melvina Martin
R861	Joe Martin	13	Charles & Eliza Martin
R965	John Martin	32	Lewis & Sarah Martin

R780	John Martin	1	William & Sarah Martin
R856	Jordan Martin	8	Harvey & Gurtie Martin
R587	Josephine Martin	38	
R960	Lee Martin	11	James Martin & Ida Jones
R596	Lewis Martin	37	William & Neatie Martin
R857	Lewis Martin	64	Harry & Celia Martin
R204	Lillie Martin	14	Payton & Amanda Martin
R691	Lindsey Martin	19	Otto & Frances Martin
R1032	Lloyd Martin	5	William & Jennette Martin
R621	Lunada Martin	16	Mike Martin & Martha Hill
R656	Luther Martin	22	Wallace & Mattie Martin
R878	Luther Martin	25	John & Rachel Martin
R856	Mabel Martin	3	Harvey & Gurtie Martin
R780	Maldonia Martin	5	William & Sarah Martin
R546	Malinda Martin	21	Charles & Maggie Mayfield
R655	Mattie Martin	36	Joe Martin & Nellie May
R1032	Maude Martin	16	William & Jennette Martin
R622	Melvina Martin	36	Mumford & Annie Robinson
R548	Neatie Martin	54	Sandy & Rachel Bean
R204	Octavia Martin	2	Payton & Amanda Martin
R1269	Ostella Martin	28	John Curry & Charlotte Vann
R691	Otto Martin	52	Toney & Mary Ross
R691	Otto Jr Martin	9	Otto & Frances Martin
R204	Payton Martin	53	Harry & Celia Martin
R861	Pearl Martin	9	Mary Martin
R856	Perry Martin	6	Harvey & Gurtie Martin
R878	Rachel Martin	50+	Lige & Sylvia Musgrove
R1032	Ralph Martin	3	William & Jennette Martin
R1032	Sarah Martin	14	William & Jennette Martin
R857	Sarah Martin	54	Rachel Smith
R780	Sarah Martin	30	Thomas Frazier & Sarah Hilderbrand
R960	Stella Martin	8	James Martin & Ida Jones
R780	Thomas Martin	11	William & Sarah Martin
R595	Tobe Martin	30	William & Neatie Martin
R584	Vinita Martin	21	Richard Sorrel & Dicy Tinnon
R1032	William Martin	38	Lewis & Sarah Martin
R780	Willie Martin	3	William & Sarah Martin
R696	Willis Martin	30	Otto & Frances Martin
R448	William Martin	25	David & Jane Martin
R72	Amanda Masir	46	Rector & Polly Landrum

R72	Henry Masir	55	Charity Masir
R72	Mattie Masir	13	Henry & Amanda Masir
R50	Jackson Matthews	50	Pricilla Matthews
R993	Elizabeth May	37	Daniel & Harriet Rowe
R388	Elmer May	2	John & Lizzie May
R388	Ettie May	6	John & Lizzie May
R993	Henry May	43	Dave May & Mariah Reynolds
R388	Idella May	16mos	John & Lizzie May
R388	John May	46	Dave & Sophia May
R750	Lizzie May	30	
R388	Minnie May	4	John & Lizzie May
R388	Nellie May	8mos	John & Lizzie May
R388	Sophia May	7	John & Lizzie May
R405	Andrew Mayes	9	Lew Mayes & Sarah Hines
R834	Bettie Mayes	45	Nero Irons & Winnie Mayfield
R405	Blanche Mayes	11	Lew Mayes & Sarah Hines
R1043	David Mayes	40	David & Susan Mayes
R405	Homer Mayes	14	Lew Mayes & Sarah Hines
R1043	Jennetta Mayes	5	David & Gertrude Mayes
R1038	Josiah Mayes	44	David & Susan Mayes
R405	Louvena Mayes	13	Lew Mayes & Sarah Hines
R405	Nona Mayes	8	Lew Mayes & Sarah Hines
R1043	Richard Mayes	3	David & Gertrude Mayes
R297	William Mayes	34	John Mayes & Flora Bryant
R544	Alice Mayfield	8	Charles & Maggie Mayfield
R5	Amos Mayfield	57	Handy Starr & Sylia Mayfield
R544	Charles Mayfield	47	Thomas & Emily Mayfield
R408	Cornelia Mayfield	15	Thomas & Ella Mayfield
R206	Dollie Mayfield	20	Blake & Ann Johnson
R1248	Dora Mayfield	8	
R517	Ella Mayfield	38	Edmond & Susan Martin
R409	Emberry Mayfield	38	Miles & Sallie Mayfield
R408	Emmett Mayfield	9	Thomas & Ella Mayfield
R408	Fannie Mayfield	12	Thomas & Ella Mayfield
R206	George Mayfield	23	Charles Mayfield & Fannie Rogers
R408	Hattie Mayfield	10	Thomas & Ella Mayfield
R408	Houston Mayfield	19	Thomas & Ella Mayfield
R544	James Mayfield	6	Charles & Maggie Mayfield
R408	John Mayfield	16	Thomas & Ella Mayfield
R408	Lenard Mayfield	5	Thomas & Ella Mayfield

R544	Lillie Mayfield	11	Charles & Maggie Mayfield
R70	Louisa Mayfield	16	Thomas Mayfield & Ary Lynch
R5	Luther Mayfield	5	Maggie Campbell
R544	Maggie Mayfield	48	Ben & Jane Ross
R5	Mannie Mayfield	9	Maggie Campbell
R1147	Mathews Mayfield	30	
R408	Milert Mayfield	20	Thomas & Ella Mayfield
R206	Ollie Ann Mayfield	5mos	George Dollie Mayfield
R544	Richard Mayfield	13	Charles & Maggie Mayfield
R357	Robert Mayfield	62	Mariah Mayfield
R407	Sallie Mayfield	60	Maria Mayfield
R409	Sallie Mayfield	20	Emberry & Josephine Mayfield
R408	Thomas Mayfield	40	Miles & Sallie Mayfield
R408	Thomas Jr Mayfield	6	Thomas & Ella Mayfield
R541	Thomas Mayfield	86	
R544	Thomas Mayfield	14	Charles & Maggie Mayfield
R1248	Thomas Mayfield	6	
R1218	William Mayfield	6	
R892	Abbie Mayhew	58	Charity Stover
R1188	Eve Mays	47	
R245	Charles McAwee	6	John & Emma McAwee
R245	Ella McAwee	12	John & Emma McAwee
R245	Emma McAwee	28	Anderson & Nancy Madison
R245	Evaline McAwee	10	John & Emma McAwee
R245	Nettie McAwee	4	John & Emma McAwee
R356	John McClure	14	Jesse McClure & Caroline Starr
R455	William McClure	35	Jesse & Ary McClure
R588	Jack McConnell	46	Lewis & Eliza McConnell
R86	Lewis McConnell	43	Lewis & Eliza McConnell
R963	Bertha McCormick	14	Calvin & Bettie McCormick
R963	Bettie McCormick	40	Charley Rogers & Sarah London
R963	Clara McCormick	12	Calvin & Betttie McCormick
R963	Dewey McCormick	1	Calvin & Bettie McCormick
R963	Hattie McCormick	8	Calvin & Bettie McCormick
R963	Helena McCormick	6	Calvin & Bettie McCormick
R963	Henry McCormick	17	Calvin & Bettie McCormick
R963	O D McCormick	3	Calvin & Bettie McCormick
R1090	Jack McCoy	72	
R1187	Jenny McCoy	72	
R570	Siney McCoy	61	Bev & Hannah Martin

R17	Jake McDaniel	37	Dennis McDaniel & Lucy Smith
R694	Irving McDonald	14	John & Siney McDonald
R694	Jane McDonald	10	John & Siney McDonald
R694	John McDonald	52	James McDonald & Betsy Glass
R694	John Jr. McDonald	18	John & Siney McDonald
R841	Ethel McGhee	8	Rufus McGhee & Rachel Whitaker
R841	Thomas McGhee	16	Rufus McGhee & Rachel Whitaker
R1079	Adaline McGilbrey	48	John & Liza Cushenberry
R65	Aggie McGinnis	23	George & Rachel Baker
R65	Aurilla McGinnis	11	LD & Aggie McGinnis
R65	Daniel McGinnis	10	LD & Aggie McGinnis
R65	Granville McGinnis	4	LD & Aggie McGinnis
R65	Lucinda McGinnis	6	LD & Aggie McGinnis
R65	Mackey McGinnis	9	LD & Aggie McGinnis
R65	Rachel McGinnis	2	LD & Aggie McGinnis
R65	Sylvester McGinnis	3mos	LD & Aggie McGinnis
R968	Bennie McIntosh	11	Ben & Melissa McIntosh
R968	Bertha McIntosh	12	Ben & Melissa McIntosh
R1025	Bettie McIntosh	35	Ben Landrum & Jane Riley
R968	Melissa McIntosh	43	Aleck & Lucy Ratliff
R908	James McKinney	12	James Whitmire&Lucinda McKinney
R277	Lucinda McKinnny	40	Dave Mayes & Rose Towers
R426	Charles McLain	9	Charlie & Malinda McLain
R426	Christiana McLain	10	Charlie & Malinda McLain
R426	Ella McLain	12	Charlie & Malinda McLain
R165	Felix McLain	30	Wyatt & Caroline McLain
R426	Jennetta McLain	3	Charlie & Malinda McLain
R426	Malinda McLain	34	Collie & Martha Albert
R426	Mattie McLain	4mos	Charlie & Malinda McLain
R426	Samuel McLain	14	Charlie & Malinda McLain
R426	Turner McLain	4	Charlie & Malinda McLain
R604	Charlie McLish	9	Rafe & Lula McLish
R604	Lula McLish	27	John & Sue Tucker
R119	Alfred McNair	27	Jack & Cynthia McNair
R117	Butler McNair	50	George & LeeAnn McNair
R1036	Chaney McNair	42	Bob & Vina Drew
R76	Floyd McNair	19	Lewis & Rosie McNair
R119	George McNair	18	Jack & Cynthia McNair
R76	John McNair	12	Lewis & Rosie McNair
R76	Lewis McNair	50	Jacob & Maria McNair

R117	Matilda McNair	59	
R677	Rosa McNair	4	Alfred McNair & Dora Rider
R119	Willie Jane McNair	15	Jack & Cynthia McNair
R1014	Bessie McRea	22	Charles & Martha Phillips
R1014	Llewelyn McRea	2mos	A.S. & Bessie McRea
R823	Elizabeth Meigs	71	Mary Daniels
R820	Fleming Meigs	21	George & Lucinda Meigs
R822	George Sr. Meigs	60	Peter & Elizabeth Meigs
R822	George Jr Meigs	19	George & Lucinda Meigs
R819	Henry Meigs	14	Simon & Fannie Meigs
R821	John Meigs	27	George & Lucinda Meigs
R819	Katie Meigs	17	Simon & Fannie Meigs
R92	Matilda Meigs	24	Joshua & Madaline Ward
R819	Nathan Meigs	19	Simon & Fannie Meigs
R139	Bessie Melton	13	Henry Melton & Matilda Gibson
R512	Frances Melton	25	James & Annie Teal
R139	Iola Melton	7	Henry Melton & Matilda Gibson
R139	Joe Melton	12	Henry Melton & Matilda Gibson
R347	Lula Melton	31	
R526	Cassie Midleton	32	John & Mary Crowder
R345	Gertrude Miller	29	Elias & Margaret Hickle
R9	Jennie Miller	41	Banger & Hannah Lasley
R961	Sallie Miller	59	Jack Miller & Easter Holt
R932	Herbert Milton	11	Richard Milton & Phoebe Johnson
R932	Joseph Milton	18	Richard Milton & Phoebe Johnson
R932	Pearl Milton	8	Richard Milton & Phoebe Johnson
R932	Percy Milton	16	Richard Milton & Phoebe Johnson
R932	Serena Milton	10	Richard Milton & Phoebe Johnson
R133	Catherine Mix	37	Duncan Vann & Jane Blackwell
R133	Samuel Mis	16	Sam & Catherine Mix
R1146	Jo-kah Mixtedwater	28	
R972	Cretwell Montgomery	10	Henry & Julia Montgomery
R972	Ethel Montgomery	12	Henry & Julia Montgomery
R972	Eva Montgomery	14	Henry & Julia Montgomery
R972	Hart Montgomery	3	Henry & Julia Montgomery
R972	Marion Montgomery	16	Henry & Julia Montgomery
R972	Ruth Montgomery	7	Henry & Julia Montgomery
R868	Altha Moore	17	Mike Moore & Fannie Brice
R1022	Andrew Moore	18	Stewart Neeley & Winnie Mackey
R792	Fred Moore	16	Arch Moore & Jane Daniels

R1045	Joseph Moore	28	Steward Neely & Winnie Mackey
R1045	Mamie Moore	8	Joseph & Minnie Moore
R868	Oscar Moore	17	Mike Moore & Fannie Brice
R1039	Robert Moore	24	Steward Neeley & Winnie Mackey
R721	Cynthia Morgan	58	Jack Ridge & Chaney Ross
R580	Jennie Morgan	14	Mary Morgan
R721	John Morgan	64	Alsey Morgan
R751	John Morrell	23	Henry & Malinda Morrell
R1016	Charles Morris	2	Cleave & Cora Morris
R1016	Clarence Morris	6	Cleave & Cora Morris
R1016	Cora Morris	24	Charles & Jane Smith
R1016	David Morris	4	Cleave & Cora Morris
R568	David Morris	49+	Wyly & Louisa Morris
R1016	Helen Morris	7mos	Cleave & Cora Morris
R319	Willie Morris	14	Will Morris & Lizzie Johnson
R910	Dwight Moss	6	Richard & Sarah Moss
R910	Elmira Moss	8	Richard & Sarah Moss
R913	George Moss	22	Richard & Sarah Moss
R910	Howard Moss	15	Richard & Sarah Moss
R910	Julia Moss	19	Richard & Sarah Moss
R910	Rutherford Moss	10	Richard & Sarah Moss
R910	Samantha Moss	13	Richard & Sarah Moss
R910	Sanford Moss	17	Richard & Sarah Moss
R910	Sarah Moss	43	Nathan & Frances Duffin
R910	Willie Moss	4	Richard & Sarah Moss
R734	Henry Murrell	57	Joe Flowers & Judy Murrell
R734	Jessie Murrell	20	Henry & Malinda Murrell
R734	Malinda Murrell	46	Harden & Saphronia Wilson
R922	Nelson Murrell	77	Robert Ross & Mariah Nave
R734	Nola Murrell	14	Henry & Malinda Murrell
R734	Willie Murrell	18	Henry & Malinda Murrell
R369	Clara Musgrove	17	Jack & Sallie Musgrove
R369	Frank Musgrove	24	Jack & Sallie Musgrove
R87	Pearly Musgrove	13	Jack & Sallie Musgrove
R369	Sidney Musgrove	13	Jack & Sallie Musgrove
R369	Turner Musgrove	8	Jack & Sallie Musgrove
R247	Elijah Muskrat	13	Robert & Emma Muskrat
R247	Eugene Muskrat	17	Robert & Emma Muskrat
R247	Kaiser Muskrat	19	Robert & Emma Muskrat
R247	Lucy Muskrat	8	Robert & Emma Muskrat

R247	Robert Muskrat	68	Lucy Muskrat
R247	Smith Ann Muskrat	11	Robert & Emma Muskrat
R299	Gracie Nash	5	Lem & Minta Nash
R299	Minta Nash	24	Ephriam & Flora Bryant
R130	Arthur Nave	15	John Nave & Laura Cloid
R460	Charles Nave	45	Charles Timberlake & Katie Nave
R486	Clyde Nave	8	Charles Nave
R486	Cora Nave	18	Charles Nave
R486	Dewitt Nave	13	Charles Nave
R135	Earl Nave	2	Ellis Nave & Jessie Brown
R486	Fannie Nave	14	Charles Nave
R1092	Louis Nave	49	
R745	Maggie Nave	50	John & Vicey Cooper
R486	Mattie Nave	11	Charles Nave
R1219	Moses Nave	9	
R747	Neoma Nave	79	Jim Terry
R22	Joanna Neal	8	Louis Neal & Emma Brown
R22	Ora Neal	10	Louis Neal & Emma Brown
R783	Sarah Nelson	63	Mariah Nave
R783	Willie Nelson	19	William & Sarah Nelson
R1249	Mollie Nero	28	Nero Irons & Fannie Miller
R1249	Richard Nero	32	Nero Irons & Fannie Miller
R718	Daniel Newman	6	Taylor & Kizzie Newman
R718	Edna Newman	4mos	Taylor & Kizzie Newman
R718	Kizzie Newman	40	Mose & Nancy Ross
R718	Ralph Newman	7	Taylor & Kizzie Newman
R718	Taylor Jr Newman	4mos	Taylor & Kizzie Newman
R718	Willie Newman	3	Taylor & Kizzie Newman
R1046	Bessie Nicholson	7	Lee & Fannie Nicholson
R1046	Ethel Nicholson	12	Lee & Fannie Nicholson
R1046	Fannie Nicholson	31	Rhoda Bean
R1046	Howard Nicholson	1mo	Lee & Fannie Nicholson
R1046	Justinie Nicholson	5	Lee & Fannie Nicholson
R1046	Mabel Nicholson	2	Lee & Fannie Nicholson
R940	Eliza Nivens	50	David & Susan Mays
R36	Elnora Nivens	1	Harrison Nivens & Bertha Irons
R940	Rosella Nivens	40	Santa & Cynthia Nivens
R940	Santa Nivens	66	Jennie Smith
R644	Emily Nolen	50	William Pollard & Matilda Lacey
R767	Cairo Norman	14	Horace & Susan Norman

R767	Charles Norman	12	Horace & Susan Norman
R767	Harry Norman	16	Horace & Susan Norman
R768	Henry Norman	10	Hudson Norman & Irene Cannon
R767	Horace Norman	45	Jack Norman & Lucy Brown
R915	Mary Norwood	60	Ed Humphries & Ann May
R470	Jesse Oar	58	Stella Oar
R1093	Margaret Orr	72	
R1093	Tom Orr	52	
R1041	Esther Owen	11	Earnest Owen & Anna Butler
R143	Squire Owens	44	John & Malinda Owens
R479	Alberta Pack	11	Thomas & Emma Pack
R30	Arthur Pack	14	Jackson & Ellen Pack
R30	Bertie Pack	10	Jackson & Ellen Pack
R479	Howard Pack	13	Thomas & Emma Pack
R30	Jackson Jr Pack	5	Jackson & Ellen Pack
R30	Jackson Pack	44	Jack & Marsha Pack
R30	Jessie Pack	8	Jackson & Ellen Pack
R30	Lillie Pack	12	Jackson & Ellen Pack
R30	Mattie Pack	5	Jackson & Ellen Pack
R479	Thomas Pack	39	Lem Cowitt & Kate Pack
R479	Thomas Jr Pack	14	Thomas & Emma Pack
R788	Dennis Paden	15	Ben Paden & Judy Chambers
R389	Nellie Parris	25	Samuel & Ellen Roberts
R1221	Ellen Payne	43	Thomas Still & Harriet Woodall
R318	George Peevy	2	George & Tennessee Peevy
R318	Tennessee Peevy	45	Sam & Louisa Catherine
R39	James Perry	55	George & Harriet Perry
R96	Lou Peters	33	Henry & Mary Ragins
R449	Fred Peterson	17	Sam Peterson & Mary Leek
R639	Lena Peterson	17	McLain
R449	Mary Peterson	10mos	Fred & Lena Peterson
R1004	Alice Phillips	15	Charles & Martha Phillips
R1004	Benjamin Phillips	11	Charles & Martha Phillips
R1004	Charles Phillips	17	Charles & Martha Phillips
R323	Lonnie Phillips	9	William Mathis & Rosa Phillips
R1004	Martha Phillips	50	Jack Thompson & Emily Vann
R323	Rosa Phillips	56	Jim Canana & Mary Phillips
R323	Walter Phillips	12	William Mathis & Rosa Phillips
R1004	William Phillips	13	Charles & Martha Phillips
R246	Amelia Pickett	57	Ellis Buffington & Sarah Alberty

R1017	Samuel Pinder	44	Daniel & Jane Pinder
R59	Bossie Pigee	8	Aaron & Diana Pigee
R59	Diana Piqee	35	George. & Rachel Baker
R59	Edgar Pigee	12	Aaron & Diana Pigee
R59	William Pigee	11	Aaron & Diana Pigee
R59	Wilson Pigee	4	Aaron & Diana Pigee
R831	Annie Polston	2	Wiley & Nettie Polston
R831	Callie Polston	3mos	Wiley & Nettie Polston
R831	Sallie Polston	3mos	Wiley & Nettie Polston
R831	Wiley Polston	50	Eli Ridge & Lydia Tucker
R374	Agnes Porter	5	Cuffy Porter & Katie Rowe
R502	John Porter	57	Hannah Lessley
R336	Charlotte Potts	48	Myra Scott
R904	Eddie Powell	5	Larces & Emma Powell
R904	Emma Powell	40	Ben & Rhoda Alberty
R906	Harold Powell	6mos	Will & Nettie Powell
R904	Jessie Powell	6	Larces & Emma Powell
R702	Larkin Powell	56	Charley & Mary Powell
R904	Mamie Powell	9	Larces & Emma Powell
R906	Nettie Powell	19	Lewis Ross & Emma Powell
R904	Ora Powell	2	Larces & Emma Powell
R904	Willie Powell	1mo	Larces & Emma Powell
R1220	Ellis Powers	6	
R695	Etta Prophet	8	Harry Prophet & Pauline Turk
R556	Emma Purtle	46	Riley & Maria McNair
R1070	Ben Qualls	3	John & Mary Qualls
R1070	Emperor Qualls	5	John & Mary Qualls
R1070	James Qualls	13	John & Mary Qualls
R1070	John Qualls	11	John & Mary Qualls
R1070	Mary Qualls	30	Jac & Harriett Vann
R1070	Sarah Qualls	3	John & Mary Qualls
R1070	Westly Qualls	7	John & Mary Qualls
R494	Thomas Rankin	28	Thomas Dilwood & Wren Rankin
R493	Wren Rankin	50	Anthony & Mollie Rankin
R698	Eliza Ratcliff	60	Ned Whitson & Celia Ratcliffe
R700	Ellis Ratcliff	37	Eliza Ratcliffe
R700	Irvin Ratcliff	15	Ellis & Lida Ratcliff
R124	Nathan Ratcliff	20	Ellis Ratcliff & Ann Salisberry
R700	Oscar Ratcliff	18	Ellis & Mollie Ratcliff
R63	Susan Ratliff	50	Johnson & Vina Ratliff

R366	Arre Ray	23	Jess & Permelia Rowe
R366	Ina Ray	5	Randall & Arre Ray
R175	Jeff Ray	15	Charley Ray & Lucy Barker
R169	Charlie Rector	15	Richard & Laura Rector
R169	Emma Rector	13	Richard & Laura Rector
R169	Laura Rector	46	Armstead & Jane Ray
R169	Mary Rector	12	Richard & Laura Rector
R169	Record Rector	18	Richard & Laura Rector
R236	William Rector	45	
R404	Betsy Reed	70	Aggie Melton
R593	George Sr Reed	45	Lafayette & Mary Reed
R608	John Reese	59	Dick Brown & Sarah Ross
R364	Savannah Reese	20	Jess & Permelia Rowe
R28	Binnie Reeves	16	Bass & Winnie Reeves
R28	Charlie Reeves	15	Bass & Winnie Reeves
R272	Charlie Reeves	12	Aleck & Georgeanna Reeves
R28	Estella Reeves	12	Bass & Winnie Reeves
R272	Georgeanna Reeves	52	Rector & Mariah Buffington
R272	Lula Reeves	16	Aleck & Georgeanna Reeves
R272	Sellie Reeves	20	Aleck & Georgeanna Reeves
R28	Sylvester Reeves	20	Bass & Winnie Reeves
R28	Winnie Reeves	40	Dred & Caroline Foreman
R743	Mariah Reynolds	49	Henry Ridge & Susie Woodard
R1159	Eliza Richard	40	
R503	Alice Richardson	37	James & Minerva Vann
R503	Amy Richardson	6	Charley & Alice Richardson
R503	Anna Richardson	18	Charley & Alice Richardson
R503	Ellen Richardson	14	Charley & Alice Richardson
R885	George Richardson	1	Will & Laura Richardson
R503	Jesse Richardson	7	Charley & Alice Richardson
R503	Julia Richardson	12	Charley & Alice Richardson
R503	Malinda Richardson	10	Charley & Alice Richardson
R1066	Martha Richardson	76	Edward & Annie Humphries
R503	Nicodeus Richardson	8	Charley & Alice Richardson
R885	Will Richardson	30	Will Richardson & Caroline Ratley
R503	Willie Richardson	6wks	Charley & Alice Richardson
R200	Andy Rider	41	Willis Rider & Nancy Still
R1160	Emma Rider	22	
R740	John Rider	17	Enoc Durant & Mary Rider
R1097	Lucy Rider	22	

R520	Sallie Rider	36	Angeline Brady
R1096	Sallie Rider	26	
R931	Cornelius Ridge	49	Henry & Katie Ridge
R954	Henry Ridge	23	Cornelius & Laura Ridge
R931	Jesse Ridge	12	Cornelius & Laura Ridge
R858	Katie Ridge	84	Phoebe Fields
R931	Laura Ridge	45	Lewis & Patience Gray
R931	Myrtle Ridge	8	Cornelius & Laura Ridge
R931	Pearl Ridge	14	Cornelius & Laura Ridge
R1168	David Riley	18	
R925	Hannah Riley	38	Lewis & Susie Taylor
R937	Jane Riley	50	Martha Downing
R1168	Louisa Riley	42	
R677	Mary Riley	37	Robert Foster & Martha Thompson
R692	Mary Riley	30	Sam & Lizzie Mathews
R769	Mary Riley	81	Richard & Clara James
R933	Maud Riley	25	Bill Townsend & Phoebe Milton
R930	Ruth Riley	32	Henry & Katie Thornton
R432	Samuel Riley	64	William Ross & Diana Riley
R414	Sedalia Riley	5	Dave Riley & Lottie Lynch
R559	Blue Risby	10days	Thomas & Mary Risby
R559	Mary Risby	18	Richard Thompson & Laura Gross
R720	Jesse Roach	40	Jesse Roach & Katie Blackwell
R1211	Joseph Roach	6	
R1262	Mary Robbins	50	Jennie Roach
R1222	Jennie Roberson	38	
R294	Ellen Roberts	40	Nellie Lynch
R624	Amanda Robinson	12	William & Millie Robinson
R905	Andy Robinson	1	Elijah & Sarah Robinson
R528	Anna Robinson	12	Charlie & Eliza Robinson
R699	Annie Robinson	35	Otto & Frances Martin
R528	Arthur Robinson	9	Charlie & Eliza Robinson
R528	Benjamin Robinson	18	Charlie & Eliza Robinson
R532	Charles Robinson	24	Charles & Eliza Robinson
R624	Charles Robinson	14	William & Millie Robinson
R528	Daniel Robinson	15	Charlie & Eliza Robinson
R528	Eliza Robinson	57	Isaac Baldwin & Mary Bolden
R905	Fred Robinson	8	Elijah & Sarah Robinson
R532	Geneva Robinson	6mos	Charles & Johanna Robinson
R528	George Robinson	17	Charlie & Eliza Robinson

R531	Henry Robinson	2	Isaac & Georgia Robinson
R531	Isaac Robinson	28	Charles & Eliza Robinson
R531	Isaac Jr. Robinson	4	Isaac & Georgia Robinson
R975	James Robinson	40	Mumford & Annie Robinson
R624	James Robinson	18	William & Millie Robinson
R624	Jennetta Robinson	16	William & Millie Robinson
R624	John Robinson	10	William & Millie Robinson
R905	Katie Robinson	7mos	Elijah & Sarah Robinson
R699	Luckey Robinson	2mos	James & Annie Robinson
R905	Lucy Robinson	4	Elijah & Sarah Robinson
R531	Lydia Robinson	1	Isaac & Georgia Robinson
R528	Maggie Robinson	16	Charlie & Eliza Robinson
R528	Mattie Robinson	13	Charlie & Eliza Robinson
R624	Millie Robinson	42	Thomas & Manerva Hill
R624	Ollie Robinson	8	William & Millie Robinson
R905	Sarah Robinson	21	Lewis Ross & Emma Powell
R699	Thomas Robinson	4	James & Annie Robinson
R625	Tobe Robinson	40	Mumford & Annie Robinson
R699	Willie Robinson	2	James & Annie Robinson
R532	Willie Robinson	2	Charles & Johnanna Robinson
R624	William Robinson	49	Mumford & Annie Robinson
R624	William Robinson	3	William & Millie Robinson
R1071	Neatie Rodgers	31	Warren & Isabella Adams
R1263	Albert Rogers	23	Tassie Rogers & Mary Robbins
R37	Alonzo Rogers	6mos	Lewis & Adaline Rogers
R1212	Annie Rogers	9	
R319	Arthur Rogers	15	Isaac Rogers & Lizzie Johnson
R149	Bessie Rogers	20	Samuel & Jane Rogers
R1190	Betsy Rogers	38	
R12	Bettie Rogers	45	Charles & Sarah Rogers
R12	Bertha Rogers	15	Bettie Rogers
R12	Clara Rogers	12	Bettie Rogers
R1262	Dollie Rogers	15	Charlie Atkins & Fannie Rogers
749	Eddie Rogers	21	Isaac & Alice Rogers
R11	Ella Rogers	37	Edward Lunday & Sarah Rogers
R129	Fannie Rogers	37	
R150	Gracie Rogers	8	William & Eliza Rogers
R12	Hattie Rogers	6	Bettie Rogers
R12	Helena Rogers	5	Bettie Rogers
R12	Henry Rogers	17	Bettie Rogers

R832	James Rogers	34	Loss Rogers & Mary Robbins
R355	Jennie Rogers	46	Dave Hendricks & Becky Parris
R355	Lennox Rogers	18	Jennie & Fannie Rogers
R37	Lewis Rogers	25	Isaac & Rachel Rogers
R719	Mary Rogers	30	Vida Bates
R150	Myrtle Rogers	11	William & Eliza Rogers
R1191	Nancy Rogers	37	
R12	Odee Rogers	4	Bettie Rogers
R1210	Rachel Rogers	6	
R37	Sallie Rogers	11mos	Lewis & Adaline Rogers
R78	Sam Rogers	35	Joe Rogers & Sarah Clines
R781	Sam Rogers	36	Poor Rogers & Phillis Hayes
R149	Samuel Rogers	41	Dick Rogers & Rachel Turk
R801	Sarah Rogers	40	Alec & Martha Reed
R149	Velva Rogers	5	Samuel & Mariah Rogers
R150	William Rogers	43	Dick Rogers & Rachel Turk
R963	William Rogers	21	Clem Dixon & Bettie McCormack
R651	Charles Rose	29	John Rose & Emily Nolen
R132	Daisy Rose	5	William Rose & Allie Rainfrow
R636	James Rose	12	John & Emily Rose
R644	Jessie Rose	7	John Rose & Emily Nolen
R636	John Rose	55	Isaac & Caroline May
R636	Robert Rose	15	John & Emily Rose
R744	William Rose	24	John Rose & Emily Nolen
R1095	Alberty Rosey	22	
R1094	Nig Rosey	47	
R119	Alfred Ross		John & Mary Ross
R739	Alva Ross	3	David & Mary Ross
R988	Amanda Ross	15	Calvin & Maggie Ross
R715	Arthur Ross	20	Mose & Nancy Ross
R988	Artie Ross	9	Calvin & Maggie Ross
R715	Bert Ross	17	Cyrus Ross
R988	Calvin Ross	49	Andy & Chaney Fields
R387	Carrie Ross	49	Jacob & Lillie Ross
R664	Chaney Ross	48	Peggy Looney
R736	Cynthia Ross	25	George May & Annie Foster
R646	Dave Ross	49	George & Peggy Ross
R739	David Ross	41	Joe & Sarah Ross
R646	Effie Ross	13	Dave & Nancy Ross
R917	Ella Ross	20	Jacob & Mariah Ross

R753	Ellen Ross	26	
R35	Elnora Ross	11	John Ross & Dora Rogers
R715	Emma Ross	18	Mose & Nancy Ross
R760	Emma Ross	17	Jefferson & Sylvia Ross
R1002	Emma Ross	2	Willie & Rosa Ross
R158	Eva Ross	14	Edward Carris & Sadie Ross
R760	Frank Ross	10	Jefferson & Sylvia Ross
R988	Frank Ross	5	Calvin & Maggie Ross
R918	Fred Ross	6	George & Rose Ross
R717	George Ross	37	Mose & Nancy Ross
R918	George Ross	33	Jacob & Mariah Ross
R715	Georgia Ross	14	Cyrus Ross
R760	Gertie Ross	15	Jefferson & Sylvia Ross
R904	Gertie Ross	13	Lewis Ross & Emma Powell
R1018	Hannah Ross	34	Burgess & Sallie Williams
R739	Harry Ross	13	David & Mary Ross
R646	Hattie Ross	15	Dave & Nancy Ross
R904	Hattie Ross	17	Lewis Ross & Emma Powell
R988	Henry Ross	14	Calvin & Maggie Ross
R739	Herbert Ross	11	David & Mary Ross
R1149	Hester Ross	49	
R917	Jacob Ross	73	Moses & Phillis Ross
R760	Jefferson Ross	55	Jacob & Lydia Ross
R1148	Jess Ross	8	
R660	Joe Ross	70	Moses & Philis Ross
R739	John Ross	1	David & Mary Ross
R988	John Ross	8	Calvin & Maggie Ross
R739	Joseph Ross	15	David & Mary Ross
R254	John Ross	15	John Ross & Rhodie Ford
R1002	Lee Etta Ross	2wks	Willie & Rosa Ross
R665	Lewis Ross	42	James & Sarah Ross
R715	Lewis Ross	15	Cyrus Ross
R904	Lillie Ross	12	Lewis Ross & Emma Powell
R904	Lula Ross	14	Lewis Ross & Emma Powell
R714	Maggie Ross	30	Andrew & Mary Watie
R988	Maggie Ross	45	Ned & Mahala Williams
R714	Mamie Ross	3	Nelson & Maggie Ross
R917	Mariah Ross	56	William & Charity Melton
R739	Mary Ross	31	Sallie Musgrove
R988	Mary Ross	13	Calvin & Maggie Ross

R714	Melvin Ross	14mos	Nelson & Maggie Ross
R715	Minnie Ross	12	Cyrus Ross
R988	Minnie Ross	7	Calvin & Maggie Ross
R1189	Mose Ross	44	
R434	Moses Ross	41	Jacob & Lydia Ross
R919	Moses Ross	31	Jacob & Mariah Ross
R715	Nancy Ross	60	Cyrus & Winnie Ross
R646	Nancy Ross	47	John & Monday Hill
R715	Nancy Ross	9	Martha Ross
R716	Nelson Ross	32	Mose & Nancy Ross
R739	Nelson Ross	6	David & Mary Ross
R385	Peter Ross	54	Willis & Mariah Ross
R1002	Rosa Ross	21	Thomas & Delsie Archer
R918	Rose Ross	24	Lewis & Mary Gibson
R715	Roy Ross	14	Martha Ross
R726	Rufus Ross	24	David & Nancy Ross
R1148	Ruth Ross	26	
R158	Sadie Ross	28	Edward Harris & Caroline Ross
R380	Sandy Ross	76	Willis & Merca Ross
R918	Stella Ross	3	George & Rose Ross
R114	Thomas Ross	53	Moses & Phillis Ross
R577	Thomas Ross	18	Frank Ross & Katie Blackwell
R1213	Thomas Ross	10	
R739	Vernie Ross	8	David & Mary Ross
R1002	Willie Ross	26	Jacob & Mariah Ross
R760	Wilson Ross	20	Jefferson & Sylvia Ross
R895	Abbie Rowe	7	Eddie & Abbie Rowe
R895	Abbie Rowe	27	George Adair & Celia Chamber
R451	Aleck Rowe	9mos	Perry & Lourena Rowe
R162	Alex Rowe	12	Billy & Katie Rowe
R946	Angeline Rowe	22	Esau & Nancy Fox
R16	Annie Rowe	17	George & Peggy Rowe
R895	Arthur Rowe	11	Eddie & Abbie Rowe
R1078	Belle Rowe	28	John Tyler & Delilah Rowe
R162	Billy Rowe	51	Jess & Lela Rowe
R360	Clarinda Rowe	5	Joseph & Pollie Rowe
R361	Colis Rowe	12	Jesse & Permelia Rowe
R20	Cully Rowe	28	George & Becky Rowe
R372	Cully Rowe	30	George & Peggy Rowe
R709	Delilah Rowe	50	Daniel & Hariett Rowe

R709	Daniel Rowe	14	Andrew Thompson & Delilah Rowe
R374	Dinah Rowe	20	George & Peggy Rowe
R711	Eddie Rowe	36	Boliver Wadkins & Delilah Rowe
R451	Elizabeth Rowe	2mos	Perry & Lourena Rowe
R709	Eva Rowe	12	Ben Ward & Delilah Rowe
R752	Fred Rowe	23	Andrew Thompson & Lilah Rowe
R373	Freeman Rowe	23	George & Peggy Rowe
R1052	George Rowe	38	Daniel & Harrriet Rowe
R946	Grant Rowe	29	Dan & Mina Rowe
R973	Grant Rowe	19	Jeff & Betsy Rowe
R709	Harvey Rowe	7	Ben Ward & Delilah Rowe
R451	Inola Rowe	3	Perry & Lourena Rowe
R973	Jeff Rowe	46	Daniel & Harriet Rowe
R362	Jesse Rowe	55	James Foreman & Katie Starr
R367	Jesse Jr Rowe	28	Jesse & Permelia Rowe
R162	Johnathan Rowe	6mos	Billy & Katie Rowe
R162	Joseph Rowe	6	Billy & Katie Rowe
R300	Joseph Rowe	62	David & Katie Rowe
R360	Joseph Rowe	33	Jesse & Permelia Rowe
R16	Katie Rowe	20	George & Peggy Rowe
R973	Leola Rowe	16	Jeff & Betsy Rowe
R162	Lewis Rowe	13	Billy & Katie Rowe
R947	Lewis Rowe	23	Dan & Mina Rowe
R360	Loma Rowe	3mos	Joseph & Pollie Rowe
R709	Loubertha Rowe	19	Andrew Thompson & Delilah Rowe
R451	Lourena Rowe	23	Sam Peterson & Mary Leek
R162	Lula Rowe	3	Billy & Katie Rowe
R789	Maggie Rowe	50	Hannah Bramson
R895	Minnie Rowe	9	Eddie & Abbie Rowe
R361	Nancy Rowe	16	Jesse & Permelia Rowe
R162	Onie Rowe	2	Billy & Katie Rowe
R360	Osa Rowe	2	Joseph & Pollie Rowe
R16	Peggy Rowe	57	Rufus & Delia Vann
R374	Peggy Rowe	53	Rufus Vann & Delilah Archer
R361	Permelia Rowe	58	Calis & Phillis Jones
R360	Pollie Rowe	21	Ben Paden & Judy Chamber
R16	Ruthie Rowe	12	George & Peggy Rowe
R361	Salona Rowe	14	Jesse & Permelia Rowe
R973	Viola Rowe	17	Jeff & Betsy Rowe
R1010	Rebecca Royal	18	Ellis & Rebecca Webber

R91	Ira Sales	32	Pleasant Sales & Martha Hudson
R670	Amanda Sanders	35	Houston & Malinda Martin
R468	Clarinda Sanders	2	John & Lula Sanders
R1056	Clifton Sanders	2	Isaac & Lizzie Sanders
R468	Ethel Sanders	8	John & Lula Sanders
R1098	G.M. Sanders	22	
R1056	Grover Sanders	7	Isaac & Lizzie Sanders
R1150	Jack Sanders	44	
R468	John Sanders	55	Mike Whitmire & Amy Pettit
R468	Lee Sanders	13	John & Lula Sanders
R325	Lillie Sanders	24	Willie & Queenie Sanders
R1056	Lizzie Sanders	26	Mack Davis & Easter Woodard
R468	Lula Sanders	36	Shadrick & Polly Wind
R1056	Margaret Sanders	5	Isaac & Lizzie Sanders
R38	Mary Sanders	35	Prince & Lucy Albert
R468	Maude Sanders	12	John & Lula Sanders
R468	Ona Sanders	9	John & Lula Sanders
R468	Saphronia Sanders	6mos	John & Lula Sanders
R1223	Ted Sanders	32	Squire Sanders & Katie Vann
R468	Viola Sanders	6	John & Lula Sanders
R1150	Winnie Sanders	50	
R1172	Clinton Scales	51	
R1224	Mary Scales	86	
R111	Lela Schrimsher	10	Henry Schrimsher & Mary Tucker
R607	Ab Scott	32	Lewis & Hariett Scott
R522	Elnora Scott	9	Jim & Oma Scott
R522	Jim Scott	37	Lucy Scott
R642	John Scott	39	Lewis & Harriett Scott
R606	Lewis Scott	89	Moses & Celia Scott
R68	Mary Scott	30	Thomas Harlin & Rachel LeFlore
R522	Rosa Scott	10	Jim & Oma Scott
R362	Adami Seals	18	Joshua & Lizzie Seals
R362	Alverta Seals	16	Joshua & Lizzie Seals
R362	Clifford Seals	12	Joshua & Lizzie Seals
R362	Pearley Seals	14	Joshua & Lizzie Seals
R660	John Shadd	12	Albert & Ida Shadd
R396	Arlena Shafer	1mo	Henry & Arlena Shaffer
R396	Lizzie Shafer	20	John Newton & Nancy Daniels
R505	Carrie Shannon	18	Edward & Hannah Shannon
R505	Hannah Shannon	43	Burgess Williams & Emily Mann

R507	Mary Shannon	21	Edward & Hannon Shannon
R506	Minnie Shannon	23	Edward & Hannah Shannon
R229	Anderson Shaw	13	Abe & Ann Shaw
R229	Augustus Shaw	11	Abe & Ann Shaw
R229	Emanuel Shaw	12	Abe & Ann Shaw
R230	George Shaw	24	Abe & Ann Shaw
R229	Wooster Shaw	8	Abe & Ann Shaw
R461	Claude Sheppard	16	Sam & Rachel Sheppard
R461	Clint Sheppard	2mos	Sam & Rachel Sheppard
R461	Edna Sheppard	6	Sam & Rachel Sheppard
R337	Ellen Sheppard	32	Mary Stone
R462	Grace Sheppard	21	Sam & Rachel Sheppard
R461	Henry Sheppard	8	Sam & Rachel Sheppard
R1250	Joel Sheppard	14	
R461	Keller Sheppard	14	Sam & Rachel Sheppard
R461	Morris Sheppard	12	Sam & Rachel Sheppard
R461	Ollie Sheppard	3	Sam & Rachel Sheppard
R461	Rachel Sheppard	42	Sam & Rena Vann
R461	Sam Sheppard	57	Jesse Foreman & Peggie Sheppard
R982	Amy Shields	58	Harry & Celia Martin
R981	Blanche Sheilds	12	Frank & Sophia Shields
R981	Frank Shields	37	Isaac & Amy Shields
R488	George Shields	3wks	Frank & Mary Shields
R981	Grace Shields	10	Frank & Sophia Shields
R944	Eugene Shobe	5	Alfred & Rosa Shobe
R944	Rosa Shobe	30	Joe & Peggy Durant
R944	Viola Shobe	10	Alfred & Rosa Shobe
R374	Clarence Simmons	4	Jake Simmons & Katie Rowe
R23	Janie Simmons	43	Jordan & Lila Thompson
R1171	Lost Simons	26	
R322	Willis Simpson	65	Ed Gibson & Jerusia Simpson
R921	Rosanna Skaggs	25	Jacob & Mariah Ross
R662	William Skaggs	42	Frank Skaggs & Harriett Scott
R623	Josie Slaughter	26	William & Millie Robinson
R951	Alfred Smith	19	Robert & Frances Smith
R487	Annie Smith	18	Alfred & Lucinda Smith
R951	Arthur Smith	2	Robert & Frances Smith
R487	Belle Smith	19	Alfred & Lucinda Smith
R647	Bertha Smith	15	Charles & Jane Smith
R170	Bertha Smith	3	Jess & Johnnie Smith

R926	Bessie Smith	11	Moses & Nancy Smith
R647	Catherine Smith	12	Charles & Jane Smith
R647	Charles Smith	55	Benj & Catherine Smith
R926	Charley Smith	15	Moses & Nancy Smith
R314	Charlotte Smith	50	Griffin & Eliza Davis
R647	Chester Smith	19	Charles & Jane Smith
R926	Cicero Smith	17	Moses & Nancy Smith
R170	Clay Smith	11	Jess & Johnnie Smith
R487	Clem Smith	8	Alfred & Lucinda Smith
R170	Clif Smith	8	Jess & Johnnie Smith
R647	Curtis Smith	8	Charles & Jane Smith
R487	Eddie Smith	4	Alfred & Lucinda Smith
R825	Elmer Smith	10	Joseph & Eliza Smith
R1015	Elnora Smith	30	Charles & Jane Smith
R926	Elsie Smith	9	Moses & Nancy Smith
R487	Fannie Smith	12	Alfred & Lucinda Smith
R951	Frances Smith	44	Boson & Jane Looney
R647	Frank Smith	17	Charles & Jane Smith
R825	Fred Smith	17	Joseph & Eliza Smith
R487	George Smith	10	Alfred & Lucinda Smith
R779	Hattie Smith	30	Milton & Lucy Williams
R1195	Isabell Smith	34	
R312	Isola Smith	23	Joseph & Charlotte Smith
R170	Ivory Smith	5	Jess & Johnnie Smith
R928	Jackson Smith	25	Moses & Nancy Smith
R49	James Smith	46	
R845	James Smith	45	Emily Vann
R647	Jane Smith	45	Walter & Matilda Dannenberg
R729	Jessie Smith	11	Jim & Queenie Smith
R170	Johnnie Smith	29	Tuls & Ann Carter
R825	Joseph Smith	45	Caesar & Matilda Smith
R487	Katie Smith	13	Alfred & Lucinda Smith
R825	Laura Smith	14	Joseph & Eliza Smith
R951	Lawrence Smith	7	Robert & Frances Smith
R729	Linwood Smith	9	Jim & Queenie Smith
R487	Lizzie Smith	14	Alfred & Lucinda Smith
R825	Lovely Smith	6	Joseph & Eliza Smith
R729	Lucille Smith	4	Jim & Queenie Smith
R487	Lucinda Smith	44	Dan & Mandy Ross
R729	Mabel Smith	5	Jim & Queenie Smith

R1099	Malinda Smith	39	
R729	Mamie Smith	1	Jim & Queenie Smith
R649	Matilda Smith	22	C.C. & Jane Smith
R647	Melvola Smith	5	Charles & Jane Smith
R926	Nancy Smith	50	David & Susan Mays
R729	Robert Smith	13	Jim & Queenie Smith
R648	Pearl Smith	26	C.C. & Jane Smith
R951	Queen Smith	17	Robert & Frances Smith
R729	Queenie Smith	41	Fannie Sanders
R623	Sadie Smith	8	Walter Smith & Josie Slaughter
R729	Sonnie Smith	3	Jim & Queenie Smith
R1003	Thomas Smith	23	Mose & Nancy Smith
R926	Tollie Smith	6	Moses & Nancy Smith
R928	Ulysses Smith	3	Jackson & Mary Smith
R523	William Smith	22	Alfred & Lucinda Smith
R1049	Kitt Snaden	9mos	Alf & Luella Snaden
R1049	Luella Snaden	17	George Meigs & Lucinda McKinney
R1225	Milo Snow	23	
R1192	John Sofkee	62	
R1194	Lewis Sofkee	26	
R1192	Minta Sofkee	47	
R1193	William Sofkee	28	John & Minta Sofkee
R537	Morris Sorril	25	Morris Sorril & Dicey Tinnen
R1169	John Spaniard	59	
R1170	Nannie Spaniard	24	
R1169	Susie Spaniard	46	
R218	Barbara Starr	88	Margie Starr
R356	Caroline Starr	46	Barbara Starr
R863	Charley Starr	40	Jack & Charlotte Starr
R1023	Charlotte Starr	3	Elijah & Morning Starr
R1026	Eddie Starr	29	Jack & Charlotte Starr
R1023	Elijah Starr	25	Jack & Charlotte Starr
R478	Emma Starr	20	Willis & Julia Starr
R890	Jack Starr	66	Jim & Mary Starr
R67	Jerry Starr	70	Easter McNair
R478	Jimmie Starr	9	Willis & Julia Starr
R217	Josh Starr	48	Phil Mayes & Barbara Starr
R334	Lafayette Starr	44	Jesse Ratliff & Gracie Starr
R945	Lizzie Starr	33	Jack & Charlotte Starr
R478	Lucy Starr	10	Willis & Julia Starr

R1023	Morning Starr	22	Henry & Rachel Steele
R478	Nora Starr	13	Willis & Julia Starr
R1080	Reuben Starr	21	Josh Starr & Lucy Alberty
R1033	Sarah Starr	52	Simps Bean & Caroline Rider
R471	Toby Starr	56	Mose & Mary Starr
R478	Tyra Starr	15	Willis & Julia Starr
R478	Willis Starr	55	George Adair & Grace Starr
R1151	James Stealer	47	
R971	Claude Steele	21	Harry Steele & Rachel Adair
R949	Joe Steele	13	Harry & Rachel Steele
R949	Mary Steele	16	Harry & Rachel Steele
R949	Myrtle Steele	8	Harry & Rachel Steele
R949	Roxie Steele	19	Harry & Rachel Steele
R949	Willie Steele	10	Harry & Rachel Steele
R196	Levi Stroud		
R238	Maggie Stroud	30	Lewis Gunter & Rachel Rector
R311	John Sumpter	51	Henry & Anna Davis
R701	Henry Sykes	47	John & Katie Sykes
R1152	Aggie Talley	102	
R450	Charity Taylor	18	Sam Peterson & Mary Leek
R693	Emanuel Taylor	56	Clarisa Hamilton
R1100	Fred Taylor	10	Henry & Mary Taylor
R1100	Henry Taylor	32	
R989	Joann Taylor	55	George Wilson & Sina Lindsey
R847	John Taylor	46	Isaac Vann & Malinda Smith
R1100	Mary Taylor	37	Henry & Mary Taylor
R147	Poriesteene Taylor	9	Jeff & Laura Taylor
R147	Prince Taylor	11	Jeff & Laura Taylor
R560	Albert Thomas	34	Abraham & Narcissas Thomas
R83	Annie Thomas	21	Gibb & Millie White
R680	Fred Thomas	46	Fred & Maggie Thomas
R504	Henry Thomas	53	Harry & Celia Thomas
R208	Willie Thomas	26	Charlie Thomas & Carrie West
R605	Belle Thompson	34	Moses & Margaret Foster
R757	Bertha Thompson	18	James & Cornelia Thompson
R943	Bessie Thompson	6mos	George & Mary Thompson
R1251	Carrie Thompson	11	
R891	Celia Thompson	58	
R943	Clarence Thompson	4	George & Mary Thompson
R722	Daniel Thompson	29	Albert Thompson & Katie Blackwell

R941	Daniel Thompson	74	George & Millie Bean
R1252	Earthy Thompson	22	
R943	Ethel Thompson	2	George & Mary Thompson
R757	Fred Thompson	17	James & Cornelia Thomnpson
R757	GeorgeSr Thompson	66	Mary Thompson
R1059	GeorgeJr Thompson	26	George Sr & Rhoda Thompson
R757	Georgia Thompson	9	James & Cornelia Thompson
R757	Jesse Thompson	17	George & Rhoda Thompson
R757	Joe Thompson	7	James & Cornelia Thompson
R1060	John Thompson	24	George Sr & Rhoda Thompson
R265	Johnson Thompson	42	Riley Thompson & Tisha Harnage
R1226	Judah Thompson	28	
R757	Leviticus Thompson	12	James & Cornelia Thompson
R1251	Lydia Thompson	22	
R330	Mariah Thompson	35	Harris & Mary Allen
R943	Mary Thompson	22	John & Nettie Fuman
R846	Nancy Thompson	20	Abbie Blythe
R161	Nellie Thompson	23	Robert & Mollie Love
R10	Polly Thompson	47	Jake & Peggy Martin
R757	Rhoda Thompson	63	Harry & Celia Martin
R757	Robert Thompson	15	James & Cornelia Thompson
R757	Sadie Thompson	18	George & Rhoda Thompson
R974	Sandy Thompson	40	Daniel & Patience Thompson
R413	Eliza Thornton	22	Henry & Katie Thornton
R410	Emma Thornton	17	Henry & Katie Thornton
R412	Ethel Thornton	1	Joseph & Hattie Thornton
R710	Hattie Thornton	21	Ed Brown & Delilah Rowe
R412	James Thornton	2mos	Joseph & Hattie Thornton
R412	Joseph Thornton	25	Henry & Katie Thornton
R410	Katie Thornton	70	Edmond & Lydia Ross
R410	Millie Thornton	19	Henry & Katie Thornton
R1020	Elizabeth Tinnon	26	Joe & Millie Duncan
R577	Fannie Tinnon	12	Horace & Dicey Tinnon
R577	Gertie Tinnon	16	Horace & Dicey Tinnon
R537	Luie Tinnon	16	Horace & Dicey Tinnon
R1020	Mary Tinnon	4	Willie & Elizabeth Tinnon
R629	Henrietta Todd	12	William & Rachel Todd
R629	Julia Todd	6	William & Rachel Todd
R629	Louisa Todd	10	William & Rachel Todd
R629	Minnie Todd	8	William & Rachel Todd

R629	Opelia Todd	1	William & Rachel Todd
R629	Rachel Todd	27	Nelson & Henny Martin
R629	Viola Todd	3	William & Rachel Todd
R224	William Todd	36	Ira Todd & Jane Landrum
R276	Annie Towers	40+	Susie Eaton
R1035	Edward Towers	16	Richard & Maggie Towers
R293	John Towers	51	Nellie Towers
R145	Mary Towers	12	Richard Towers & Mahala Ward
R1035	Richard Towers	40	Rose Towers
R276	Wilson Towers	75	Jim & Jennie Towers
R952	William Townsend	24	William Townsend & Phoebe Melton
R453	Charity Trow	23	Wash & Louisa Ross
R202	Ann Tucker	48	Daniel Ashby & Peggie Clay
R386	George Tucker	100	Joe Tucker & Betsy Reed
R604	Joe Tucker	17	John & Sue Tucker
R920	Oscar Tucker	14	Willis Tucker & Sarah Allen
R148	Anderson Turk	67	
R152	Bettie Turk	24	Anderson & Rachel Turk
R153	John Turk	21	Anderson & Rachel Turk
R695	Paulina Turk	36	Charlie Steward & Nancy Still
R148	Rachel Turk	64	William Melton & Aggie Brown
R151	Willis Turk	30	Anderson & Rachel Turk
R141	Cornelius Tyeskey	46	Jeff Tyeskey & Nancy Bell
R140	Della Tyeskey	12	Eli & Amanda Tyeskey
R140	Eli Tyeskey	10	Eli & Amanda Tyeskey
R140	Jeff Jr. Tyeskey	17	Eli & Amanda Tyeskey
R140	Jeff Tyeskey	85	Tyeskey & Cynthia Harnage
R140	Wahhahchia Tyeskey	20	Eli & Amanda Tyeskey
R140	Willie Tyeskey	9	Eli & Amanda Tyeskey
R384	Dollie Umphuris	54	Sibby Adair
R611	Lewis Vanderpool	58	Julia Vanderpool
R689	Albert Vann	11	March & Laura Vann
R483	Amy Vann	34	
R1062	Ann Vann	10	Young & Josephine Vann
R349	Areminta Vann	8	Wesley & Katie Vann
R181	Belle Vann	21	Seaton & Ellen Blair
R483	Bessie Vann	12	Richard & Amy Vann
R122	Bettie Vann	36	
R1173	Buster Vann	43	
R66	Buster Vann	5	James Vann & Georgergia Estrich

R94	Callie Vann	41	
R807	Carrie Vann	17	Dennis & Charlotte Vann
R1227	Carrie Vann	9	
R1063	Catherine Vann	1	Isaac & Bell Vann
R986	Chaney Vann	27	John & Amanda Buckner
R1253	Charley Vann	33	
R483	Charlie Vann	10	Richard & Amy Vann
R689	Chesley Vann	16	March & Laura Vann
R349	Dollie Vann	4	Wesley & Katie Vann
R295	Early Vann	4	Mandy Vann
R280	Ed Vann	30	William & Emaline Vann
R1106	Ed Vann	28	
R508	Ella Vann	24	John & Lucy Mayo
R113	Elnora Vann	18	Jesse Ridge & Ary Lynch
R844	Emily Vann	70	Joe & Debbie Halfbreed
R689	Ernest Vann	16mos	March & Laura Vann
R689	Essie Vann	14	March & Laura Vann
R349	Ethel Vann	7mos	Wesley & Katie Vann
R358	Fannie Vann	47	Sam & Sallie Brewer
R1155	Fannie Vann		
R1063	Felix Vann	3	Isaac & Bell Vann
R349	Florence Vann	5	Wesley & Katie Vann
R302	Frank Vann	19	Jesse Vann & Emma Pertle
R1062	Gant Vann	8	Young & Josephine Vann
R473	George Vann	60	Henry & Matilda Vann
R836	George Vann	87	Joshua McCaney & Charlotte Brown
R1254	George Vann	52	
R349	George Vann	3	Wesley & Katie Vann
R66	Gipton Vann	4	James Vann & Georgia Estrich
R349	Granville Vann	12	Wesley & Katie Vann
R689	Guy Vann	9	March & Laura Vann
R836	Harrison Vann	19	George & Mary Vann
R836	Harrison Vann	10	William Thomas & Lucy Vann
R483	Harry Vann	16	Richard Vann & Jennie Glasgon
R1103	Henry Vann	34	
R1063	Isaac Vann	23	Newton & Charlotte Vann
R1196	Isaac Vann	26	
R754	James Vann	26	John Bishop & Jennie Vann
R382	James Vann	16	Jesse & Bettie Vann
R836	James Vann	9	Winfield Pratchet & Lucy Vann

R836	Jane Vann	11	George & Mary Vann
R754	Jennie Vann	40	James Vann
R302	Jesse Vann	50	William & Peggy Vann
R54	Jodie Vann	9	Andy Vann & Sallie Brooks
R836	John Vann	14	George & Mary Vann
R836	John Vann	16	Lucy Vann
R26	Joseph Vann	48	John Rowe & Emily Vann
R934	Josephine Vann	1	Ed & Rosa Vann
R349	Katie Vann	34	Tobe & Ellen Martin
R668	Kizzie Vann	29	William & Lucinda Hopkins
R689	Laura Vann	38	Charley & Mandy Jones
R127	Lieutenant Vann	15	Charley Vann & Susan Melton
R497	Lottie Vann	22	Elias & Annie Campbell
R349	Lou Vann	15	Wesley & Katie Vann
R302	Lovat Vann	11	Jesse Vann & Emma Pertle
R1266	Lucille Vann	7	Eli Vann & Martha Virgel
R1153	Lucy Vann	72	
R483	Lucy Vann	4	Richard & Amy Vann
R349	Lydia Vann	6	Wesley & Katie Vann
R797	Maggie Vann	28	Sam & Mary J Crawley
R807	Mamie Vann	14	Dennis & Charlotte Vann
R295	Mandy Vann	21	Cornelius & Laura Ridge
R689	March Vann	40	Dave & Jane Vann
R168	Mariah Vann	50	Armstead & Jane Ray
R641	Martha Vann	23	Daniel & Elizabeth Sims
R516	Mary Vann	46	
R1161	Mary Vann	23	
R704	Matilda Vann	69	
R382	Mattie Vann	4	Jesse & Bettie Vann
R1214	May Vann	6	
R689	McKinley Vann	4	March & Laura Vann
R89	Minta Vann	47	Peter & Manda Vann
R519	Mollie Vann	25	Caroline Skipper
R591	Nicey Vann	40	Dave Brown & Mary High
R836	Peter Vann	6	Winfield Pratchet & Lucy Vann
R115	Polly Vann	90	Jack Brown
R632	Rachel Vann	40	William & Neatie Martin
R1081	Rachel Vann	38	Davis
R1154	Rachel Vann	44	
R483	Richard Vann	61	Dick Vann & Susie Thompson

R843	Richard Vann	30	George & Altamira Vann
R836	Richard Vann	14	Lucy Vann
R54	Rider Vann	10	Andy Vann & Sallie Brooks
R302	Riley Vann	15	Jesse Vann & Emma Pertle
R349	Robert Vann	14	Wesley & Katie Vann
R934	Rosa Vann	21	Richard & Phoebe Milton
R1008	Ruth Vann	23	Anderson & Dinah Johnson
R1102	Sam Vann	27	
R296	Samantha Vann	18	James & Matilda Childers
R1101	Sarah Vann	27	
R1104	Sissie Vann	35	
R483	Stella Vann	18	Richard Vann & Jennie Glasgon
R13	Susan Vann	80	Benjamin & Harriet Vann
R465	Susan Vann	70	Ben & Harriett Vann
R836	Thomas Vann	12	Lucy Vann
R689	Vernice Vann	18	March & Laura Vann
R675	Walter Vann	22	Jess Vann & Emma Purtle
R675	Waneta Vann	1	Walter & Elnora Vann
R18	Wesley Vann	37	Tobe & Mary Vann
R154	William Vann	43	Neal Vann & Betsy Rider
R474	William Vann	104	George Bruner & Katie Vann
R573	William Vann	45	William Vann & Peggy Lynch
R1227	William Vann	10	
R1105	William Vann	30	
R884	Willie Vann	7mos	Samuel Vann & Bertha Bean
R1062	Young Vann	28	Jim & Mollie Vann
R689	Zack Vann	7	March & Laura Vann
R476	Joseph Venton	36	Lish & Melvina Stover
R804	Calwest Vinson	6	Yancy & Lizzie Vincent
R804	Elijah Vinson	15	Yancy & Celia Vinson
R804	Essie Vinson	3mos	Yancy & Lizzie Vinson
R804	Orra Vinson	8	Yancy & Lizzie Vinson
R804	Pink Vinson	3	Yancy & Lizzie Vinson
R804	Tildy Vinson	13	Yancy & Celia Vinson
R804	Yancy Vinson	38	Charlotte Johnson
R984	Martha Virgel	29	Warren Adams & Ibbie Vann
R477	Alline Walker	17	Thomas & Lucy Walker
R375	Bertha Walker	17	Fred & Emily Walker
R1004	Charles Walker	29	William Walker & Martha Phillips
R375	Emily Walker	60	Jack Ratcliff & Sylvia Grimmett

R377	Emma Walker	23	Fred & Emily Walker
R375	Flora Walker	19	Fred & Emily Walker
R375	Fred Walker	20	Fred & Emily Walker
R477	Hattie Walker	19	Thomas & Lucy Walker
R1197	Liza Walker	37	
R477	Lucy Walker	47	William Lockard & Louisa Going
R80	Amanda Walton	50	Demps Handle & Jennie Landrum
R80	John Walton	13	Charles & Amanda Walton
R80	Nellie Walton	11	Charles & Amanda Walton
R80	Rosetta Walton	18	Charles & Amanda Walton
R80	William Walton	16	Charles & Amanda Walton
R283	Abraham Ward	55	Peter & Louisa Ward
R289	Alonza Ward	35	Abraham & Caroline Ward
R948	Amanda Ward	40	Daniel & Patience Thompson
R283	Artes Ward	15	Abraham & Caroline Ward
R284	Ben Ward	43	Peter & Louisa Ward
R291	Berry Ward	23	Abraham & Caroline Ward
R225	Berthena Ward	14	Manuel Ward & Matty Hill
R213	Catherine Ward	40	Sam Mosely & Fannie Vann
R897	Charley Ward	2	Howard & Julia Ward
R948	Dan Ward	12	Elick & Amanda Ward
R287	David Ward	39	Peter & Louisa Ward
R948	Effie Ward	9	Elick & Amanda Ward
R948	Elick Ward	47	Aleck McFail & Hannah Fields
R285	Eliza Ward	13	Squire & Mary Ward
R156	Ella Ward	12	Joshua & Magdaline Ward
R156	Ellen Ward	12	Joshua & Magdaline Ward
R289	Elnora Ward	3	Alonzo & Mahala Ward
R226	Emanuel Ward	33	Berry & Harriett Ward
R282	Eva Ward	10	Ben Sanders & Martha Ward
R289	Ezra Ward	5	Alonzo & Mahala Ward
R290	Frances Ward	1mo	Will & Belle Ward
R288	George Ward	36	Peter & Louisa Ward
R290	Gracie Ward	2	Will & Belle Ward
R948	Harry Ward	16	Elick & Amanda Ward
R897	Helen Ward	10	Howard & Julia Ward
R948	Henrietta Ward	20	Elick & Amanda Ward
R1162	Horace Ward	47	
R948	Irvin Ward	18	Elick & Amanda Ward
R225	Isabella Ward	13	Manuel Ward & Matty Hill

R156	Jefferson Ward	10	Joshua & Magdaline Ward
R285	Jennie Ward	16	Squire & Mary Ward
R948	Jesse Ward	3	Elick & Amanda Ward
R897	Jodie Ward	3	Howard & Julia Ward
R897	John Ward	5	Howard & Julia Ward
R285	Joseph Ward	18	Squire & Mary Ward
R156	Joshua Ward	58	Joe Buffington & Eliza Ward
R282	Louisa Ward	65	
R676	Mahala Ward	25	Pleasant Sales & Martha Hudson
R948	Mamie Ward	2	Elick & Amanda Ward
R156	Minnie Ward	16	Joshua & Magdaline Ward
R282	Peter Ward	75	Abraham & Isabel Ward
R948	Roy Ward	14	Elick & Amanda Ward
R286	Sadie Ward	22	Squire & Mary Ward
R897	Sarah Ward	9	Howard & Julia Ward
R289	Savannah Ward	10	Alonza & Mahala Ward
R285	Squire Ward	40	Peter & Louisa Ward
R948	Troy Ward	7	Elick & Amanda Ward
R156	Turner Ward	17	Joshua & Magdaline Ward
R290	Will Ward	32	Abraham & Caroline Ward
R472	Abraham Ware	77	Major Pack & Annie Ware
R1055	Beatrice Warren	3	Willie & Jessie Hicks
R758	Callis Warren	20	Ellis & Amanda Warren
R64	Dinah Warren	1	Simon & Lucinda Warren
R683	Ellis Warren	49	Jane Warren
R64	Georgia Warren	6	Simon & Lucinda Warren
R64	Henry Warren	4	Simon & Lucinda Warren
R64	Jennie Warren	3	Simon & Lucinda Warren
R64	Lucinda Warren	26	George & Rachel Baker
R790	Rufus Warren	38	Warren Little & Judy Chambers
R64	Samuel Warren	10	Simon & Lucinda Warren
R758	Willis Warren	26	Ellis & Amanda Warren
R343	Martha Washington	59	Jerry & Rhoda Foreman
R131	William Washington	56	William & Mariah Washington
R383	Alfred Waters	5	James & Eliza Waters
R383	Eliza Waters	25	Robert & Emeline Muskrat
R383	Jimmie Waters	2mos	James & Eliza Waters
R712	Andrew Watie	48	Daniel Thompson & Patience Watie
R712	Cora Watie	13	Andrew & Mary Watie
R778	Elijah Watie	57	Charlotte Tinnon

R712	Hannah Watie	7	Andrew & Mary Watie
R712	Joe Watie	15	Andrew & Mary Watie
R712	Louella Watie	17	Andrew & Mary Watie
R712	Mary Watie	43	Dick Whitmire & Louisa Gray
R713	Rufus Watie	22	Andrew & Mary Watie
R75	Frank Watkins	31	Boliver Watkins & Amanda Masir
R586	Howard Watson	44	Benjamin & Evaline Watson
R604	Lee Watson	11	John & Mary Watson
R864	Mary Watson	42	Joshua Martin & Harriett Lynch
R604	May Watson	9	John & Mary Watson
R435	Emma Weaver	8mos	Eddie & Lizzie Weaver
R435	Lizzie Weaver	20	Reuben & Nellie Hall
R1005	Arthur Webber	13	Ellis & Rebecca Webber
R889	Becky Webber	65	Mose & Hannah Webber
R315	Bert Webber	26	Isaac & Delilah Webber
R1228	Betsy Webber	18	
R923	Beulah Webber	3mos	Lewis & Mattie Webber
R923	Cora Webber	10	Lewis & Sarah Webber
R816	Edward Webber	21	Ellis & Harriett Webber
R1006	Ellis Webber	42	Rebecca Webber
R923	Floyd Webber	9	Lewis & Sarah Webber
R806	Frank Webber	37	Robert & Margaret Webber
R1255	George Webber	21	
R813	Harriett Webber	40	Peter & Elizabeth Meigs
R813	Hattie Webber	3	Wesley Webber & Missy Rowe
R633	Joe Webber	22	John & Lou Webber
R633	John Webber	28	John & Lou Webber
R923	Lewis Sr Webber	41	Rebecca Webber
R923	Lewis Jr Webber	15	Lewis & Sarah Webber
R1005	Louella Webber	16	Ellis & Rebecca Webber
R1005	Mabel Webber	6	Ellis & Rebecca Webber
R475	Malinda Webber	37	Robin & Hannah Webber
R808	Margaret Webber	66	
R690	Mary Webber	34	John McGee
R813	Milly Webber	15	Ellis & Harriett Webber
R818	Moses Webber	24	Ellis & Harriett Webber
R1005	Rebecca Webber	47	Frank Crossland & Zilpha Holt
R817	Wesley Webber	23	Ellis & Harriett Webber
R45	Isaac Welch	42	Jacob & Eliza Welch
R510	Samuel Welcome	48	Peter & Elizabeth Welcome

R187	Bell Welton	10	Lee & Ellen Welton
R187	Ellen Welton	41	Lawson Neal & Ruthie Starr
R187	Joe Welton	4	Lee & Ellen Welton
R187	Lovey Welton	14	Lee & Ellen Welton
R187	Neal Welton	12	Lee & Ellen Welton
R187	Nimmie Welton	16	Lee & Ellen Welton
R187	Sy Welton	19	Lee & Ellen Welton
R187	Tensie Welton	9mos	Lee & Ellen Welton
R799	Bessie West	18mos	Joe & Mary West
R207	Callis Jr West	16	Callis & Carrie West
R207	Carrrie West	12	Callie & Carrie West
R207	Carrie West	40	Jack Comer & Martha Thompson
R207	Charlie West	14	Callis & Carrie West
R207	Cornelius West	15	Callis & Carrie West
R207	Ella West	11	Callis & Carrie West
R799	George West	5	Joe & Mary West
R456	Hannah West	67	
R207	Henry West	17	Callis & Carrie West
R785	James West	3mos	George & Lizzie West
R799	Joe West	28	David West & Judy Chambers
R791	John West	33	Rose & Millie West
R209	Laura West	24	Charlie Thomas & Carrie West
R785	Lizzie West	28	Allen & Mary Haynes
R207	Martha West	4	Callis & Carrie West
R207	Sadie West	6	Callis & Carrie West
R207	Vinita West	1	Callis & Carrie West
R207	Walter West	7	Callis & Carrie West
R207	Watie West	9	Callis & Carrie West
R374	Roger Wheat	14mos	David Wheat & Katie Rowe
R841	Rachel Whitaker	40	George & Paulina Bryant
R983	Addie White	40	Warren Adams & Jennie McNair
R424	Amos White	5mos	Henry & Lillie White
R320	Birdie White	3	Jim & Sarah White
R320	Etta White	2	Jim & Sarah White
R321	Harry White	23	Gib & Millie White
R320	Jim White	24	Gib & Millie White
R424	Lillie White	23	Collie & Martha Albert
R1199	Lucinda White	52	
R248	Lula White	25	Lewis Johnson & Sarah Wilson
R424	Mattie White	3	Henry & Lillie White

R317	Millie White	48	Charlotte Johnson
R424	Nancy White	1	Henry & Lillie White
R320	Samantha White	5	Jim & Sarah White
R320	Sarah White	23	
R317	Viola White	14	Gib & Millie White
R1075	Allie Whitmire	9	Jess Whitmire & Lucinda Anderson
R1257	Caroline Whitmire	43	
R888	Daniel Whitmire	44	Dick Whitmire & Betsy Davis
R1109	Harriet Whitmire		
R1009	Harry Whitmire	4	Jesse & Lucinda Whitmire
R1075	Henry Whitmire	8	Jess Whitmire & Lucinda Anderson
R1108	Jack Whitmire	23	
R1009	Jesse Whitmire	40+	Fox Holt & Hannah Whitmire
R1047	Josie Whitmire	26	Mack Davis & Easter Carter
R1110	Levi Whitmire		
R554	Lucinda Whitmire	29	William Tucker & Lottie Whitmire
R994	Lydia Whitmire	40	Becky Webber
R1107	Margaret Whitmire	24	
R1111	Marshall Whitmire		
R354	Phyllis Whitmire	65	Nat Alberty & Rose Wright
R955	Roseta Whitmire	29	Boson & Jane Looney
R897	Sallie Whitmire	52	Jackson Davis & Julia Furch
R214	Sam Whitmire	29	Jesse Whitmire & Catherine Ward
R215	Samuel Whitmire	26	Jesse Whitmire & Catherine Ward
R84	Sophia Whitmire	18	Lilah Rowe
R371	Sophia Whitmire	17	William & Delilah Rowe
R121	Ibis Wickliff	13	Lewis & Lucinda Wickliff
R121	John Wickliff	16	Lewis & Lucinda Wickliff
R121	Lewis Wickliff	51	Isaac & Rachel Wickliff
R121	Lewis Jr Wickliff	6	Lewis & Lucinda Wickliff
R121	Lon Wickliff	12	Lewis & Lucinda Wickliff
R186	Ira Wickliffe	3	Kenny Wickliffe & Ada Taylor
R186	Olin Wickliffe	7	Kenny Wickliffe & Ada Taylor
R186	Oscar Wickliffe	5	Kenny Wickliffe & Ada Taylor
R186	Rachel Wickliffe	11	Kenny Wickliffe & Ada Taylor
R186	Thomas Wickliffe	14	Ken Wickliff & Ada Taylor
R842	Alberta Wiggins	10	K.W. & Elmira Wiggins
R842	Elmira Wiggins	30	Joe Vann & Harriett Peters
R842	Herbert Wiggins	6	K.W. & Elmira Wiggins
R796	Mary Wiley	52	Armstead & Jane Ray

R292	Malinda William	20	Abraham & Caroline Ward
R972	Abbie Williams	18	Henry & Julia Montgomery
R25	Alice Williams	14	Dan & Easter Williams
R328	Alonzo Williams	16	John & Orrena Williams
R582	Ann Williams	26	Albert Thompson & Katie Blackwell
R328	Anna Williams	17	John & Orrena Williams
R328	Arlesta Williams	11	John & Orrena Williams
R736	Beatrice Williams	8	Andrew Williams & Cynthia Ross
R195	Benny Williams	14	Sandy & Elizabeth Williams
R413	Bessie Williams	5	Jesse Williams & Eliza Thornton
R635	Charles Williams	75	Sylvia Ware
R41	Daniel Williams	25	Daniel Williams&Martha Washington
R615	David Williams	19	David Williams & Louisa Riley
R292	Delois Williams	7mos	William & Malinda Williams
R972	Dorothy Williams		Jesse & Abbie Williams
R25	Easter Williams	40	Jack & Sylvia Ratcliffe
R359	Ed Williams	37	Pomp & Charity Williams
R341	Eddie Williams	13	Harrison & Mary Williams
R1021	Emma Williams	24	Joe & Millie Duncan
R328	Eugene Williams	8	John & Orrena Williams
R341	Fred Williams	18	Harrison & Mary Williams
R1021	Lee Williams	1	Walter & Emma Williams
R635	Lizzie Williams	54	Fannie Blunt
R428	Maggie Williams	10	Marcus Williams & Sarah Brown
R341	Maggie Williams	15	Harrison & Mary Williams
R972	Major Williams	10mos	Jesse & Abbie Williams
R88	Marsha Williams	21	James & Nancy Vann
R244	Mary Williams	40	Sarah Foster
R341	Mary Williams	62	
R195	Mattie Williams	12	Sandy & Elizabeth Williams
R292	Monroe Williams	5mos	William & Malinda Williams
R1157	Ned Williams	42	
R328	Orrena Williams	44	Henry & Emma Harlan
R61	Sallie Williams	49	Ellis Carter & Eliza Arnold
R25	Silvia Williams	15	Dan & Easter Williams
R342	Ulysses Williams	23	Dan Williams & Martha Washington
R328	Willie Williams	18	John & Orrena Williams
R1031	Lloyd Willis	9	Emmanuel Wilson & Maggie Willis
R1031	Maggie Willis	29	Merrett Willis & Chaney Ross
R755	Steve Willis	10	John Baldridge & Emma Brown

R991	Amelia Wilson	2mos	John & Lizzie Wilson
R991	Annie Wilson	19	Eli & Millie Wilson
R365	Claude Wilson	6	Charlie & Mary Wilson
R55	Easter Wilson	15	Ebeneezer Wilson& Frances Johnson
R995	Edward Wilson	23	Eli & Amanda Wilson
R55	Ephraim Wilson	20	Ebenezer Wilson & Frances Johnson
R365	Flossie Wilson	2mos	Charlie & Mary Wilson
R996	Frances Wilson	22	Eli & Amanda Wilson
R992	George Wilson	26	Eli & Millie Wilson
R1156	Harriett Wilson	56	
R252	Jacob Wilson	43	Allen & Angeline Wilson
R991	Jesse Wilson	16	Eli & Millie Wilson
R991	John Wilson	27	Eli & Millie Wilson
R365	Joseph Wilson	3	Charlie & Mary Wilson
R55	Laura Wilson	14	Ebeneezer Wilson& Frances Johnson
R365	Mary Wilson	31	Jess & Permelia Rowe
R251	Oliver Wilson	48	Allen & Angeline Wilson
R467	Blanche Winfield	14	Douglas & Leah Winfield
R467	Emma Winfield	18	Douglas & Leah Winfield
R467	Leah Winfield	50	Joe Pack & Sophia Lowrey
R467	Pleas Winfield	17	Douglas & Leah Winfield
R250	Leanna Wolfe	24	Joe & Eliza Smith
R1000	Paulina Wolfe	32	Robert & Zilfra Kirk
R332	Eliza Woolridge	47	Mike Whitmire & Lila Alberty
R332	McKinley Woolridge	5	D.E. & Eliza Woolridge
R332	Verrilee Woolridge	15	D.E. & Eliza Woolridge
R332	Vidalee Woolridge	8	D.E. & Eliza Woolridge
R727	Della Wortham	21	David & Nancy Ross
R397	Anna Wright	11	Edmond & Ruthie Wright
R570	Dempsey Wright	50+	Harry Chouteau & Hannah Martin
R397	Henry Wright	18	Edmond & Ruthie Wright
R814	John Wright	28	Edward & Mary Wright
R397	Minnie Wright	14	Edmond & Ruthie Wright
R397	Nora Wright	17	Edmond & Ruthie Wright
R397	Ruthie Wright	42	John Wolfe & Susan Bright
R376	Caroline Young	11	Albert Dotey & Ida Young
R376	Emma Young	8	Albert Dotey & Ida Young
R376	Ida Young	31	Fred & Emily Walker
R376	Pet Young	14	Albert Dotey & Ida Young
R725	Samuel Young	27	Isaac & Chaney Young

R839	Coralee Youngblood	9	Frank & Mary Youngblood
R839	Curie Youngblood	5	Frank & Mary Youngblood
R839	Mary Youngblood	40	George & Narcissa Vann
R839	Richard Youngblood	2	Frank & Mary Youmgblood
R839	Wash Youngblood	2mos	Frank & Mary Youngblood

INDEX THREE

FREEDMEN MINORS

NATIONAL ARCHIVES PUBLICATION
MICROFILM
M1186 Rolls 26, 27

CARD #	NAME	AGE	PARENTS
84	Bill Adair	2	William & Emma Adair
83	Roosevelt Adair	2	Robert & Ida Adair
385	Harry Adams	2	George & Katie Adams
460	Myrtle Adams	4	Squire & Lillie Adams
86	Sammy Adams	1	Samuel & Hattie Adams
479	Anderson Alberty	1	Alexander & Lizzie Alberty
435	Birdie Alberty	3	Moses & Amanda Alberty
87	Frankie Alberty	2	Jay & Hannah Alberty
492	Josephine Alberty	4	John Thompson & Lelia Alberty
146	Katy Alberty	1	Andrew & Elizabeth Alberty
42	Lillian Alberty	3	Noah & Mary Alberty
318	Myrtle Alberty	1	Lee Ross & Malinda Alberty
231	Rachel Alberty	1	Jerry & Hessie Alberty
479	Robert Alberty	1	Alexander & Lizzie Alberty
42	Theodore Alberty	1	Noah & Mary Alberty
199	Vernon Alberty	1	Joshua & Fannie Alberty
414	Maggie Aldrich	1	William & Darthulia Aldrich
417	Marion Aldrich	3	James & Linniebell Aldrich
417	Martha Aldrich	1	James & Linniebell Aldrich
85	Frank Allen	2	John & Lucy Allen
329	Loyd Allen	1	Clinton & Ella Allen
9	Ottorein Allen	1	Allen & Dollie Jones
375	Dennis Alrid	2	Amos & Mary Alrid
147	Clarence Alwell	2	Will & Emma Alwell
147	Peaches Alwell	1	Will & Emma Alwell
246	Jewell Anderson	1	J W & Sarah Anderson
309	Wilbert Anderson	1	Sterling & Octa Anderson
387	Catherine Arnsby	3	Lewis & Julia Arnsby
22	Goldie Bailey	1	Fred & Rose Bailey
201	Franky Baker	2	Nat & Melinda Baker
201	Freddie Baker	1	Nat & Melinda Baker
438	Edith Baldridge	1	Russell & Viola Baldridge
66	Rachel Baldridge	1	Wheat & Emma Baldridge
66	Sallie Baldridge	2	Wheat & Emma Baldridge
451	Stephen Baldridge	15	John Baldridge & Emma Brown
282	Lydia Banks	1	William & Frances Banks
202	Adda Barden	1	Luny & Etta Barden
272	Clifford Barker	1	Harrison & Hettie Barker

151	Elizabeth Barker	3	Billie & Susie Barker
433	Emmett Barker	1	William & Susie Barker
429	Beaulah Barnes	2	Robert & Sarah Barnes
429	Freeley Barnes	1	Robert & Sarah Barnes
195	Amy Bean	1	Joseph & Hattie Bean
319	Carrie Bean	1	Patum & Eartha Bean
88	Goldie Bean	1	Lewis & Sarah Bean
25	Leona Bean	2	N A & Mary Bean
8	Thomas Bean	1	Thomas & Lewi Bean
239	Tobitha Bean	2	Jacob & Addie Bean
169	Frank Beattie	2	Frank & Lillian Beattie
347	James Beck	3	Benjamin & Ida Beck
332	Peggie Beck	2	William & Jane Beck
200	Willard Beck	2	Dallas & Eliza Beck
495	Booker Bell	1	George & Maggie Bell
255	Calasure Bell	2	George & Annie Bell
437	Jesse Bell	1	Arthur & Alice Bell
494	Joe Bell	2	George & Margaret Bell
495	Thomas Bell	2	George & Maggie Bell
4	Hugh Benge	2	Charles & Mary Benge
4	Jennie Benge	1	Charles & Mary Benge
461	Clarence Benton	2	Isaiah & Minnie Benton
331	Edgar Benton	1	Aaron & Lena Benton
233	Eliza Benton	3	David & Vina Benton
233	Mama Benton	1	David & Vina Benton
3	Bessie Bethel	1	Arthur & Tannie Bethel
3	Jethro Bethel	2	Arthur & Tannie Bethel
348	Chanie Blackwell	1	Frank & Lucinda Blackwell
401	Eliza Blackwell	3	Efton & Rebecca Blackwell
439	David Blue	1	Mansom & Carrie Blue
219	Joe Bolden	2	Osborne Bolden & Malinda Rogers
436	Catharine Bonds	1	Henry & Mary Bonds
247	Earl Bradford	1	Thomas & Fannie Bradford
247	Plinnie Bradford	2	Thomas & Fannie Bradford
122	Catherine Brewer	6	Samuel & Leah Brewer
122	Henry Brewer	4	Samuel & Leah Brewer
122	Margaret Brewer	2	Samuel & Leah Brewer
122	Willey Brewer	1	Samuel & Leah Brewer
60	Millie Brewer	1	Jackson & Clara Brewer
427	Catherline Briggs	3	Ezra & Nannie Briggs

427	John Briggs	1	Ezra & Nannie Briggs
427	Robin Briggs	1	Ezra & Nannie Briggs
45	Alberta Brown	1	Samuel & Ellen Brown
45	Beatrice Brown	3	Samuel & Ellen Brown
238	George Brown	1	Richard & Lilly Brown
130	Hartents Brown	3	William & Lettie Brown
90	James Brown	2	Richard & Claire Brown
140	Jerome Brown	2	Pearl & Easter Brown
5	Joseph Brown	2	Richard & Lillie Brown
194	Katie Brown	2	George & Lulu Brown
513	Lewis Brown		James & Julia Brown
149	Lige Brown	2	David & Florence Brown
513	Lucy Brown	1	James & Julia Brown
91	Luther Brown	2	Joseph & Lula Brown
465	Robert Brown	3	Charley & Nellie Brown
513	Roosevelt Brown	3	James & Julia Brown
149	Tass Brown	1	David & Florence Brown
269	Thomas Brown	2	Silas & Jane Brown
493	Washington Jr Brown	3	Washington & Lillie Brown
39	William Brown	2	Edward & Mamie Brown
43	Della Bruce	3	George & Dora Bruce
43	Joseph Bruce	1	George & Dora Bruce
89	Sophia Bruner	2	Matthew & Bessie Bruner
153	Blanchie Buffington	3	Ernest & Saphronia Buffington
153	Eva Buffington	1	Ernest & Saphronia Buffington
152	Love Buffington	4	John & Mary Buffington
152	Ollie Buffington	2	John & Mary Buffington
150	Philip Buford	2	Philip & Jennie Buford
232	Carmen Butler	2	John & Minnie Butler
44	Jessie Butler	1	Elsa Novels & Lillie Butler
313	Lucile Butler	3	Lewis Butler & Fannie Beck
65	Robert Byrd	1	Henry & Susie Byrd
270	Earl Cabbell	3	Frank & Annie Cabbell
440	Clifford Campbell	4	Thomas & Alena Campbell
46	Emla Campbell	2	Henry & Julia Campbell
440	Wesley Campbell	1	Thomas & Alena Campbell
333	Lono Carbin	1	Lee & Frances Carbin
250	Maydie Carbin	2	Sanford & Eliza Carbin
154	Effa Carson	3	Jason & Laura Carson
402	Genevia Carson	2	Tom & Lillie Carson

402	Lelia Carson	4	Tom & Lillie Carson
154	Wilson Carson	1	Jason & Laura Carson
287	Clifton Carter	2	Mose & Oma Carter
287	Elnora Carter	1	Mose & Oma Carter
497	Luie Carter	4	John & Minnie Carter
523	Marguerite Carter	1	John & Minnie Carter
523	Myrtle Carter	2	John & Minnie Carter
1	Moses Carter	1	Jerry & Roxey Carter
295	Willie Carter	3	Joseph & Angeline Carter
93	Lula Castleberry	3	Fred & Ida Castleberry
93	Theotia Castleberry	1	Fred & Ida Castleberry
249	Ed Chambers	1	Matt & Allie Chambers
249	Elsie Chambers	2	Matt & Allie Chambers
92	William Chambers	1	Ed & Polly Chambers
271	Flossie Chatman	3	William Chatman & Sarah Burell
271	Willie Chatman	1	William Chatman & Sarah Burell
257	Rose Chouteau	1	William & Mary Chouteau
24	Aaron Claggett	3	John & Nancy Claggett
23	John Claggett	1	Charles & Ruth Claggett
23	Uren Claggett	2	Charles & Ruth Claggett
225	Ruby Clay	3	George & Rachel Clay
480	Charlie Colbert	1	James & Susie Colbert
480	Elizabeth Colbert	3	James & Susie Colbert
452	Irine Colbert	1	Johnny & Maggie Colbert
69	Lonnie Coody	2	Henry & Lue Coody
68	Rebecca Coody	1	William & Jennetta Coody
94	Della Cook	3	Bud Cook & Bettie McCormick
67	Lolah Cotton	2	Robert & Cynthia Cotton
131	Clarence Cravens	1	William & Lucinda Cravens
540	Henry Crittenden	1	Anthony & Jane Crittenden
256	Hattie Crossland	3	Lewis & Sallie Crossland
361	Rennie Crossland	1	George Jr & Primmie Crossland
361	Susie Crossland	3	George Jr & Primmie Crossland
496	Julious Curls	2	Riley & Nancy Curls
196	Alice Daniels	1	Enoch & Laura Daniels
158	Clifford Daniels	1	Ransom & Nellie Daniels
196	Dorthy Daniels	1	Enoch & Laura Daniels
196	Katherine Daniels	3	Enoch & Laura Daniels
57	Emma Davis	1	Joseph & Henrietta Davis
388	Lawrence Davis	1	M H & Annie Davis

211	Marcia Davis	2	John & Katie Davis
211	Richard Davis	1	John & Katie Davis
157	Thlemer Davis	2	Joe & Belle Davis
132	Addie Day	4	William & Sarah Day
132	Charley Day	2	William & Sarah Day
132	Janie Day	1	William & Sarah Day
47	John Deckman	2	John & Amanda Deckman
47	Joseph Deckman	3	John & Amanda Deckman
171	Dora Dehart	1	William & Ruth Dehart
470	Foreman Delwood	1	Thomas & Fannie Delwood
470	Geneva Delwood	3	Thomas & Fannie Delwood
70	Shannon Dennis	1	James & Bertha Dennis
95	Raymond Dent	5	Rolla & Gertrude Dent
314	Henry Dickson	3	G W & Mattie Dickson
314	Leslie Dickson	1	G W & Mattie Dickson
314	Letitia Dickson	1	G W & Mattie Dickson
97	Thesla Dotson	1	Wilson & Susan Dotson
97	Zack Dotson	2	Wilson & Susan Dotson
156	Elmirah Downing	1	Walter & Rachel Downing
251	Emmet Downing	3	Johnson & Mary Downing
156	Henryetta Downing	3	Walter & Rachel Downing
155	Hooley Downing	1	Solomon & Mary Downing
234	Mandy Downing	2	Manuel Downing & Artie Ross
155	Roy Downing	3	Solomon & Mary Downing
334	Sophia Downing	1	Alex & Martha Downing
212	Theodore Downing	1	Emanuel & Salona Downing
334	Willie Downing	3	Alex & Martha Downing
362	Bessie Drew	3	Joshua & Susan Drew
362	Jake Drew	1	Joshua & Susan Drew
498	Paul Drew	4	Thomas & Ruth Drew
14	Richard Drew	2	Benjamin & Hattie Drew
363	Robert Drew	1	Isaac & Mary Drew
96	Willie Drew	2	Henry & Mary Drew
418	Jake Duncan	3	Charley & Ella Duncan
418	Mary Duncan	1	Charley & Ella Duncan
364	Calella Elliott	3	William & Annie Elliott
364	Frank Elliott	1	William & Annie Elliott
499	William Elliott	2	Robert & Mary Elliott
464	Addie Fields	3	John & Nellie Fields
353	Charley Fields	2	Mike & Carrie Fields

288	Cordelia Fields	1	Jackson & Lucrecie Fields
377	Fanny Fields	3	James & Lucinda Fields
288	Oliver Fields	3	Jackson & Lucrecie Fields
99	Ollie Fields	2	Thomas & Vinnie Fields
377	Ross Fields	1	James & Lucinda Fields
500	Tyre Finley	3	Tyre & Eva Finley
432	Viola Finwick	1	Milton & Lula Finwick
38	Alvert Flemmings	5	Alfred & Mary Flemmings
38	Truman Flemmings	3	Alfred & Mary Flemmings
100	Myrtle Ford	2	Ollie & Ettie Ford
213	Sammie Ford	2	John & Lutetia Ford
349	Willie Ford	1	W H & Nona Ford
393	Lillian Foreman	3	Abe & Lizzie Foreman
365	Christina Foster	1	Thomas & Nellie Foster
406	Odell Foster	1	Robert & Hester Foster
442	George Freeman	1	Osa & Gertie Freeman
335	John Freeman	2	Irven Freeman & Millie Webber
384	Eugene French	1	Aleck & Viola French
159	Edgar Frye	1	Leander & MaryAnn Frye
159	Florence Frye	3	Leander & MaryAnn Frye
383	Harvel Fulsom	2	Jess & Florence Fulsom
98	Sallie Funkhouser	1	Lee & Julia Funkhouser
98	Wallace Funkhouser	1	Lee & Julia Funkhouser
381	Florence Gains	1	Ed & Eliza Gains
534	James Gaskins	1	Sam & Amanda Gaskins
162	Glennie Gibson	1	Harvey & Lena Gibson
203	Odesia Gibson	1	Moses & Susie Gibson
203	Ramond Gibson	1	Moses & Susie Gibson
161	Cynthia Glass	4	Randall & Blanch Glass
520	Ethel Glass	2	Neal Glass & Amanda Drew
235	Polly Glass	1	Joseph & Mattie Glass
360	Lawrence Graves	2	Eli & Edna Graves
214	Luther Grimmet	3	Sandy & Sophie Grimmet
133	Otha Grimmet	2	John & Hannah Grimmet
214	Sadie Grimmet	1	Sandy & Sophie Grimmet
160	Pansey Grimmett	1	Harry Grimmett & Mamie Voe
133	Sam Grimmet	1	John & Hannah Grimmet
58	Solomon Grimmett	1	Henderson & Mary Grimmett
296	Leone Gunter	4	Lewis & Alice Gunter
296	Margree Gunter	1	Lewis & Alice Gunter

350	Stephen Gunter	1	William & Mary Gunter
419	Clarinda Hall	3	Richard Thompson & Josephine Hall
252	Crisella Hanks	1	Steven & Irene Hanks
252	Ralph Hanks	2	Steven & Irene Hanks
252	Willie Hanks	3	Steven & Irene Hanks
515	Clyde Hardrick	3	William & Annie Hardrick
2	Flossie Hardrick	1	Silas & Celia Hardrick
330	Jefferson Hardrick	3	Nelson & Mary Hardrick
2	Roy Hardrick	3	Silas & Celia Hardrick
2	Ruthie Hardrick	3	Silas & Celia Hardrick
330	Samuel Hardrick	1	Nelson & Mary Hardrick
258	Alleena Harlan	1	Neely & Caroline Harlan
258	Ernesteen Harlan	3	Neely & Caroline Harlan
366	Creola Harlin	2	Joseph & Charlotte Harlin
102	Lena Harlin	2	Benjamin & Daisy Harlin
389	Lula Harlin	2	Clem & Jeannette Harlin
366	Millard Harlin	1	Joseph & Charlotte Harlin
102	Terry Harlin	1	Benjamin & Daisy Harlin
26	Ambrose Harris	1	J W & Sallie Harris
16	Armon Harris	1	Toney & Belle Harris
16	Arthur Harris	3	Toney & Belle Harris
21	Arthur Harris	4	Alex & Carrie Harris
259	Berdena Harris	1	Robert & Nancy Harris
407	Cal Harris	1	Henry & Ada Harris
33	Dora Harris	1	W M & Carrie Harris
21	James Harris	1	Alex & Carrie Harris
26	Lawrence Harris	2	J W & Sallie Harris
390	Luther Harris	2	Silas & Lucy Harris
103	Robert Harrison	1	John & Susie Harrison
444	Bernice Hawkins	1	Arther & Eliza Hawkins
521	Rosa Haynes	2	Tinker & Lizzie Haynes
320	Clayford Herrel	4	Bud Herrel & Mary Keys
10	Neoma Hicks	3	Leroy Hicks & Saphronia Worley
502	Albert Hill	5	James & Bertha Hill
453	Clarence Hill	1	James & Bertha Hill
530	Ella Hill	2	Hayes & Elsie Hill
514	Herman Hill	1	John & Nettie Hill
338	Jenita Hill	2	Perry & Rebecca Hill
135	Lagus Hill	2	Lucinda Bell
163	Roxie Hill	2	Andy & Mary Hill

514	Russel Hill	3	John & Nettie Hill
204	Clarence Holmes	3	John & Charlotte Holmes
204	Mary Holmes	1	John & Charlotte Holmes
71	Alex Holt	1	Edmond & Ibby Holt
315	Jacob Holt	2	James & Pearl Holt
501	Edward Hopkins	1	Randolph & Laura Hopkins
471	Kizzie Hopkins	2	Alfred & Delilah Hopkins
471	Ollie Hopkins	3	Alfred & Delilah Hopkins
472	Pleasant Hopkins	3	Florence Hopkins
471	William Hopkins	1	Alfred & Delilah Hopkins
101	Elizabeth Howard	1	Tom & Anna Howard
101	Irene Howard	3	Tom & Anna Howard
358	Ben Howell	1	George & Maria Howell
443	Vernon Huddleston	2	Lewis & Ella Huddleston
123	Elmer Hudson	3	William & Eliza Hudson
123	Mercy Hudson	1	William & Eliza Hudson
337	Esterie Huff	1	Presley & Pearl Huff
164	Lucile Huff	3	Presley & Pearl Huff
164	Newell Huff	5	Farist Wilson & Pearl Huff
32	John Humphrey	1	James & Ethel Humphrey
240	Noris Hunter	2	William & Mary Hunter
481	James Huston	3	Sam & Almeda Huston
481	Mary Huston	1	Sam & Almeda Huston
215	Caroline Irons	1	Andy & Josie Irons
529	Charley Irons	1	Alexander & Lydia Irons
321	Joe Irons	3	George & Jenanna Irons
321	Roseburn Irons	2	George & Jenanna Irons
380	Williard Irons	2	Ned & Julia Irons
134	Clarence Irven	1	Samuel & Mamie Irven
134	Henry Irven	2	Samuel & Mamie Irven
434	Bertha Jackson	4	Dick Anderson & Ellen Jackson
434	Charlie Jackson	2	K S & Ellen Jackson
434	Tom Jackson	1	K S & Ellen Jackson
104	Willie Jackson	3	William & Fannie Jackson
503	Carrie James	6	Archie James & Ida Muskrat
503	Frances James	3	Archie James & Ida Muskrat
105	Henry James	1	Allen & Eavie James
105	Leolia James	2	Allen & Eavie James
167	Leon Jamison	1	Monday Jamison & Nancy Glass
379	Irena Jenkins	1	Sam & Patsy Jenkins

504	Annie Johnson	1	John & Mamie Johnson
136	At Johnson	1	Minnie Johnson
165	Carrie Johnson	3	Lewis & Malinda Johnson
216	Catherine Johnson	3	Leander & Minnie Johnson
217	Clarence Johnson	2	Nathan & Martha Johnson
166	Ellen Johnson	3	Robert Buckmaster & Lottie Johnson
286	Eva Johnson	2	Frank & Missouri Johnson
216	Frank Johnson	3	Leander & Minnie Johnson
297	Frankie Johnson	3	Frank & Charlotte Johnson
217	Jessie Johnson	4	Nathan & Martha Johnson
482	Lacey Johnson	3	John & Mamie Johnson
367	Leroy Johnson	1	Samuel & Flora Johnson
121	Lucile Johnson	1	Lee Tucker & Lizzie Johnson
165	Mamie Johnson	1	Lewis & Malinda Johnson
166	Mary Johnson	3	Robert Buckmaster & Lottie Johnson
367	McKinley Johnson	2	Samuel & Flora Johnson
217	Nelson Johnson	3	Nathan & Martha Johnson
205	Raymond Johnson	4	Sam Johnson & Emma Ford
297	Ross Johnson	5	Frank & Charlotte Johnson
36	Charley Jones	1	William & Josephine Jones
491	Clarence Jones	3	George Jones & Bettie Irons
260	Harry Jones	3	Spencer & Georgia Jones
491	Jeff Jones	1	George Jones & Bettie Irons
505·	Maude Jones	1	William & Elizabeth Jones
260	Roosevelt Jones	1	Spencer & Georgia Jones
516	Theodore Jones	1	Marion & Lena Jones
506	Louisa Kelly	5	George Kelly & Nellie Graves
206	Clarence Keys	4	Frank Keys & Martha Tabb
137	Dan Keys	4	Maria Keys
168	John Keys	2	George & Lizzie Keys
206	Watie Keys	1	Frank & Luveney Keys
7	George Jr King	2	George & Mary King
7	Lizzie King	3	George & Mary King
148	Archie Laflace	1	Robert & Frances Laflace
148	Walter Laflace	5	Robert & Frances Laflace
148	Zelius Laflace	3	Robert & Frances Laflace
242	Bessie Landrum	4	Sam & Fearbey Landrum
234	Clarence Landrum	3	John Landrum & Artie Ross
242	Daniel Landrum	1	Sam & Fearbey Landrum
339	Joseph Landrum	3	Joseph & Rachel Landrum

339	Lillie Landrum	5	Joseph & Rachel Landrum
518	Nicholas Jr Landrum	1	Nicholas & Florence Landrum
339	Paralee Landrum	6	Joseph & Rachel Landrum
454	Russell Landrum	2	Lone & Cherry Landrum
242	Sammie Landrum	2	Sam & Fearbey Landrum
351	Clifford Lasley	1	Charles & Lillie Lasley
170	Georgie Ledman	3	Buck & Eliza Ledman
253	Elizabeth Leek	1	Ed & Amanda Leek
59	Stella Lett	1	J B & Minerva Lett
298	Bethel Lewis	2	Earl & Lula Lewis
207	Robert Lewis	2	William & Emma Lewis
207	William Lewis	3	William & Emma Lewis
391	Jessie Liggins	2	Felix Liggins & Jennetta Vann
273	William Lonien	1	Jackson & Rebecca Lonien
409	Bessie Love	1	Frank & Anna Love
409	Toles Love	2	Frank & Anna Love
408	James Lowe	1	Willie & Lillie Lowe
408	Willie Lowe	3	Willie & Lillie Lowe
517	Thomas Loyd	2	Claud & Vida Loyd
328	Flora Luther	2	Richard Trent & Ada Luther
336	Lonnie Lynch	3	William & Mary Lynch
48	Roosevelt Lynch	3	Andrew & Mary Lynch
226	Sammie Lynch	3	Cyrus & Lula Lynch
171	Tilman Lynch	3	Will Lynch & Ruth Dehart
20	Malinda Mabry	2	William & Mary Mabry
484	Bennie Mackey	1	Dennis & Nancy Mackey
376	Charlie Mackey		John & Julia Mackey
369	Eli Mackey	2	Eli & Mulsie Mackey
376	Enias Mackey	2	John & Julia Mackey
376	Lorena Mackey	2	John & Julia Mackey
483	Mattie Mackey	15	James & Nettie Mackey
74	Naomi Mackey	3	Ellis & Peggie Mackey
369	Oscar Mackey	1	Eli & Mulsie Mackey
227	Edith Madden	2	William Jr & Amanda Madden
227	Elmer Madden	1	William Jr & Amanda Madden
107	Clarence Maken	3	Thomas & Henryetta Maken
107	Roy Maken	1	Thomas & Henryetta Maken
368	Alice Malone	3	Paton & Mary Malone
457	Mamie Manuel	2	Sam & Sallie Manuel
457	Willie Manuel	1	Sam & Sallie Manuel

111	Eulalah Markham	1	Nancy Markham
209	Fleta Markham	1	William & Cora Markham
110	Hattie Markham	2	Sig & Mary Markham
209	William Markham	3	William & Cora Markham
420	Cordia Martin	3	Joshua Sr & Ellen Martin
109	Daniel Martin		Solomon & Eva Martin
173	Elvaloyd Martin	1	Michael & Ida Martin
139	George Martin	2	Fred & Martha Martin
218	Gertha Martin	2	Jake & Burty Martin
522	Gladdis Martin	3	Blunt & Louie Martin
294	Israel Jr Martin	3	Israel & Lizzie Martin
109	Jennie Martin	1	Solomon & Eva Martin
174	Josephine Martin	1	Joshua & Florence Martin
522	Joy Martin	1	Blunt & Louie Martin
340	Lottie Martin	2	Willis & Gracie Martin
218	Loued Martin	1	Jake & Burty Martin
139	Oscar Martin	1	Fred & Martha Martin
531	Rosel Lee Martin	3	William & Jeanette Martin
188	Viola Martin	1	Sam & Melvina Martin
473	Viola Martin	1	Harvey & Gurtie Martin
509	Wiley Martin	1	William & Carrie Martin
509	Willie Martin	3	William & Carrie Martin
49	Frankie Mathews	1	William & Florence Mathews
241	Helen Mathews	1	John & Lena Mathews
316	Floyd Maxey	1	Guss & Kate Maxey
316	Rayburn Maxey	2	Guss & Kate Maxey
322	Louanna Mayberry	2	Thomas & Ellen Mayberry
306	Clem Mayes	4	Gippy & Ellen Mayes
306	Emma Mayes	1	Gippy & Ellen Mayes
403	Adam Mayfield	1	Houston & Bertha Mayfield
403	Annie Mayfield	2	Houston & Bertha Mayfield
75	Artice Mayfield	2	Charles & Lizzie Mayfield
50	Lucinda Mayfield	1	George & Ella Mayfield
478	Maria Mayfield	2	E M & Joana Mayfield
50	Ora Mayfield	3	George & Ella Mayfield
17	William Maynard	1	Wilson & Annie Maynard
142	Cornelius McClane	2	John & Sarah McClane
208	Abe McClendon	1	George & Mary McClendon
138	May McClure	1	William & Ibby McClure
138	Natholean McClure	3	William & Ibby McClure

124	Theodore McConnell	1	Andrew & Beatrice McConnell
274	Henry McCoy	2	Waddie & Carrie McCoy
312	Isaac McDaniels	3	Jake & Sophie McDaniels
108	Minnie McGruder	1	Wiley & Matilda McGruder
108	Rosena McGruder	3	Wiley & Matilda McGruder
76	Julius McLain	2	Felix & Nellie McLain
397	Mack McLain	1	Mack McLain & Josephine Sheppard
289	Thelma McMullan	1	Charlie & Lily McMullan
400	Bertha McNack	3	Wallace & Elizabeth McNack
404	Edgar McNack	3	Fannie McNack
467	Clara McWaters	1	Sherman & Hannah McWaters
467	Clyde McWaters	1	Sherman & Hannah McWaters
106	Clementine Meigs	4	Samuel & Ida Meigs
106	Viola Meigs	1	Samuel & Ida Meigs
72	Roosevelt Meigs	1	Flemons & Mattie Meigs
141	Birtie Merrell	3	George & Elmira Merrell
410	Elnora Merrell	3	Lewis & Mattie Merrell
410	Lucinda Merrell	1	Lewis & Mattie Merrell
533	Howard Moats	3	Henry & Sarah Moats
507	Geraldin Montgomery	1	Marion & Annie Montgomery
466	Alfred Moore	2	Ellis Vann & Sophia Moore
466	Drew Moore	1	Ellis Vann & Sophia Moore
73	Everett Moore	1	William & Etta Moore
175	Garland Moore	3	Readus & Emma Moore
175	Octava Moore	1	Readus & Emma Moore
172	John Morris	2	Charles & Alice Morris
275	Schuylor Morris	2	Wiley & Mary Morris
519	David Mozee	6	David & Carrie Mozee
13	William Muck	1	H C & Katie Muck
392	Ralph Mundis	1	J C & Sarah Mundis
508	Georgia Murry	7	Ed Murry & Mary Ross
352	Leona Musgrove	2	Willie & Susie Musgrove
341	Allen Nalls	1	Anthony & Sarah Nalls
341	Mathew Nalls	3	Anthony & Sarah Nalls
19	Alfred Nash	1	Perry & Luberta Nash
19	Henry Nash	4	Perry & Luberta Nash
254	Cullus Nave	1	Ulysses & Maggie Nave
176	Lewis Nave	9	Edward & Minnie Nave
228	Robert Nave	1	Cornelius & Florence Nave
342	Castella Neal	1	Carl & Ellen Neal

342	Marrea Neal	2	Carl & Ellen Neal
342	Pasco Neal	1	Carl & Ellen Neal
143	Albertie Nelson	1	William & Henrietta Nelson
539	Carrie Nero	2	Abe & Sarah Nero
248	Willis Newton	3	Harry Newton & Rosie Rogers
511	Becky Nivens	1	July & Sallie Nivens
511	Berry Nivens	2	July & Sallie Nivens
61	Nannie Nivens	1	Samuel & Julia Nivens
61	Nola Nivens	4	Samuel & Julia Nivens
61	Roseville Nivens	1	Samuel & Julia Nivens
311	Callis Nivins	1	Callis & Emma Nivins
62	Douglas Nivins	1	Richard & Annie Nivins
112	Alexander Oates	3	Alexander & Gracie Oates
112	Ora Oates	1	Alexander & Gracie Oates
421	John Owens	1	Squire & Lizzie Owens
370	Ella Parker	3	Spain & Malinda Parker
370	Robin Parker	1	Spain & Malinda Parker
395	Charlotte Parris	1	David & Fannie Parris
538	Eddie Parris	4	Robert & Nellie Parris
283	Clifton Patterson	1	Arthur & Matilda Patterson
510	James Payne	7	Wallace & Irene Payne
485	Minnie Peace	3	William & Mary Peace
485	Robert Peace	2	William & Mary Peace
317	Levie Perry	2	HW Perry & Sallie McConnell
177	Clemtory Phillips	3	Clem Phillips & Susan Morris
474	Anna Pinder	4	Daniel & Nancy Pinder
431	Louisa Pitts	1	Henry & Luversa Pitts
431	Wellington Pitts	2	Henry & Luversa Pitts
524	Clarinda Porter	2	William & Flora Porter
394	Dewy Porter	3	Sam & Charlotte Porter
524	Ernestine Porter		William & Flora Porter
524	Orchid Porter	3	William & Flora Porter
394	Violet Porter	1	Sam & Charlotte Porter
261	Hester Powell	2	Charles & Ella Powell
261	Myrtle Powell	4	Charles & Ella Powell
541	Stella Price	3	Jake & Emma Price
236	Walter Rainey	1	Samuel & Pearl Rainey
323	Johnie Ray	2	William & Jane Ray
15	David Reed	3	Frank & Mollie Reed
125	Myrtle Reed	3	George & Harriet Reed

15	Susie Reed	1	Frank & Mollie Reed
525	Gertrude Reese	8	Banks & Martha Reese
262	Blanchie Reynolds	3	Harrison & Losie Reynolds
180	Eli Reynolds	1	Washington & Nancy Reynolds
262	Kathrine Reynolds	1	Harrison & Losie Reynolds
445	Robert Reynolds	3	Peter & Amanda Reynolds
445	Vice Reynolds	1	Peter & Amanda Reynolds
52	Willard Rhea	2	George Rhea & Ruth Fletcher
326	Ivy Richardson	1	Charlie & Alice Richardson
276	Emma Rider	1	Sam & Bertha Rider
51	James Rider	2	John & Mattie Rider
284	Alice Riley	2	Frank & Louberthia Riley
34	Ethel Riley	1	Arthur & Blanche Riley
488	Flossie Riley	1	Tom & Lutitia Riley
34	Homer Riley	2	Arthur & Blanche Riley
487	Jesse Riley	1	Jesse & Ruth Riley
468	Morris Riley	3	Ed & Mary Riley
526	Rosella Riley	3	Ephram Riley & Lula Dabney
178	Crawford Roach	1	Tuxie & Ella Roach
263	Glover Roach	1	Henry & Rebecca Roach
263	Henry Roach	2	Henry & Rebecca Roach
300	Betty Robinson	1	Lucky & Rosa Robinson
300	Mady Robinson	3	Lucky & Rosa Robinson
371	Opel Robinson	1	Tobe & Lizzie Robinson
12	Rachel Robinson	1	Sherman & Belle Robinson
12	William Robinson	2	Sherman & Belle Robinson
486	Addie Rogers	1	Gussie & Jennetta Rogers
535	Alma Rogers	2	Anderson & Martha Rogers
181	Clarence Rogers	1	Cooey & Clara Rogers
181	Edna Rogers	2	Cooey & Clara Rogers
459	Fannie Rogers	1	Andrew & Tebie Rogers
396	George Rogers	1	Daniel & Ella Rogers
396	Henry Rogers	4	Daniel & Ella Rogers
396	Ida Rogers	2	Daniel & Ella Rogers
224	Katie Rogers	1	Joseph & Sylva Rogers
354	Leroy Rogers	3	Reuben & Mattie Rogers
382	Stella Rogers	1	Bud & Nanie Rogers
299	Creola Rose	1	John & Mamie Rose
114	Ann Ross	1	Malcolm & Nolie Ross
397	Christian Ross	3	John Ross & Josephine Sheppard

285	Clara Ross	2	Lee Hicks & Amanda Ross
378	Esau Ross	3	Willie & Rose Ross
11	Ewing Ross	3	Nathan & Sarah Ross
113	Georgia Ross	2	Austin & Lena Ross
179	Janie Ross	2	Samuel & Josie Ross
378	Johnie Ross	1	Willie & Rose Ross
113	Leroy Ross	3	Austin & Lena Ross
463	Sadie Ross	6	Joseph & Jane Ross
325	Thelma Ross	1	Lewis & Alice Ross
355	Tommy Ross	2	Henry Funkhouser & Caroline Vann
77	Trim Ross	1	James & Oner Ross
27	Willie Ross	3	Edward Ross & Henrietta Thornton
18	Jesse Rouse	2	John & Patsie Rouse
458	Lewis Rowe	1	Perry & Laurena Rowe
512	Alberta Sanders	3	John & Lula Sanders
302	Alberty Sanders	2	Daniel Jr & Malinda Sanders
117	Annie Sanders	3	Sam & Fannie Sanders
307	Fannie Sanders	1	Allen & Annie Sanders
126	Florence Sanders	1	Ben & Lizzie Sanders
302	Leona Sanders	1	Daniel Jr & Malinda Sanders
117	Napolian Sanders	1	Sam & Fannie Sanders
185	Pearl Sanders	1	Bessie Sanders
446	Ray Sanders	1	Benjamin & Fluten Sanders
446	Theodore Sanders	3	Benjamin & Fluten Sanders
126	Willard Sanders	3	Ben & Lizzie Sanders
512	Willie Sanders	1	John & Lula Sanders
37	Alberta Scarborough	1	George & Laura Scarborough
37	Mabelle Scarborough	3	George & Laura Scarborough
542	Lucy Scott	2	James & Mary Scott
527	Elmer Shafer	3	Henry & Lizzie Shafer
527	Roosevelt Shafer	1	Henry & Lizzie Shafer
229	Willie Shankling	2	Richard & Mary Shankling
183	Clem Sheppard	2	Clem & Lula Sheppard
411	Hazel Shields	4	Frank & Mary Shields
469	Leroy Shields	2	Isaac Shields & Eliza Cannon
411	Olander Shields	2	Frank & Mary Shields
79	Jim Siek	4	John & Matt Siek
398	Alice Silk	1	Squire & Emma Silk
398	Annie Silk	2	Squire & Emma Silk
398	William Silk	3	Squire & Emma Silk

27	Augustus Simmons	1	Lon Simmons & Henrietta Thornton
489	Minerva Sissle	1	Henry Sissle & Minnie Mackey
222	Beulah Smith	2	Chester & Keller Smith
528	Clark Smith		Jack & Lucy Smith
116	Conday Smith	1	Joseph & Alice Smith
310	Ibbie Smith	1	Jesse Adair & Pearl Smith
184	Lingo Smith	3	Joe & Sarah Smith
264	Loyd Smith	3	Charley & Millie Smith
265	Lucy Smith	3	Sonny & Hattie Smith
412	Maggie Smith	2	Aaron & Ella Smith
184	Morea Smith	1	Joe & Sarah Smith
144	Raymond Smith	2	John & Lucy Smith
264	Sarah Smith	1	Charley & Millie Smith
144	Sarbra Smith	1	John & Lucy Smith
182	Sylvester Smith	3	Thomas & Belle Smith
222	Thelma Smith	1	Chester & Keller Smith
265	Willie Smith	1	Sonny & Hattie Smith
476	Eugene Snaden	2	Alf & Luella Snaden
476	Lucinda Snaden	1	Alf & Luella Snaden
35	Eva Sorril	2	Morris & Ida Sorril
35	Ruby Sorril	3	Morris & Ida Sorril
115	Bernice Spight	3	Don & Delilah Spight
41	Norris Stanton	2	Calvin & Lucy Stanton
41	Robert Stanton	1	Calvin & Lucy Stanton
356	Agatha Starr	2	Harry & Martha Starr
422	Dannie Starr	1	Daniel & Alice Starr
221	Emma Starr	3	Henry & Peggie Starr
301	Floyd Starr	1	Willis & Pearl Starr
475	Gertrude Starr	2	William & Florence Starr
80	Lannie Starr	1	Samuel & Sadie Starr
221	Loley Starr	1	Henry & Peggie Starr
80	Luthar Starr	3	Samuel & Sadie Starr
301	Marion Starr	3	Willis & Pearl Starr
210	Robert Starr	1	Charlie & Hannah Starr
210	Viola Starr	2	Charlie & Hannah Starr
53	Lula Stephens	1	Peter & Betsie Stephens
220	Ollie Stidmon	1	Charles & Daisy Stidmon
127	Pearlie Summer	2	Sylvester Summer & Ida Humphrey
78	Clover Swepston	1	Perry & Jane Swepston
244	Archie Taylor	1	John & Ada Taylor

303	Elijah Taylor	2	Frank & Lucy Taylor
230	Herman Taylor	2	Mack Taylor & Annie Tyner
186	Leonetta Terry	1	S H & Eliza Terry
186	Margie Terry	4	S H & Eliza Terry
40	Jerry Thomas	2	John Davis & Florence Thomas
243	Abbie Thompson	1	Jordan & Nancy Thompson
423	Alex Thompson	4	Edward & Susan Thompson
292	Amy Thompson	1	Steven & Mary Thompson
423	Clifford Thompson	3	Edward & Susan Thompson
477	Clyde Thompson	2	Henry & Lucinda Thompson
423	Eddie Thompson	1	Edward & Susan Thompson
291	Georgie Thompson	2	William & Victoria Thompson
223	Jesse Thompson	2	Daniel & Eliza Thompson
54	Julius Thompson	1	Jack & Sarah Thompson
243	Louie Thompson	3	Jordan & Nancy Thompson
280	Oliver Thompson	1	John & Lelia Thompson
223	Teetsy Thompson	4	Daniel & Eliza Thompson
63	Lottie Thornton	2	Robert & Dollie Thornton
290	Lucy Tucker	1	Lewis & Carrie Tucker
118	Clara Turner	2	Harry & Maude Turner
118	Evrett Turner	3	Harry & Maude Turner
118	Leon Turner	1	Harry & Maude Turner
324	Minnie Tyner	3	Prince & Martha Tyner
230	Zevelina Tyner	1	John & Annie Tyner
28	Garnett Tyson	1	William Tyson & Myrtle Martin
424	Ardella Vann	1	Daniel & Susie Vann
455	Bennie Vann	2	George & Minerva Vann
441	Buddie Vann	1	William & Maggie Vann
187	Charley Vann	1	Robert & Fannie Vann
447	Clara Vann	1	William Foreman & Lillie Vann
190	Clyde Vann	3	Moses & Lottie Vann
424	Ella Vann	2	Daniel & Susie Vann
399	Elmore Vann	3	Riley Vann & Lilly Riley
30	Emma Vann	2	Rufus & Sallie Vann
441	Emma Vann	4	William & Maggie Vann
305	Fannie Vann	3	Sank & Fannie Vann
448	Frank Vann	1	Lonnie & Jocy Vann
64	Georgia Vann	3	Jacob & Florence Vann
344	Gladys Vann	3	George & Mary Vann
428	Hanner Vann	1	Reed & Maud Vann

119	Heriel Vann	1	Jesse & Mary Vann
357	Homer Vann	1	Reed & Kittie Vann
190	Jessie Vann	1	Moses & Lottie Vann
245	Joe Vann	3	Ellis Vann & Bertha Bean
304	Joseph Vann	2	William & Lovie Vann
425	Josie Vann	1	Jesse & Minnie Vann
344	Larneil Vann	5	George & Mary Vann
64	Lena Vann	1	Jacob & Florence Vann
372	Lenard Vann	1	James & Bessie Vann
386	Lillie Vann	3	William Jones & Ellen Childers
30	Lorena Vann	1	Rufus & Sallie Vann
428	Lottie Vann	7	Reed & Maud Vann
197	Maude Vann	1	David & Bessie Vann
426	Ray Vann	2	Wesley & Katie Vann
278	Rena Vann	3	Berr & Sarah Vann
413	Roberta Vann	4	James Vann & Georgia Estrich
277	Rosella Vann	1	Roand & Euna Vann
189	Ruth Vann	3	Ben & Irene Vann
426	Tessey Vann	1	Wesley & Katie Vann
343	Theodore Vann	2	Lewis Vann & Virginia Little
449	Tom Vann	5	Robert Mayes & Katie Vann
428	Tommy Vann	2	Reed & Maud Vann
293	Victoria Vann	1	Bishop & Lillie Vann
344	Willa Vann	1	George & Mary Vann
55	William Vann	2	Henry & Callie Vann
266	Willie Vann	1	Eddie & Emma Vann
308	Carnlyer Vestel	2	Isaac & Eliza Vestel
536	William Vinson	2	Yancy & Lizzie Vinson
405	Oak Wagoner	3	S A & Cora Wagoner
416	Alice Waitie	1	Walter Waitie & Dallie Williams
128	Elizabeth Walker	3	Moses & Peggy Walker
6	George Walker	1	David & Lucinda Walker
128	Girtrue Walker	1	Moses & Peggy Walker
281	Nancy Walker	1	Daniel & Frances Walker
532	Robert Walker	2	Isaac & Fannie Walker
281	Smith Walker	2	Daniel & Frances Walker
56	Walter Walker	1	Daniel & Aggie Walker
31	Lillian Ward	1	William & Belle Ward
31	Lydia Ward	3	William & Belle Ward
359	Booker Watkins	4	Lee & Nannie Watkins

359	Julius Watkins	1	Lee & Nannie Watkins
267	Beatrice Webber	2	Aaron & Annie Webber
29	Ellie Webber	1	Josh & Mary Webber
430	James Webber	2	Edward & Hallie Webber
430	Jossieline Webber	1	Edward & Hallie Webber
129	Leander Webber	3	Moses & Ellen Webber
129	Melvine Webber	1	Moses & Ellen Webber
462	Arthur Whitmire	2	Joe & Hattie Whitmire
145	Elnora Whitmire	1	Dave & Carrie Whitmire
193	Ernest Whitmire	1	Isaac & Susie Whitmire
82	Flora Whitmire	3	Charles & Maggie Whitmire
145	Lawrence Whitmire	2	Dave & Carrie Whitmire
373	Mariton Whitmire	2	Nathan & Patsy Whitmire
193	Silvertia Whitmire	2	Isaac & Susie Whitmire
82	Teddie Whitmire	2	Charles & Maggie Whitmire
198	Guthrie Wickliff	1	Jackson & Cynthia Wickliff
198	Louie Wickliff	3	Jackson & Cynthia Wickliff
237	Nathaniel Wickliff	5	Lewis & Lucinda Wickliff
450	Arthur Williams	3	Augustus & Martha Williams
191	Lois Williams	2	Chester & Nettie Williams
490	Rockwell Williams	3	Riley & Fannie Williams
279	Rhoberta Wilson	3	Reed & Alice Wilson
345	Samuel Wilson	4	Manuel Wilson & Maria Jones
346	Teddy Wilson	1	Henry & Lizzie Wilson
327	Carrie Winters	1	Charlie & Rachel Winters
327	Frank Winters	3	Charlie & Rachel Winters
192	Henryetta Wofford	2	Alma & Amanda Wofford
81	Oatas Wolfe	3	Solomon & Leanna Wolfe
415	Eliza Woods	2	Israel & Rilda Woods
268	Samuel Workman	2	Alfred & Jennie Workman
456	Roseburn Wright	3	John & Maggie Wright
374	Augusta Young	1	Bethel & Isa Young
374	Uzella Young	3	Bethel & Isa Young
120	Willie Young	1	John & Lucinda Young

www.ingramcontent.com/pod-product-compliance
Lightning Source LLC
Chambersburg PA
CBHW071118280326
41935CB00010B/1050